Oral Interpretation of Literature in American Colleges and Universities

ORAL INTERPRETATION OF LITERATURE IN AMERICAN COLLEGES AND UNIVERSITIES

A Historical Study of Teaching Methods

BY

MARY MARGARET ROBB

Professor of Speech and Drama
University of Colorado

Revised Edition

JOHNSON REPRINT CORPORATION

New York and London

1968

© 1941 by Mary Margaret Robb
© 1968 by Johnson Reprint Corporation

Reprinted with the permission of Mary Margaret Robb

This volume reproduces in part the edition originally published in 1941
by the H. W. Wilson Company.

Library of Congress Catalog Card Number: 68-29050

Printed in the United States of America

PREFACE

It will always be important for teachers and students to be aware of the historical background of the subject they are studying. Without knowledge of the history, they often claim as new techniques or concepts so old and worn as to have been discarded. It is impossible to see clearly where we are going unless we know where we have been; and we can often adjust or add to that which, pedagogically speaking, is old as the hills.

When this book first appeared in 1941, the field of research in the history of speech education was a relatively new one. Although there is still work to be done, much has been accomplished since then. In the last part of this edition and in the appendix, the progress made in exploring the historical background of the teaching of oral interpretation and in establishing it as an important subject in the liberal arts curriculum is described.

The revision of the text is chiefly through additions, in an effort to bring the history up to date. Few changes are made in the first three parts of the book. There is a softening of the emphasis on the two schools—natural and mechanical—since they never were mutually exclusive, and the tendency to label teachers is not one that should be encouraged. The *liberal* is usually very *conservative* in some of his ideas; in the same way, the teachers who relied upon *mechanical* rules were usually trying to teach speakers to speak naturally.

There is no pretension to an intensive treatment of the subject. An attempt has been made instead to give an extensive view, to acquaint the reader with the most important teachers and writers in the field and the methods which they used. In addition, the author has tried to show the major trends in teaching speech and their relation to the general background of the period. The material is arranged in five different parts so that the reader may easily see the pattern which the evolution of speech education took from 1750 to the present time, especially that of the teaching of oral interpretation. Each part has an introductory section which presents the background of the period in an effort to assist the reader in understanding the reasons for the changes that took place. It is hoped that the continuity of the history will give readers, especially teachers, a feeling of pride and security. This is not a new or untried field of study but one with a history.

In the first preface, the writer stated that it was hoped that the book would open up the field and encourage the writing of "many more chapters of the as yet unwritten history of speech." This has been done. *Speech Education in America,* 1954, edited by Karl Wallace, is the most notable contribution to the teachers of speech. The author claims for this book only a small part in encouraging the sizeable amount of research that has been done since 1941 and finds the results most gratifying.

I am deeply indebted to colleagues throughout the country who have sent me interesting materials, have corrected errors, and have encouraged me to attempt this revision (without their gentle prodding I'm sure I would not have done it). A special debt of gratitude is due Dr. Magdalene Kramer and Dr. Lester Thonssen for suggestions and criticisms.

M.M.R.

September 1966

TABLE OF CONTENTS

Preface 5

List of Illustrations 9

Introduction 11

Part I.   The Influence of English Elocutionists: 1760-1827
    Chapter I.   English Influence on Colonial Education 17
    Chapter II.   English Teachers Develop Elocution 30
    Chapter III. An Analysis of the Methods Used in Teaching .. 44

Part II.   Dr. Rush and the Scientific Method: 1827-1870
    Chapter I.   The Period of Expansion 71
    Chapter II.   Dr. James Rush 81
    Chapter III. Important Teachers of the Period 103

Part III.   Psychology and Oral Interpretation: 1870-1915
    Chapter I.   New Concepts of American Culture 123
    Chapter II.   The Delsarte System 142
    Chapter III. The Tradition of Walker, Austin, and Rush Remains Unbroken 153
    Chapter IV. Psychological Sanction for the Natural School .. 163

Part IV.   The Speech Program Is Enlarged: 1915-1940
    Chapter I.   Speech Education Becomes More Extensive 187
    Chapter II.   Methods Used in Teaching Oral Interpretation .. 197

Part V.   Oral Interpretation Improves Its Academic Status: 1940-1965
    Chapter I.   Arts and Humanities in a Scientific Age 211
    Chapter II.   Oral Interpretation Strengthens Its Position in the Liberal Arts 218

Conclusion 230

Appendix 233

Bibliography 239

Index 253

LIST OF ILLUSTRATIONS

PAGE

CHART SHOWING INFLECTION 48
From *The Elements of Elocution* by John Walker

EXAMPLE OF SIR JOSHUA STEELE'S NOTATIONS 52
From *Prosodia Rationalis*

AUSTIN'S SYSTEM OF GESTURE 64
From *Chironomia*

AUSTIN'S USE OF NOTATION FOR GESTURE 66
From *Chironomia*

NOTATIONS USED BY DR. RUSH 89
From *The Philosophy of the Human Voice*

CHART SHOWING THE DELSARTE SYSTEM 145
From *The Delsarte System*

CRITERION OF THE LEGS 146
From *The Delsarte System*

THE FULTON AND TRUEBLOOD SYSTEM 161
From *Practical Elements of Elocution*

INTRODUCTION

The educator is continually evaluating the courses offered in the curriculum, examining their purpose and the methods used in teaching them. Above all, he is interested in establishing a compatibility between the subject and his own philosophy of education. Pressures from the academic environment and also from the world itself unite to produce changes in the educational process. A study of these changes and of the evolution of any one subject offered in the curriculum reveals many interesting and significant relationships and trends. It is the purpose of this book to trace the historical development of the methods used in teaching the oral interpretation of literature in the colleges and universities in the United States, and to show the relationship between this development and the general educational pattern.

The study shows a long and continuous development which is replete with experiment and variation in method. The evolution from the declamation and student oration to an elective subject, designed to teach a better understanding and appreciation of literature, covers a period of more than a hundred years. This growth is synchronous with the development from the small denominational college, created to educate the few, to the large university of the present day with its multiplicity of offerings.

In investigating the different methods which have been used in teaching oral interpretation of literature, an attempt is made to identify major trends. The study is divided, therefore, into five rather arbitrary periods: (1) The English elocutionists develop the Natural and Mechanical schools, 1760–1827, (2) Dr. James Rush introduces the "scientific method" into the teaching of elocution, 1827–1870, (3) Psychology exerts an influence upon the teaching of oral interpretation, 1870–1915, (4) An extensive program of speech becomes a part of the curriculum of higher education, 1915–1940, and (5) Oral interpretation improves its academic status, 1940–1965.

In analyzing these five periods, particular attention has been given to the purposes and organization of the work, teaching methods, and the relationships established with other subjects. A short survey of the background of each period and the influence of environmental changes precedes the discussion of the development of oral interpretation of literature as a course in the curriculum of higher education.

It is impossible to appraise and to compare methods in a completely detached and unbiased manner. However, it is possible to present the facts concerning the teaching of the subject as recorded by the writers of the period and to note variations in emphasis and innovations in organization and method.

Four men stand out as being the most important in directing the evolution of the teaching of the oral interpretation of literature. Thomas Sheridan and John Walker, two English elocutionists, are credited with initiating two conflicting schools of thought concerning the methods which are most effective in teaching speech. Sheridan believed in following natural laws as demonstrated in animated conversation, while Walker believed in devising mechanical rules and notations to guide the student. Dr. James Rush introduced scientific procedure as a necessary part of the teaching of vocal techniques, and Samuel Silas Curry placed the stimulating of mental processes first in his method of teaching. The whole study of historical development rests most heavily upon these men and the contributions which they made.

The factual material has been gathered from textbooks, college catalogues and reports, newspapers and periodicals, research studies, public addresses, and letters. Histories, memoirs and diaries, critical essays, letters, and documents have yielded the material for the general background for each section.

The studies which deal with the growth of speech education in the United States have proved very helpful in this study of the methods used in the teaching of oral interpretation. Fritz's study,[1] which traces the teaching of speech in America before 1850, and Coulton's study[2] of trends in speech education between 1835 and 1935 have contributed information concerning the textbooks and their usage. Other studies were: *An Introductory Study in the History of the Teaching of Public Speaking in the United States* by Anthony F. Blanks,[3] and Porter Gale Perrin's *The Teaching of Rhetoric in the American Colleges before 1750.*[4]

Oral Interpretation is defined as oral reading, with or without memorization, which has as its purpose communication of the intellectual and emotional content of literature to an audience. There are many other terms which enter into this study which are either synonymous with Oral Interpretation or may be considered a specific part of the term.

Elocution is used more often than any other term in the early history. It was always closely related to the training of voice and gesture, the

[1] Fritz, Charles Andrew. *The Content of the Teaching of Speech in the American College before 1850.* Unpublished Ph.D. dissertation, New York University, 1928.
[2] Coulton, Thomas E. *Trends in Speech Education in American Colleges 1835–1935.* Unpublished Ph.D. dissertation, New York University, 1935.
[3] Blanks, Anthony F. Unpublished Ph.D. dissertation, Stanford University, 1928.
[4] Perrin, Porter Gale. Unpublished Ph.D. dissertation, Chicago University, 1936.

delivery and technique of reading. *Declamation, Oral Expression, Spoken English,* and in some cases, *Oratory,* were also used. *Declamation* may be defined as the speaking of memorized "pieces," either prose or poetry. *Oratory* meant either the presentation of original compositions or the interpretation of orations by famous men, and occasionally it was used as generic term instead of *Public Speaking. Oral Expression* and *Spoken English* were used rather loosely and often referred to all the speech offerings in the curriculum, especially during the period 1870 to 1915. *Rhetoric* was originally considered the all-inclusive term but eventually became a specialized study, and *Public Speaking* or *Speech* were used instead.

Because the teacher's work is usually evaluated in terms of the methods used, a study of past methods should be of value to him. It is always well to recognize the traditional strings with which new theories or methods are tied, and it seems logical to believe that the knowledge of the historical background of a subject will contribute to more versatile and intelligent teaching.

It is difficult to view educational problems sympathetically or wisely except in the light of their origin and the environment which developed them. Therefore, it seems necessary for the teacher to have a knowledge of the past in order to protect himself against senseless mistakes and to keep him from labeling old ideas as new and original. For the student, a historical background is useful because it gives color and breadth to the subject studied.

PART I

THE INFLUENCE OF ENGLISH
ELOCUTIONISTS: 1760-1827

CHAPTER I

ENGLISH INFLUENCE ON COLONIAL EDUCATION

ENGLISH INFLUENCE ON COLONIAL EDUCATION. The English cultural influence which naturally predominated throughout the early years of American colonial education persisted as a determinative until well after the War of 1812. It brought to the new country the impact of European ideas, some of them well aged in tradition, others vibrant with iconoclastic tendencies. The transplanted culture drew strength from its new environment and in the next century was able to stand upon its own feet, but in the period under consideration was most dependent upon the old world.

In order to understand the different forms in which speech education appeared, it is necessary to analyze briefly the educational system which we inherited. Butts, in *The College Charts Its Course*, traces the development of the seven liberal arts as a core of higher education in the American college and university and finds that "the seeds of election" were not sown until about 1776-1860.[1] This program, in which rhetoric was an integral part, was the only acceptable one until late in the eighteenth century because it satisfied the theological and humanistic needs of the time and was therefore impregnable until secular interests wedged in and made new demands.

A religious interest was particularly evident in our higher education. Beard says:

> The intellectual life of the colonies, like their hierarchy of classes, their social tastes, and their domestic institutions, sprang from the British heritage of the seventeenth century, developed under the influence of local circumstances, and was modified by the currents of new opinion from the Old World that from time to time touched their shores. Inevitably the dominant interest in the beginning was theology. From the breakup of the Roman Empire to the beginning of the colonial era, the clergy had been the leaders in thought and instruction. As a rule they were the makers of books, the teachers in schools and universities, the compilers of laws, the guardians of all things of the spirit.[2]

The purpose in founding the majority of the early colleges was religious in nature, and instruction in speaking fitted nicely into a program designed to educate ministers. To speak and read well was important.

There was criticism of English oratory, especially that of the clergy, in the early part of the eighteenth century and a demand for

[1] Butts, R. Freeman. *The College Charts its Course*. p. 32.
[2] Beard, Charles A. and Mary. *The Rise of American Civilization*. vol. 1. p. 145.

rhetoric that was practical. Sandford gives the details of this criticism in *English Theories of Address 1530-1828:*

> The inertness and colorlessness of delivery, prevalent at the time, were criticized severely. More attention was urged to correctness of pronunciation, vocal expressiveness, and the like. Similarly, the absence of proper gestures was noted. Addison, for instance, in a passage often quoted by the elocutionists, makes merry at the expense of orators who lack action in their speaking: . . . "It proceeds perhaps, from our national virtue (modesty) that our orators are observed to make use of less gesture or action than those of other countries. Our preachers stand stock still in the pulpit, and will not so much as move a finger to set off the best sermons in the world." [8]

In addition to Addison, Swift and Chesterfield criticized the oratory of the day—the first in his *Letter to a Young Clergyman,*[4] and the latter in *Letters to his Son.*[5] Not only was the manner of speaking deplored, but also the manner of reading the sermons.

The clergymen themselves were not satisfied with their education in this field. In 1771, Anselm Bayly, a sub-dean of his Majesty's Chapel-Royal, wrote a treatise in which he lamented the fact that elocution was not an important part of education in the schools and that the ministers were not equal to the ancient orators. "If a Demosthenes, a Cicero, can with the arts of speaking, and mere worldly arguments," he says, "prevail in the senate and at the bar; how much more powerfully may a Preacher influence his audience with the same weapons in one hand and the Word of God in the other?" He says further that England can boast more good writers and fewer good speakers than any other country and places the blame upon the schools.[6]

No doubt, the same kind of criticism was made in the colonies because the training given in rhetoric, as in England, emphasized the style of composition at the expense of the other parts of classical rhetoric. Classical rhetoric with its five parts: *inventio* (discovery of material), *dispositio* (organization), *elocutio* (style), *memoria* (store of illustrative material), and *pronuntiatio* (delivery) was emasculated until *elocutio* with its ornamentation of figures of speech dominated. Perrin says that the first two parts became the property of logic, *memoria* was ignored, and style and delivery remained with emphasis upon style until after 1720. Our return to the classical concept of rhetoric in reply to humanistic demands for classical studies he places as late as 1748.[7] This indicates a lag in the colonial college

---

[8] Sandford, William P. *English Theories of Address 1530-1828.* p. 134.
[4] Swift, Jonathan. *Letter to a Young Clergyman.* vol. 8. p. 7-15.
[5] Chesterfield, Philip D. S. *Letters to His Son.* p. 208, 358, 359.
[6] Bayly, Anselm. "Pronunciation or the Art of Just Speaking" in *A Practical Treatise on Singing and Playing with Just Expression and Real Elegance.* p. 25-6. A dissertation on the Art of Just Speaking appeared in *An Introduction to Language,* 1758.
[7] Perrin, Porter Gale. *The Teaching of Rhetoric in the American Colleges before 1750.* p. 52.

because Sandford places the date for the regaining of dominance by the classics in English rhetoric as 1660.[8]

Secular demands in the colonies which favored instruction in practical rhetoric appeared after the American Revolution. The new republic needed political leaders, lawyers, and educators. The tendency to veer from the purely religious function was seen in the charters of King's College (Columbia) 1754, and the College of Philadelphia (University of Pennsylvania) 1775. In commenting on this variation, Butts says: "This wider conception of a liberal education implied that college studies should contribute to the commercial and civic usefulness of the many as well as to the religious and civic leadership of the few." [9] When special instruction in elocution was introduced at Harvard in 1756, the Board of Overseers gave as their reason that good public speech makes the speaker "an honor to his country." [10]

Not only the old Aristotelian concept of rhetoric as practical speech came back into favor, but a new emphasis was made upon delivery. The English elocutionists became engrossed with questions concerning the methods of teaching the use of vocal expression and bodily action as a part of rhetoric. Perrin states that in our early colleges, a distinction was made at first between oratory and rhetoric; oratory was practical while rhetoric was theoretical. However, commencement theses [11] on rhetoric at Harvard and Yale became more and more concerned with voice and gesture. He gives several examples: one in 1744 at Harvard was titled "A proper gesture is a certain eloquence of face and body which indicates the will of the speaker hardly less than the words he utters," another in 1747, "*Pronuntiatio* is a graceful moderation of facial expression and gesture." There is some indication that the ideal was natural delivery: one thesis at Yale stated, "Everything in delivery ought to paint naturally the mind's thoughts" and one at Harvard stated that no art should appear.[12]

This new interest in delivery was no doubt a reaction to the rhetoric of "exornation" and its artificial and bookish concern with tropes and figures, but it was also a reply to the demand for more effective public speakers. *Elocution* was the name given to the study of voice and gesture. Although it was a definite part of rhetoric, it was the beginning of what was later to be known as *Oral Interpretation of Literature*.

---

[8] Sandford. *op. cit.* p. 91.
[9] Butts. *op. cit.* p. 66.
[10] Thwing, Charles F. *A History of Higher Education in America Since the Civil War.* p. 154.
[11] Commencement theses were broadsides on different subjects written by students and distributed among the audience. Some were disputed before the assembly and were so marked on the broadside.
[12] Perrin. *op. cit.* p. 116-17.

ELOCUTION DEVELOPS FROM CLASSICAL RHETORIC AND POETIC. The reading or reciting of literary forms may claim kinship with both the *rhetoric* and *poetic* of the ancients. Elocution was founded in the parts of these two forms which overlap. Baldwin says that the ancients saw no fundamental distinction between the style of composition in rhetoric and poetic because they realized that the appeal of public address, in so far as it was an appeal of style, was largely imaginative and rhythmical as was the appeal of the drama or epic. They also believed that the oral delivery of the two forms was important.[13]

The need of *pronuntiatio* both in rhetoric and poetic was recognized by Aristotle. Although he did not consider *pronuntiatio* an art, he did think it was important in terms of audience reaction. He says:

It is plain that delivery has just as much to do with oratory as with poetry. . . . It is, essentially, a matter of the right management of the voice to express the various emotions—speaking loudly, softly, or between the two; of high, low, or intermediate pitch; of the various rhythms that suit various subjects. These are the three things—volume of sound, modulation of pitch, and rhythm—that a speaker bears in mind. . . . No systematic treatise upon rules of delivery has yet been composed; indeed, even the study of language made no progress 'till late in the day. Besides, delivery is—very properly—not regarded as an elevated subject of inquiry. Still, the whole business being concerned with appearances, we must pay attention to the subject of delivery, unworthy though it is, because we cannot do without it.[14]

Cicero [15] and Quintilian added action to Aristotle's concept of *pronuntiatio*. Quintilian suggested enlisting the help of an actor and teacher of gymnastics to train the rhetorician. He explains the function of the actor as follows: "In the first place he must correct all faults of pronunciation. . . . Our actor will also be required to show how a narrative should be delivered, and to indicate the authoritative tone that should be given to advice, the excitement which should mark the rise of anger, and the change of tone that is characteristic of pathos. . . ." [16] The work of the teacher of gymnastics he describes as correcting the movement of the hands and head. "No one will deny that such details form a part of the art of delivery, nor divorce delivery from oratory; and there can be no justification for disdaining to learn what has got to be done, especially as *chironomy*, which, as the name shows, is *the law of gesture,* originated in heroic times and met with the approval of the greatest Greeks, not excepting Socrates himself. . . ." [17]

[13] Baldwin, Charles S. *Ancient Rhetoric and Poetic.* p. 247.
[14] Aristotle. *Works,* ed. by W. D. Ross (1403ᵇ23-1404ᵃ13).
[15] Cicero. *De Oratore.* I. p. 15.
[16] Quintilian. *The Institutio Oratorio.* I. xi, 4, 12.
[17] Quintilian. *op. cit.* p. 17.

Just why the English writers, who were primarily interested in this branch of rhetoric, should have called themselves *Elocutionists* is not too plain. A great number of them were grammarians and lexicographers, and that might suggest an interest which began with style or *elocutio* and developed into one in *pronuntiatio*. Sometimes both terms were used interchangeably. John Mason, a non-conformist divine in London, who trained students for the ministry, wrote an essay in 1751 entitled *An Essay on Elocution or Pronunciation intended chiefly for the Assistance of those who Instruct others in the Art of Reading and those who are often called to Speak in Publick.* Mason's definition does not sound too foreign to present-day readers:

A good pronunciation *in reading*, is the Art of managing and governing the Voice so as to express the full Sense and Spirit of your Author in that just, decent, and graceful Manner, which will not only instruct but affect the Hearers; and will not only raise in them the same Ideas he intended to convey, but the same Passions he really felt.[18]

John Quincy Adams, the first lecturer to hold the Boylston Chair of Rhetoric in Harvard, makes mention of this confusion of terms in his lecture on *elocutio.*

. . . by elocution is here understood an idea quite different from that, in which the word is now commonly used, and which is affixed to it by the modern English rhetoricians. Sheridan, Walker, and others, who have published professed treatises upon elocution, mean by that word the mode of speaking, or delivery; the same thing, which by the ancients was understood under the name of action.[19]

The declamation originated as a method used in the study of rhetoric, and was in the end closely connected with elocution. At the beginning, which Sandford assigns to the first signs of decay in the post-classical rhetoric, ca. 100-400 A.D., a declamation was a discourse composed from stock topics on subjects mainly fanciful and unreal.[20] This method of teaching rhetoric persisted through the Medieval and Renaissance periods and was handmaiden to the rhetoric of exornation. Sandford mentions John Clarke's *Formulae Oratoriae* 1632, 1637, which gave numerous formulae to be used in all parts of the oration or declamation, and also included a number of declamations which had been given in Lincoln Cathedral School in 1624.[21]

With the discarding of the rhetoric of exornation in favor of the unpolluted classical forms approved by the humanists, the declamatory method became suspect. It was too artificial and unoriginal.

---

[18] Mason, John. p. 22.
[19] Adams, John Quincy. *Lectures on Rhetoric and Oratory.* vol. 2. p. 143.
[20] Sandford. *op. cit.* p. 20-1.
[21] Sandford. *op. cit.* p. 76, 112.

The declamation eventually became a distinct kind of exercise which, with the exception of those in the early years of our colleges, interpreted unoriginal literary forms for an audience.

Rhetoric became more original and practical as it followed the classical formula of *inventio, dispositio, elocutio, memoria,* and *pronuntiatio.* In 1760, the date of the beginning of the first period of this study, Sandford finds two tendencies in the teaching of rhetoric in England: classicism and the new elocutionary movement. The elocutionists had as their purpose the improvement of rhetorical delivery but through continuous use of different literary forms, which were not written by the reader or speaker but only interpreted by him, originated the study of *Oral Interpretation of Literature.*

EARLY FORMS OF ORAL INTERPRETATION IN OUR COLLEGES. The study of Oral Interpretation appeared in different forms and in positions of varying importance in the curriculum of the American colleges and universities, but its life was continuous from the beginning until the present day. It appeared first, as could be predicted from the previous discussion, in the form of declamations and orations in Latin and Greek. There were other considerations besides communicating the material to the audience; sometimes the material was original with an emphasis on composition. But since the material was memorized and delivered before a group of people, it seems fair to consider these exercises as ancestors of the present courses that are given in oral interpretation of literature.

The following excerpt from a letter describing the first commencement of Harvard college lists the performances of the graduates.

. . . their Commencement, when the Governor, Magistrates, and the Ministers from all parts, with all sorts of Schollars, and others in great numbers were present, and did heare their Exercises; which were Latine and Greeke Orations, and Declamations and Hebrew Analysis Grammaticall, Logicall, and Rhetoricall of the Psalms; And their Answers and Disputations in Logicall, Ethicall, Physicall and Metaphysicall Questions; and so were found worthy of the first degree (commonly called Batchelour) *pro more Academiarum in Anglia. . . .*[22]

It is an interesting fact that Harvard commencement today includes student orations, one of them being in Latin.[23]   Perrin questions the

---

[22] "New England's First Fruits," in *Old South Leaflets.* vol. 3. no. 51. p. 5.
[23] Excerpt from account of Harvard orations in Boston Evening Globe, June 20, 1940:
". . . Three 'Commencement Parts,' one delivered in Latin, by students graduating with exceptionally high honors opened the ceremonies. First of these was the traditional welcome in Latin, extended by Robert A. Brooks '40 of Needham.
"Using profuse gestures to illustrate his meaning, he first welcomed Dr. Conant who was roundly applauded. Next Brooks saluted the fellows of the university, the guests, including Governor Saltonstall, and the recipients of honorary degrees.
"The youthful orator then expressed welcome and gratitude to the 'puellae' or young ladies present. Finally he urged them, in spite of the war, to use the principles and lessons of the classroom in the interpretation of all human affairs with a calm and critical mind."

conclusions of Fritz and Blanks concerning an unbroken tradition of practical rhetoric in Harvard and Yale based upon the fact that commencement orations were considered important. He says:

These commencement orations were reserved for the favored few, actually only one student of a class in this period (1636-1750), so that they can hardly be regarded as part of a regular training in rhetoric. Futhermore they were in Latin and might rather mark the climax and end of the college work than the beginning of a career of eloquence.[24]

Morison quotes from the first college book of statutes that in Harvard college "the Scholars shall never use their Mother toungue except that in publike Exercises of oratory or such like, they bee called to make them in English." [25] This law suggests that there were speeches given in English which probably were interested in persuasion rather than grammar. Thomas Clap, the fourth president of Yale states:

Twice a Week five or six deliver a Declamation memoriter from the oratorical Rostrum. The President makes some Observations upon the Manner of Delivery and sometimes upon the Subject; and sometimes gives some small Laurel to him who best acts the Part of an Orator. These Declamations are beforehand supervised by their Tutor, who corrects the Orthography and Punctuation. There are also two Orations made every Quarter-Day, upon Examinations, and frequently on special Occasions.[26]

The first catalog of Harvard College set the ninth hour of the sixth day for declamations. "So ordered that every scholler may declaime once a moneth." [27]

Perrin states that the declamation was the most persistent of all the rhetorical exercises in the early American college.   In all Harvard and Yale laws and in the William and Mary Statutes of 1727, students were to declaim at stated intervals. [28] The earliest declamations were unlike the ancient declamations on debatable subjects but merely short compositions in the ancient languages written out and delivered from memory. However, even though the chief reason for these exercises, according to Perrin, was a testing of proficiency in the languages, the delivery was criticized and the exercise often considered a preparation for the more pretentious rhetorical demonstration, the commencement oration.[29]

The declamation soon included the interpretation of orations and discourses which had been delivered by famous men. Blanks gives

[24] Perrin. op. cit. p. 147.
[25] Morison, Samuel Eliot. The Founding of Harvard College. p. 336.
[26] Clap, Thomas. The Annals or History of Yale College. p. 82.
[27] "New England's First Fruits." p. 6.
[28] Perrin. op. cit. p. 136.
[29] Ibid. p. 140-1.

no other description of them.[30]   The practice of giving declamations continued well into the nineteenth century.   These exercises were considered very important.   The following excerpts from the Scholastic Exercises described in the laws of the College of Rhode Island (Brown University) 1783, are given as typical by Snow in his study of the college curriculum in the United States.

Two of the students in Rotation shall, every evening after Prayers, pronounce a piece upon the stage, and all the members of the college shall meet every Wednesday in the afternoon in the Hall, at the ringing of the bell at 2 o'clock, to pronounce before the President and Tutors pieces well committed to memory. . . .

. . . Every student in college shall pronounce publicly on the stage, memoriter such an Oration or Piece as shall be previously approved by the President, on which occasion the two upper classes shall make use of their own composition. . . . And that the students may accomplish themselves in the art of reading, they shall, at such times as the President shall direct, prepare and read before the officers of instruction select pieces of English composition; and any student who shall particularly distinguish himself by reading well at the public examination shall, as a mark of honor, have his name entered on the records of the college.[31]

Since, in this period, there was a certain inflexibility of curriculum and also a noticeable uniformity in the institutions of higher education, it is not surprising to find similar activities in other colleges.   Fritz, in his survey of the content of the teaching of speech before 1850, reports the following examples: at Amherst, declamations were required until 1850; at Hamilton, public declamations were given every Saturday until 1842.   Princeton, Bowdoin, Rutgers, Union, and Dickinson are also mentioned as requiring declamatory work during this early period.[32]   According to Hayworth, the only speech training in the colleges until after 1760 was found in translating the ancient rhetoricians and orators and in giving Latin and Greek declamations.[33]

The lower schools imitated the colleges and not only gave programs on Wednesday afternoon, but also included elocutionary training in their "readers."   The most famous of the English readers was Lindley Murray's, entitled, *The English Reader or Pieces in Prose and Verse from the best writers designed to assist young persons to read with propriety and effect; improve their language and sentiments; and to inculcate the most important principles of Piety and Virtue.*   Rules for "the management of the voice in reading" are under the following

[30] Blanks, Anthony F. *An Introductory Study in the History of the Teaching of Public Speaking in the United States.* p. 124.
[31] Snow, Louis Franklin. *The College Curriculum in the United States.* p. 109, 111.
[32] Fritz, Charles Andrew. *The Content of the Teaching of Speech in American Colleges before 1850.* p. 22-3.
[33] Hayworth, Donald. "The Development of the Training of Public Speakers in America." *Quarterly Journal of Speech.* 14:490-4 (1928).

heads: proper loudness of the voice, distinctness, due degree of slow-
ness, propriety of pronunciation, emphasis, tones, pauses, and mode
of reading verse. There is record of an edition in 1800, and Jeremiah
Goodrich published an improved edition in Boston in 1822. There
were a great many "readers" which were imitations of Murray's.
Another very important book was an earlier one, the *Grammatical
Institutes of the English Language* published by Noah Webster in
1784. Noble, in his *A History of American Education,* speaks of the
great influence of this educator who began his book when the Revolution made it impossible to get sufficient textbooks from England.

> Part I, was the famous "blue back speller," entitled *Elementary Spelling
> Book,* a combination of primer, reader, and speller which became the first and
> only textbook that many children ever studied. . . . The blue back speller leapt
> into immediate popularity. Its fame spread through all states. For the first
> three quarters of the nineteenth century it was almost universally used in this
> country. . . . It is estimated that not less than 80,000,000 copies have been sold
> since its publication 150 years ago.
> Part II of the *Grammatical Institute* was an English Grammer. This book
> did much to popularize the teaching of a subject that was just entering the schools
> at that time. . . .
> Part III was a reader containing selections of moral and practical value
> and "pieces" for the schoolboy's declamations. The *Grammatical Institute* in its
> entirety carried out what the author conceived to be his patriotic obligation.[34]

In the next century *McGuffey's* held a comparable position.

Gradually speech education became more important in the colleges.
The first step was to appoint a special tutor for it; Harvard was probably the first to have such a tutor. Butts states that in 1767 the
greatest change since the founding of Harvard took place. The
tutorial system was revised so that each tutor taught one or only a
few subjects to each class, instead of teaching every subject to one
class.[35] Benjamin Pierce, in *A History of Harvard College,* states
that on "Friday and Saturday mornings each class shall be instructed
by a distinct tutor in Elocution, Composition in English, Rhetoric,
and other parts of the Belles Lettres." [36] A course in Oratory and
Elocution was provided for in the course of study of Brown University
in 1783.[37] Rhetoric was taught by the first president of Columbia
College, William Samuel Johnson. Sheridan's *A Rhetorical Grammar
of the English Language* was one of the textbooks used.[38] In the
second report of Amherst faculty presented December 6, 1826 it is

[34] Noble, Stuart G. *A History of American Education.* p. 101-2.
[35] Butts. *op. cit.* p. 63.
[36] Pierce, Benjamin. *A History of Harvard College.* p. 245-6.
[37] Fritz. *op. cit.* p. 25-7.
[38] *The Present State of Learning in the College of New York* (Columbia College).
p. 3.

stated that no respectable college would think itself organized without professors in Rhetoric and Oratory.[39]

Thus rhetoric became practical public speaking. Elocution continued to be a part of it but by the end of the period was concerned with methods of delivery for all forms of literature. It was particularly concerned with English poetry and prose, and the selections given in the textbooks written on the subject were without exception from English literature or English translations of the classics. In this characteristic especially can be seen the beginning of a subject distinct from rhetoric.

There were many "readers" and "speakers" published which contained collections of orations, other prose, and verse. According to Evans' *American Bibliography*, a book by Caleb Bingham, *The American Preceptor*, was published in 1794 and the *Columbian Orator* (1797) was considered the second part of it.[40] In the preface to *The American Preceptor*, Bingham states that he has given preference to American writers, and he has included orations such as the Fourth of July oration given by John Quincy Adams in 1793. In the first edition he begins with an excerpt from Blair on elocution; in later ones he tells the story of Demosthenes.[41] In the *Columbian Orator* he presumably gives his own rules for reading, but they are all taken from Blair.[42] Other collections were Alexander Thomas' *Orator's Assistant*, 1797, and the American edition of William Enfield's *Speaker*, 1798.

The first textbook in elocution to be used in the colonies, according to Fritz's study, was Sheridan's *Lectures on Elocution*. The Brown University catalog mentioned it in 1783 and continued to do so until 1826, and the University of North Carolina was using it at the beginning of the nineteenth century.[43] The records indicate that other textbooks on elocution written by Englishmen were published in this country, and although the college catalogs do not mention them they were undoubtedly used. James Burgh's *The Art of Speaking* is the first one listed by Evans' *American Bibliography*. It was published first in Philadelphia by R. Aitken in 1775. It had nine subsequent editions: Philadelphia 1780, 1781, 1786; Newbury-Port, 1781; New York, 1785, 1790; Boston, 1793, 1795; and Danbury 1795.[44]

[39] Amherst College Annals. p. 13.
[40] Evans, Charles. *American Bibliography*. vols. 9 and 11.
[41] Bingham, Caleb. *The American Preceptor*.
[42] Bingham, Caleb. *The Columbian Orator*.
[43] Fritz. *op. cit.* p. 27.
[44] The Widener Library of Harvard University possesses a copy of the first English edition with the author's autograph.

Sheridan's *Rhetorical Grammar* was published in Philadelphia in 1783 and *Lectures on Elocution* in Providence in 1796. The first mentioned was published under the inspection of Archibald Gamble, professor of English and Oratory in the University of Pennsylvania, and the book undoubtedly was used in his classes. William Scott's *Lessons in Elocution* was published in Philadelphia in 1786, 1790, 1794, 1795, 1797, 1798. A section of this book was given over to John Walker's discussion of gesture. Sometimes this section was sold separately.[45]

Although these books were used, no doubt, in other schools besides the college, the information concerning their American editions indicates that the English elocutionist was exerting an immeasurable influence in this country on the teaching of elocution.

Two Important Educational Theories. The two outstanding educational theories which were evolved during the eighteenth century were of secular design and in a way were a bifurcation of the same liberal growth. However, their developments into educational practices were, at the end of the period studied, in opposition to each other.

The period 1687-1776 is referred to as *The Period of Enlightenment*. It was an era in which the human reason was worshipped as the ultimate source of wisdom or truth as opposed to theology as the revealer of truth. John Locke articulated the educational theory of this period which is clearly explained by Preserved Smith in *A History of Modern Culture* when he says:

> The foundations of the educational theory of the Enlightenment, as of its philosophy in general, were laid by John Locke. Though somewhat influenced by Montaigne, Milton, Fénelon, and other earlier writers on the subject, he was far more indebted to his own discoveries in psychology. Thinking the mind of the child at birth "a blank page void of all character," or "wax to be fashioned and molded as one pleases," he was convinced of the great importance of early impressions. Esteeming reason sufficient for the discovery of truth, and truth as the highest possession of man, he naturally emphasized the cultivation of the rational element in man's nature.[46]

From this theory developed a redefinition of "faculty" psychology; the mind was believed to be composed of a number of faculties, such as the imagination, the memory, and the will, each capable of indefinite improvement. According to this theory, the responsibility of giving the student the proper intellectual fare so that his faculties would develop to their capacity rested upon the teacher and those administrators who designed the curriculum. As Locke's followers

[45] Evans. *American Bibliography.* vols. 5-12.
[46] Smith, Preserved. *A History of Modern Culture.* vol. 2. p. 432-3.

increased, there was a noticeable revolt against the more ornate and adulterated subjects of the Renaissance and the Reformation, and seven liberal arts were extolled as the curriculum giving the best "mental discipline."

Locke's educational theories, or rather those his followers developed, produced rather mechanical methods. From his experience as a physician, he realized that there was great variation in the bodies of men. He reasoned that there must be some variety in their mental equipment, but he saw the mind and body as separate entities. In his *Essay on Human Understanding*, he followed Descartes in emphasizing the two-fold origin of knowledge in outer and inner experience, in sensation and reflection, but he made reflection entirely dependent upon sensation.[47]

An opposing theory of education grew out of the philosophy of Rousseau. It opposed standardization of rules for education and rested heavily upon nature to direct its own development. Rousseau stated his educational theories very plainly in the *Emile*, which has been a manual for so-called "progressives" ever since. He shifted the emphasis from the subject matter to the individual being taught. To him, a teacher's function was to assist mental growth which had its impulse from within, and could not succeed unless the laws of nature were obeyed.[48]

Although Rousseau seemed to be in conflict with Locke, according to Boyd, this doctrine was an outgrowth of the theories of the Rationalists: "This is substantially the doctrine stated vaguely and hesitatingly by Locke, that education can only be effective when adapted to the learner; but whereas in Locke the reference to the internal factors in education was casual, here it is fundamental." [49]

The educators who followed Rousseau were eager to liberalize the curriculum—adding more science, modern languages and literature. They did not hold with the idea that the Classics should be held inviolate because they satisfied the need for mental discipline. Their methods of teaching were different also. They followed natural laws rather than a mental discipline which emphasized rules and mechanics.

THE RISE OF TWO SCHOOLS OF ELOCUTION. The development of conflicting educational theories had a tremendous influence on all subjects in the educational system and on culture itself. Smith has

[47] Boyd, William. *From Locke to Montessori.* p. 26, 28.
[48] Rousseau, Jean Jacques. *Emile.* tr. by Barbara Foxley. vol. 1. p. 5-7.
[49] Boyd. *op. cit.* p. 45.

aptly summarized their growth and importance in the following paragraph:

Doubtless the growing confidence in the powers of the human understanding, the enthronement of reason on the seat once held by authority and tradition, the conquest by science and politics over philosophy, and theology, the triumph of reason over superstition, intolerance, and despotism, the education of the masses in the new world-view, and the final decline of rationalism before the assault of neglected emotions and under the solvent of self-critical analysis and subjectivism —doubtless all this is the supremely important revolution of the eighteenth century.[60]

Rhetoric responded to these educational changes and allowed one of its parts, *pronuntiatio*, to develop into an important English subject called Elocution. Elocution in turn was taught by teachers adhering to the two principal theories of the day. Thus the Natural school under the leadership of Thomas Sheridan followed natural laws, and the Mechanical school under the leadership of John Walker emphasized rules and mechanics. It may be inexact to say that they followed Locke and Rousseau, but they did follow the two opposing ideas concerning methods of teaching.

It follows that the study of Oral Interpretation, because of its origins in the *rhetoric* and *poetic* of the ancients, was naturally a part of the liberal arts curriculum as it was transplanted from England to the colonies. It appeared first in the form of declamations,—as a part of college exercises which were closely related to rhetoric. Later in the period, it became a more independent form of study called *Elocution*, and was concerned with teaching techniques in reading and reciting of English prose and poetry. Two schools evolved which were alike in many ways but with different emphases in their plans for training. The Natural School followed Thomas Sheridan's ideas; the Mechanical School derived from the theories of John Walker.

[60] Smith. *op. cit.* p. 3.

CHAPTER II

ENGLISH TEACHERS DEVELOP ELOCUTION

THE TWO LEADERS

THOMAS SHERIDAN. Thomas Sheridan was born in Dublin in 1719. His father was a schoolmaster and aspired to make his son one also. Sheridan's first interest was the stage. However, he spent a good many years as a teacher of elocution. Although he was both actor and manager in theaters in Dublin and London, his name is famous in the theater chiefly as the father of Richard Brinsley Sheridan who wrote the comedies of manners, *The School for Scandal* and *The Rivals*.

In 1756, he became a teacher of elocution. He lectured successfully for ten years in London, Bristol, Bath, Oxford, Cambridge, and Edinburgh. Later he appeared occasionally on the stage and also gave programs of readings for the entertainment of London audiences.[1]

His books on elocution were written in connection with his work as a lecturer. The earliest writing was a pamphlet entitled, *Discourse Delivered in the Theatre at Oxford . . . being Introductory to his Course of Lectures on Elocution and the English Language.* In this introduction he made mention of the earlier writers, among them Dryden, Milton, Clarendon, Locke, Addison, Berkeley, and Swift, who had complained about the neglect of the English language but had suggested few remedies. The fault, Sheridan felt, lay in the fact that the English did not study their language and did not study elocution. They taught Latin but not English speech and did not realize that spoken language was more important than written language. Prejudice he felt had prevented the development of "just rules for elocution" and in his lectures, he proposed to state such rules as the art required [2]

His *Course of Lectures on Elocution* was published in 1763 and became a popular textbook in England and America. In Lecture I, Sheridan sets forth his thesis that good delivery is based upon natural conversational style:

There cannot be a better clue to guide us to the source of the malady complained of, (poor delivery) than a due attention to an observation before made: "That there are few persons, who, in private company, do not deliver their sentiments with propriety and force in their manner, whenever they speak in earnest." Consequently here is a sure standard fixed for propriety and force

---

[1] *Dictionary of National Biography.* vol. 18. p. 887-8.
[2] Sheridan, Thomas. *Discourse Delivered in the Theatre at Oxford. . . Being Introductory to his Course of Lectures on Elocution and the English Language.* p. 1-45 *passim.*

in public speaking; which is, only to make use of the same manner in the one, as in the other.[3]

Throughout the lectures, Sheridan warns against artificialities in speaking. In the opening lecture, he expresses regret that there are no proper symbols to designate changes in inflection, or to indicate pauses and stops exactly, but he is of the opinion that such symbols are of assistance chiefly to children and not to adults.[4]

His *Lectures on the Art of Reading* appeared in 1775 and included an analysis of the sounds of the English language. He, in a way, anticipated the theories that were later proposed as explanatory of the origin of language, such as the "bow-wow" theory. He was extremely sensitive to the expressiveness of different sounds as will be seen in the following discussion:

> Besides these properties in words of sweetness or harshness, strength or weakness, there is another quality to be attended to which is, expression; or the peculiar aptness of some words to stand as symbols of certain ideas preferably to others. And this aptness arises from different causes: the first and most striking is that of imitation; from which proceed those that may be called mimical sounds; such as the baa of sheep, the hiss of serpents, the mew and purr of cats. . . . After these mimical words whose whole sounds are nearly the same with those formed by the several animals from which they were taken, there is another class which bears a fainter resemblance, merely from some letters contained in them, which were borrowed from the animal world. Thus among the vowels, the *aw* was borrowed from the crow, the *a* from the goat. . . .[5]

This interest in words and sounds was continued and in 1780 he published the *General Dictionary of the English Language,* which was the first to give attention to pronunciation. He showed interest in Dr. Johnson's dictionary which was published in 1775 and even succeeded in getting a grant of money for the work. In the *Dictionary of National Biography,* Sheridan is listed as an actor and orthoepist and, no doubt, he was better known in England, at least, in these two capacities than as an elocutionist.

His *Rhetorical Grammar* was published in 1781 and the *Works of Swift with Life* in eighteen volumes was published in 1784. Swift was his godfather and exerted great influence upon him. In fact, he seems to have had contact with most of the eminent men of his day.[6]

[3] Sheridan, Thomas. *Course of Lectures on Elocution.* p. 19.
[4] *Ibid.* p. 22-34 *passim.*
[5] Sheridan, Thomas. *Lectures on the Art of Reading.* vol. 1. ſ. 75, 76.
[6] *Dictionary of National Biography.* vol. 20. p. 531.

JOHN WALKER. John Walker's life paralleled Sheridan's in many ways. He was an actor and lexicographer, and he too gave lectures on elocution.

Walker was born in 1732 in Middlesex. His parents died when he was very young and he suffered no interference when he decided to become an actor. He played with Garrick as the second lead in Drury Lane while Garrick was manager there. He also played in Dublin where his *Brutus* and *Cato* were spoken of in terms of high commendation. His wife was an actress and they played together in Covent Garden in 1762.

In 1771, he began to give lectures on elocution, and from that time on made this his chief profession. He made professional tours of Scotland and Ireland as well as England. He met with such success at Oxford that the heads of the houses invited him to give private lectures in the university. He wrote a half dozen books on speaking and a grammar and a dictionary, which along with his lectures, were said to have made him a fortune.[7]

His most famous book on elocution was *Elements of Elocution* published in 1781. It is filled with rules for pause, inflection, modulation, and gestures, and shows clearly the great interest which Walker had in developing a mechanical·system for speech. In 1783 *Hints for Improvement in the Art of Reading* appeared. *The Rhetorical Grammar* was published in 1785 and dedicated to Dr. Johnson. Although Walker considered his book a great contribution to rhetoric, it was chiefly interested in delivery, and according to Sandford, was not important to rhetoric. In Sandford's summary of it he says:

The Rhetorical Grammar, 1785, was claimed by Walker to be, with the additions from Ward, Gibbons, and Blair, "the most perfect of its kind in the language." The first edition contained, in addition to the material on delivery taken from the *Elements of Elocution*, an explanation of the tropes and figures of speech, taken from Gibbons, to which was added, of course, a set of rules for the correct delivery of each. The third edition contained additional material, as follows: a discussion of the circumflex inflection, based on Walker's *Melody of Speaking Delineated,* a series of excerpts from Ward and Priestley on invention, and a discussion of the parts of speech, abstracted from Blair. This hodge-podge of material constituted Walker's so-called "perfect work."[8]

In the *Melody of Speaking Delineated or Elocution Taught Like Music by Visible Signs,* 1787, Walker discussed inflection at length and added the circumflex which he claimed to have discovered. He also proposed a system of marks which he used in the later editions of *Elements of Elocution. The Academic Speaker,* a collection of

[7] *Dictionary of National Biography.* p. 532.
[8] Sandford. *op. cit.* p. 179.

"parliamentary debates, orations, odes, scenes, and speeches from the best writers, proper to be read and recited by youth at school," was published in 1801. *The Teachers' Assistant in English Composition* appeared in 1802, and *Outlines in English Grammar* in 1810.

Walker was a lexicographer and probably best known for his dictionary, *A Critical Pronouncing Dictionary of the English Language* which was published in 1791 and went into the 28th edition in 1826.[9]

COMMON BACKGROUND AND DIVERGENT DEVELOPMENT OF THEORIES.   Many parallels can be seen in the lives of these two men who are now considered to be the leaders of the two schools of speech, the Natural and the Mechanical.   They had the same background— they were both actors, lexicographers, and teachers of elocution. Their motivation for contributing toward the growth of the Elocutionary Movement was the same.   They attempted to answer the criticisms directed toward rhetoric, which indicated a neglect of the English language especially in its oral form; they were interested in making the language more permanent.   Sandford mentions both influences and says of the latter:

Another influence which aided in beginning the movement was the eighteenth-century interest in the study of the language, and particularly in correct pronunciation.   It was an age of dictionary-making, when men were trying to fix the language and to determine correct pronunciation, and it is not surprising that two of the leading elocutionists, Sheridan and Walker, were also dictionary-makers.   The marking of correct accent and vowel sounds in the dictionaries naturally led to the attempt to make correct inflections, pauses, and the like, in selections for drill in speaking.[10]

They both considered speech to be an art and the formulation of rules necessary for improving the techniques used.   There was no exact language with which to describe effective speaking and reading. The fact that they were both actors probably made them especially sensitive to the ephemeral character of speech and the relative impermanence of the art of the theater in comparison with other art forms.

Sheridan would have been content to find the basic principles and to work from them.   In the discourse introductory to his lectures he says:

Since therefore, nothing can be done without art, and all art is founded upon principles, and should be taught by rules, the first necessary step is, to trace the principles of elocution.   Those once discovered, to establish upon them a system of rules, peculiarly adapted to the English tongue, whereby the art

9 *Dictionary of National Biography.* p. 532.
10 Sandford. *op. cit.* p. 169-70.

of elocution may be as regularly acquired as any other art now is, and a knowledge of English, so far as regards elocution, methodically obtained.[11]

Walker demanded a much more detailed system of rules as is indicated in the following excerpt from *The Rhetorical Grammar*:

> Speaking, it is presumed, cannot be more successfully taught, than by referring us to such rules as instruct in the art of reading. The art of reading is that system of rules which teaches us to pronounce written composition with justness, energy, variety, and ease. Agreeably to this definition, reading may be considered as that species of delivery which not only expresses the sense of an author, so as barely to be understood, but which, at the same time, gives it all that force, beauty, and variety, of which it is susceptible: the first of these considerations belongs to grammar, and the last to rhetoric.[12]

Walker would probably have agreed with Sheridan's definition of a "just delivery," which consisted in "a distinct articulation of words, pronounced in proper tones, suitably varied to the sense, and the emotions of the mind; with due observation of accent; of emphasis, in its several gradations; of rest or pauses of the voice in proper places and well-measured degrees of time; and the whole accompanied with expressive looks and significant gesture."[13] Nevertheless, his methods for directing students in developing a good delivery seem to differ greatly from those of Sheridan who took his cues from nature. Walker's rules for inflection and pause, for example, are based on grammatical forms used in the English language.

It would seem, however, that the antithesis which later teachers and textbook writers saw between the theories of the two men and the schools which developed from them was not so evident at the beginning. Walker merely contributed to the development of the Elocutionary Movement in the teaching of rhetoric. His many rules for the slightest variation in inflection or in bodily action were purported to come from a study of nature. His notations, which attempted to record permanently the variations in inflection, were in line with earlier efforts, especially those of Joshua Steele, to transcribe speech in a fashion similar to that used in recording music. Walker's theories developed from those of Sheridan rather than entirely in opposition to them. A theory evolved until in its flowering it looked so dissimilar to its original self that those who interpreted it found two distinct and opposing theories.

[11] Sheridan, Thomas. *Discourse Delivered in the Theatre at Oxford. . . Being Introductory to his Course of Lectures on Elocution and the English Language.* p. 50.
[12] Walker, John. *The Rhetorical Grammar.* p. 48.
[13] Sheridan, Thomas. *Course of Lectures on Elocution.* p. 25-6.

OTHER ELOCUTIONISTS OF THE PERIOD

There were other elocutionists besides Sheridan and Walker, in this early period, whose work was significant. Some of them wrote textbooks which were used in our colleges and universities; some exerted a great influence upon our American writers. Burgh, Scott, and Austin exerted the greatest influence in America. The textbooks of the first two were published in America, and Austin was quoted by practically all American writers on elocution in the next period. Rice, Cockin, and Steele, although we have no proof that they contributed directly to the teaching of speech in this country, were an important part of the Elocutionary Movement in England which should be viewed as a whole in any analysis of the influence it exerted upon our teachers and the methods they used in teaching elocution. Porter was the only American to make a significant contribution to this subject and that at the end of the period under consideration. The order which follows is chronological.

JAMES BURGH. James Burgh's one book on elocution was published in 1762, a year before Sheridan's *Course of Lectures on Elocution*. It was reprinted in 1792 and American editions for 1785, 1795, 1800, 1804 are extant, so it must have been a popular textbook. It carried the elaborate title of *The Art of Speaking, containing an Essay in which are given Rules for Expressing properly the Principal Passions and Humours, which occur in Reading, or Public Speaking, taken from the Ancients and Moderns; exhibiting a variety of matter for Practice; the Emphatical Words printed in Italics; with notes of Direction referring to the Essay*. It is usually referred to as *The Art of Reading*, but the complete title is significant because it shows the emphasis upon the expression of the passions which was Burgh's chief interest. His appeal was first to the clergy whom he felt should use what the ancients had called "pathetic proof," the appeal to the emotions of the audience.

He began in much the same manner as that which Sheridan used, deploring the fact that the English language was not spoken properly. In the following quotation he voices a plea for it since it is a superior language.

Whoever imagines the English tongue unfit for *oratory* has not a just notion of it . . . in oratory and poetry, there is no tongue, ancient or modern, capable of expressing a greater *variety* of humours, or passions, by its *sounds* (I am not speaking of its copiousness, as to *phraseology*) than the English.

* * *

It is greatly to our shame, that, while *we* do so little for the improvement of our language, and of our manner of speaking it in public, the *French* should take so much pains in both these respects, though *their* language is very much *inferior* to *ours*, both as to emphasis and copiousness.[1]

Although Sheridan and Burgh agreed as to need for training, Burgh prescribed much more mechanical methods. He felt that the child should be taught to pay as much regard to the stops as to the words; he should learn to use varied inflection, to emphasize important words, to fill the room with his voice, to read rapidly matter in parentheses, commas, or brackets, to begin in the proper key and loudness, and to increase the force and raise the pitch as the passions dictated.[2] A great amount of space in the book is devoted to the discussion of the ability of the body to express numerous different moods and emotions which range from mirth to anger, intoxication, dotage, and death. A detailed description of each one is given, as well as the injunction that every orator should practice all of them in order that he may use any one which his speech demands.

These mechanical rules for action recall a much earlier book on gesture, probably the earliest one written in English, John Bulwer's *Chirologia* and *Chironomia* published in 1644.[3] In this book sixty-four gestures of the fingers are described in the *Chirologia* or the "Naturall Language of the Hand," while in *Chironomia* or the "Art of Manual Rhetorick," fifty "canons of rhetoricians touching the Artificiall Managing of the Hand in speaking" and thirty canons of the fingers are explained. Examples of the canons of gesture are as follows:

Canon XVII. The *Hand* brought to the stomacke, and spread gently thereon, is a gesture of Rhetoricall *asseveration*.

Canon XIX. The *Hand* rais'd and stretched out with the arme, or the *Hand* waved towards the auditors, are advantageous actions for them who would imply a *generous confidence*, and their *authortie* and *abilitie to effect a thing*: it serves also to *call* for, and *demand silence*, and for the *prologue* to an act of pacification.[4]

In addition, there were cautions which rested upon traditional rules which were evidently commonly understood and practiced although not

---

[1] Burgh, James. *The Art of Speaking.* p. 6.
[2] *Ibid.* p. 8-16 *passim.*
[3] Sandford. *op. cit.* p. 115.
[4] Bulwer, John. "Chironomia" in *Chirologia . . . Chironomia*, p. 39, 41.

written into a textbook. There were thirty-two of these cautions of which the following are typical:

Caution VI. Gesture doth with most conformity to Art, begin at the left Hand, the sentence beginning together from the left side, but is put off and laid downe at the *Right Hand*, together with the end of the sentence.

Caution X. To raise the *Hand* above the Eye, or to let it fall beneath the Breast, or to fetch it down from the Head to the lower belly, are accounted vicious misdemeanors in the *Hand*: yet the masters of this faculty doe grant a toleration sometimes to raise the *Hand* above the Head, for the better expressing of a just indignation, or when we call God, the Courteours of Heaven, or the Common people of the Skies to witnesse.

Caution XII. No gesture that respects the rule of Art, directs it selfe to the hinder parts; yet other-whiles the *Hand* being as it were cast backe, is free from this prohibition: for whereas there are seven parts of motion, To the *Right Hand*, To the left, upwards, downwards, forward, backward, and circular, the first five are only allowed a Rhetorician.

Caution XXVI. The *Left Hand* of it selfe alone, is most incompetent to the performance of any perfect action. . . .[5]

According to Sandford, no one had the temerity to improve upon Bulwer until Burgh wrote his *Art of Speaking* over a century later.

Burgh noted other bodily action besides that of the hand and proceeded on the assumption that nature expressed emotion in the same manner in all people. He believed in studying nature but he standardized the action so that it could be imitated. The following example is a typical one:

Mirth, or *laughter, opens* the *mouth* still *more* toward the ears; *crisps* the *nose; lessens* the *aperture* of the *eyes,* and sometimes fills them with *tears;* shakes and *convulses* the whole *frame;* giving considerable pain, which occasions *holding* the *sides.*[6]

The selections for practice contain marginal directions for the expression of the proper emotions and italicize the important words to be emphasized.

WILLIAM COCKIN. *The Art of Delivering Written Language,* published in 1775, shows Cockin to be even more apprehensive than Sheridan concerning mechanical methods. Cockin believed that nature had made a definite distinction between original speech and "repeated speech,"—the latter being inferior to the former and much subdued emotionally in comparison. He stated, in this connection, that mimicry should be refused a place among the modes of useful delivery, and that the natural manner of reading which became a

[5] *Ibid.* p. 133-42 *passim.*
[6] Burgh. *op. cit.* p. 18.

simple and unpretentious one, in which the emotions were much diluted, should be adopted. His explanation follows:

We must then attribute this *vanishing of all gesture and expression of countenance to nature*; who in a situation of the kind alluded to, does neither require their appearance, nor that of *expressive tones* in any striking degree, if at all: for if we grant that the signs of the emotions have, and ought to have, a significant reference to our situation, we may easily see a difference in the state of a person's mind, when unfolding his warm interested sentiments, and when reading them over again to oblige a friend. . . .[7]

He did say, however, that reading was the "art of delivering written language with propriety, force, and elegance" and that the meaning determined the pauses, modulation, and the "signs of the emotions." He evidently feared artificiality which might come with too much attention to the outward expression of the meaning and for that reason demanded this very simple and natural style. The following excerpt from his definition of good reading will make clear his attitude on method:

. . . all the Signs of the Emotions are in *quality* the same as they would flow spontaneously from nature, but abated something in *quantity,* and those most, which are in themselves of the disagreeable kind: Where the Emphasis of Force, Ornamental Cadences, the quantity of the above-named variations from natural speech, pronunciation, and some other less material particulars, are directed by Taste and Custom:—and (lastly) where affectation of every sort is to be dreaded as the greatest blemish, and where Ease, Masterliness, and Genuine Grace are considered as principal beauties, and the proper substitutes for the inferior degree of warmth and energy, which the delivery of written language ought always to discover, when compared with the extemporary effusions of the heart.[8]

JOSHUA STEELE. One of the problems which early writers considered was the lack of an exact language with which to describe effective speaking and the absence of any means by which this art could be recorded and made relatively permanent. Joshua Steele's contribution was important because his *Prosodia Rationalis,* published in 1775, set forth his attempt to work out notations which would represent certain vocal phenomena. He was really looking for instruments such as the modern phonetic alphabet and the recording machines which teachers of interpretation of literature use today, when he said:

What very great advantages might arise to the lingual and literary commerce of the world, by a set of learned men sitting down under respectable authority to reform the alphabet so as to make it contain distinct elementary sounds of

[7] Cockin, William. *The Art of Delivering Written Language.* p. 12.
[8] *Ibid.* p. 141-2.

the European languages, at least; in doing which, the difficulty would be infinitely overbalanced by the great and general utility. . . . We have heard of Betterton, Booth, and Wilks, and some of us have seen Quin; the portraits of their persons are probably preserved, but no models of their elocution remain; nor any proofs except vague assertions and arbitrary opinions, to decide on the comparative merits in the way of their profession, between them and the moderns. Had some of the celebrated speeches from Shakespeare been noted and accented as they spoke them, we should be able now to judge, whether the oratory of our stage is improved or debased. If the method, here essayed, can be brought into familiar use, the types of modern elocution may be transmitted to posterity as accurately as we have received the musical compositions of Corelli.[9]

His elaborate system was based upon the notations used in music and presented symbols for accent, quantity, pause, emphasis, and force. He deserves consideration for his efforts to solve the problem of the impermanence of speech and the difficulties encountered in teaching it, even though his system and those that were patterned on it gave rise to mechanical methods which are questioned in the light of modern educational theory.

WILLIAM SCOTT. William Scott's *Lessons in Elocution, or a Selection of Pieces in Prose and Verse for the Improvement of Youth in Reading and Speaking* appeared first in England in 1779 and in America in 1795. There were later editions here in 1815 and 1817 which would indicate that it was a fairly popular textbook. Scott acknowledged both Walker and Burgh as his sources but went beyond them in working out mechanical methods. He suggested that the right arm be raised at the beginning of a sentence and lowered at the end, and the left arm be raised for the next sentence and this method of alternating action from one side to the other continued throughout the speech. He also advocated imitation of the teacher.[10] Both techniques were undoubtedly considered classroom techniques only. The following excerpt from his directions for teaching will illustrate the extreme form his methods took:

If the pupil's knees are not well formed or incline inwards, he must be taught to keep his legs at as great a distance as possible, and to incline his body so much to that side on which the arm is extended, as to oblige him to rest the opposite leg upon the toe; and this will in a great measure hide the defect of his make. . . .

At first it may not be improper for the teacher, after placing the pupil in the position, to stand some distance, exactly opposite to him in the same position, the right and left sides only reversed; while the student is speaking to show him, by example, the action he is to make use of.[11]

[9] Steele, Joshua. *Prosodia Rationalis*. p. xiii, xiv.
[10] Scott, William. *Lessons in Elocution*. p. 10.
[11] *Ibid*. p. 15, 19.

His attention to deep breathing as important to reading is rather unique for this period, and his discussion of it is much like those to be found in the books written during the next period.

In order to acquire a forcible manner of pronouncing your words, inure yourself while reading, to draw in as much air as your lungs can contain with ease, and to expel it with vehemence, in uttering those sounds which require an emphatical pronunciation; read aloud in the open air, and with all the exertion you can command; preserve your body in an erect attitude while you are speaking; let all the consonant sounds be expressed with a full impulse or percussion of the breath, and a forcible action of the organs employed in forming them; and let all the vowel sounds have a full and bold utterance. Practice these with perseverance 'till you have acquired strength and energy of speech.[12]

REV. GILBERT AUSTIN.   Rev. Gilbert Austin was interested primarily in gesture and followed the tendency of the time in devising notations for any variation in expression.   His book, *Chironomia; or a Treatise on Rhetorical Delivery: Comprehending many precepts both Ancient and Modern for the proper regulation of the Voice, the Countenance, and Gesture,* was published in 1806.   It was an expensive book because of the one hundred and twenty-two steel engravings which illustrated so handsomely all of the positions of the body indicated by symbols.   It followed very naturally Bulwer's work of 1644 and Burgh's of 1762, merely adding to their work analyses of bodily action as an expression of the passions.   Bulwer had used pictures of the hand and fingers to illustrate the different gestures described, whereas Austin progressed to the use of pictures of the whole body using different symbols to indicate the hand, arm, and foot movements.

Austin justified the primary attention being given to gesture by quoting a long list of ancient and modern authorities.   Among them were Isocrates, Demosthenes, Cicero, and Dionysius of Halicarnassus representing the ancients; and Addison, Sheridan, Walker, Burke, Blair, and Fenelon representing the moderns.   His point of view must have been accepted by many, for although his book was too expensive to be used as a textbook, it was the source for most of the discussions of gesture written during the period (1827-1870).[13]

REV. EBENEZER PORTER.   The only significant contribution to elocution by an American during this period was made by Rev. Ebenezer Porter.   Porter was the president of Andover Theological Seminary and wrote two books to be used by the students in this

[12] *Ibid.* p. 47.
[13] Austin, Gilbert. *Chironomia.* Ch. 4.

institution and other similar ones. First, a pamphlet entitled *Analysis of Vocal Inflection as used in Reading and Speaking* was written in 1824. A book, *Analysis of Principles of Rhetorical Delivery as Applied in Reading and Speaking,* published in 1826, was really an enlargement of the pamphlet. In it he states that the students who found great obscurity in Walker's *Elements of Elocution* would understand them more readily by using his simple classification of Walker's principles.[14] He adhered to the principles of Walker but quarrelled with many of his ideas and was in many ways closer to Sheridan in his methods. *The Rhetorical Reader,* according to the title page, went through its 220th edition in 1835. This fact may be more imposing than it should be, because there is no information concerning the number of books published in any of the editions. However, the conclusion that the first American textbooks were popular seems justified. They are written in a clear and readable fashion and seem less academic and more like a guide to instruction than the books previously mentioned.

Porter's definition of elocution is simply: "Elocution, which anciently embraces style, and the whole art of rhetoric, now signifies manner of delivery, whether of our own thoughts or those of others." [15]

Although he believed rules necessary and some notations helpful, he simplified the methods used as much as possible. His chief criticism of Walker was concerned with the complexity of his system.

> This is the point on which, most of all, Walker is defective. The conviction that he was treating a difficult subject, led him to the very common mistake of attempting to make his meaning plain by prolixity of remark, and multiplicity of rules. One error of this respectable writer is, that he attempts to carry the application too far. To think of reducing to exact system all the inflections to be employed in the delivery of plain language, where there is no emotion, and no emphasis, is idle indeed. Many who have attemped to follow the theory to this extreme, perplexed by the endless list of rules which it occasions, have become discouraged. Whereas the theory is of no use except in reference to the *rhetorical* principles of language, where tones express sentiment. And even in passages of this sort, the significant inflections belong only to a few words, which, being properly spoken, determine of necessity the manner of *speaking the rest.*[16]

Porter made a distinction between what he called "correct reading" and "rhetorical reading"; the first was adapted to material which

[14] Porter, Ebenezer. *Analysis of Vocal Inflections as Used in Reading and Speaking.* (pamphlet) editor's note.
[15] Porter, Ebenezer. *Analysis of Principles of Rhetorical Delivery as Applied in Reading and Speaking.* p. 19.
[16] Porter, Ebenezer. *Analysis of Vocal Inflections as Used in Reading and Speaking.* p. 9.

contained no emotion and required technique involving distinctness and intelligibility alone. Previous writers had not made that distinction clear. Since the minister had to make an emotional appeal, his interest centered on rhetorical reading. In his discussion of rules, it is clear that he believed with the Natural school that the emotion should come from within, but because of the bad training or lack of it in the preparatory schools, he found rules necessary to develop a good delivery. In the preface to his book, *Analysis of the Principles of Rhetorical Delivery as Applied in Reading and Speaking,* he makes the following statement of his position:

> As an instructor of theological students, my attention was, many years ago, called to some prevalent defects in delivery. These I ascribed chiefly to early habits, contracted in the schools; and to the want of adequate precepts in books on reading and speaking. The worst faults in elocution, originate in *want of feeling.* But when these faults become confirmed, no degree of feeling will fully counteract their influence, without the aid of analysis and patient effort to understand and correct them. Still, in the process of correction there is danger of running into formality of manner, by withdrawing the attention from that in which the soul of eloquence consists—emotion.[17]

Because he was able to make the theories of the English elocutionists practical, his textbooks were very popular. In the advertisement announcing a new and enlarged edition of *The Rhetorical Reader* in 1843, the statement is made that the book had passed through more than three hundred editions and that it was used in every state in the union. It was designed for high schools and academies, was bound in leather, contained 312 pages, and was sold for sixty-three cents. It is, according to a modern reviewer, not a curiosity, but a remarkably modern book.[18]

OTHER CONTRIBUTIONS. There were other contributions in the form of collections of selections for practice and some variations on the theories of the elocutionists which have already been considered. William Enfield's *Speaker,* 1784, resembled Scott's *Lessons in Elocution.* William Kendrick discussed the "oratorial accent" and recommended imitation, rather than the use of rules, in his *Rhetorical Grammar,* published in 1784. Thomas Knox published *Hints to Public Speakers* in 1797, and gave rules for expressing the passions and for controlling the breath. John Wilson's *Principles of Elocution,* 1799, was another book of selections prefaced with rules. William Mayor in his *New Speaker,* 1801, offered rules for enunciation or

[17] Porter, Ebenezer. *Analysis of the Principles of Rhetorical Delivery as Applied in Reading and Speaking.* preface, p. 1.
[18] Ewbank, Henry L. *"The Rhetorical Reader by Ebenezer Porter." Quarterly Journal of Speech Education.* 13:474 (1927).

delivery and a system of rhetoric which rested heavily upon Blair's *Lectures.* John Thelwall wrote a number of books with rather new theories concerning adaptation of the elocutionary theories: *Oration on the Influence of Elocution on Martial Enthusiasm,* 1805 ; *Plan and Terms of Instruction for the Cure of Impediments of Speech,* 1809 ; *Vestibule of Eloquence,* 1810 ; *Illustrations of Rhythmus, being Selections for the Illustration of the Course of Instructions in the Rhythmus and utterance of the English Language; with an Introductory Essay on the Application of Rhythmical Science to the Treatment of Impediments, and the Improvement of our National Oratory,* 1811. Thelwall's work was based upon Walker, but the emphasis upon rhythm and the therapeutic values were an interesting development which has had many successors.   Others who made contributions were: John Sabine, who wrote the *Guide to Elocution,* 1807 ; John Button, who published *Exercises in Elocution* in 1809 ; Thomas Carpenter, whose *School Speaker* appeared in 1813 ; Benjamin Smart, whose book *The Practice of Elocution,* 1826, used a system of numbering the emotions and using the numbers above the words in selections; and A. C. Bloomfield Spalding whose *Portal to Rhetorical Delivery,* 1826, emphasized attitude and gesture in the manner of Austin.   These contributions, although not important in comparison with those before mentioned, are an indication of the extent of the Elocutionary Movement in England.[19]

[19] Sandford. *op. cit.* p. 182-3.

CHAPTER III

AN ANALYSIS OF THE METHODS
USED IN TEACHING

It has been necessary to depend entirely upon textbooks of the period for information concerning the methods used in teaching. Most of the discussions of technique sound academic and impractical to the modern reader. However, when the Elocutionary School is viewed in its own background and is not compared with present-day schools too closely, the textbooks which it produced become more understandable and consequently more remarkable. It was the first school of oral expression which placed *pronuntiatio,* or delivery, in the foreground and laid a foundation for the teaching of what is now known as *Oral Interpretation of Literature.* Since it was a new development in rhetoric, it is small wonder that so much space was given over to the defense of the subject itself and to the explanation of the different aspects of speech. Five rather general divisions: accent and emphasis, pitch and modulation, pause and timing, articulation and pronunciation, and gesture can be found in most of the textbooks mentioned. These are used as the basis for analysis of the methods used in teaching.

ACCENT AND EMPHASIS. The terms *accent* and *emphasis* are common to all the early texts, but the discussions lead in different directions especially in the explanation of accent. Grammarians and elocutionists alike were interested in discovering what the grave and acute accent meant in classical poetry. Fritz states that Charles Butler, a seventeenth-century grammarian of Magdalen College, Oxford, was the first to use the words "acute" and "grave" in relation to accent.[1] This rather academic interest was evident in the textbooks of elocution and affected the methods prescribed for gaining emphasis.

Sheridan found accent as simple as an emphasis on words and disagreed with the majority of writers who were determined to make it complicated. He used only the grave accent mark which indicated stress on the syllable.

The meaning of that term (accent) was very different amongst the Ancients from what it is with us. Amongst them we know that accents marked certain inflexions of the voice like musical notes; and the grammarians to this day, with great formality inform their pupils, that the acute accent, is the raising

[1] Fritz, Charles Andrew. "From Sheridan to Rush." *Quarterly Journal of Speech.* 16:75 (1930).

of the voice on a certain syllable; the grave, a depression of it; and the circumflex, a raising and depression both, in one and the same syllable. This jargon they constantly preserve, tho' they have no sort of ideas annexed to these words; for if they are asked to shew how this is to be done, they cannot tell, and their practice always belies their precept. The truth is, the Ancients did observe this distinction, because we have it on the authority of all their writers, who have treated on the subject; but the manner in which they did it must remain for ever a secret to us; for with the living tongue, perished the tones also, which we in vain endeavor to seek for in their visible marks. . . . The term with us has no reference to inflexions of the voice, or musical notes, but only means a peculiar manner of distinguishing one syllable of a word from the rest, denominated by us accent; and the term for that reason used by us in the singular number.[2]

Sheridan related emphasis to accent and explained that emphasis discharged the same kind of office in sentences that accent did in words.[3] The suggestion of method to be used in simple emphasis is in line with the tenets of the "follow nature" school.

. . . It is certain that every man, who comprehends what he says in private discourse, never fails to lay the emphasis on the right word; when therefore he is about to read, or repeat the words of others, or his own, in public, let him only reflect on the place, where he would lay the emphasis, supposing these words had proceeded from the immediate sentiments of his own mind, in private discourse.[4]

John Rice, another English elocutionist, disagreed with Sheridan in that he included quantity as a factor in accent. He states his opinion:

That *Accent*, in English, is neither the Tone of an articulate Voice, nor simply the Time taken up in the Utterance of it: nor merely the Force or Loudness of such Voices; but the whole Momentum or Quantity of Sound emitted to produce it.

That syllables being accented as variously as the Measures of their Length and Force can be combined, and the Measures of Syllables being considered as *long, neutral*, and *short*, there are two capital Distinctions in the Mode of accenting Syllables, viz., the *loud* and *soft*: The *former* belonging to the *short* Syllables, the *latter* to *long* ones.[5]

Rice explained that accent and consequently emphasis on words and syllables had been designed by the makers of language for the particular purpose of clarity—"to convey them more forcibly to the Ear, in order to present their meaning in a Stronger light to the Understanding."[6]

[2] Sheridan, Thomas. *Course of Lectures on Elocution.* p. 56, 58.
[3] *Ibid.* p. 77.
[4] *Ibid.* p. 89.
[5] Rice, John. *An Introduction to the Art of Reading with Energy and Propriety.* p. 82, 83.
[6] *Ibid.* p. 70.

In *Prosodia Rationalis, An Essay toward the establishing the Melody and Measure of Speech, to be expressed and perpetuated by certain symbols,* Joshua Steele proposed to extend to speech the symbolic method used in recording music. Since he was quite familiar with music, his notation for speech resembled that of music in a number of ways as the example shown later demonstrates. (See page 54) Emphasis he denoted by the following symbols: Δ for heavy ∴ for light, and .. for lightest, and for a common term, he used "poize." For accent he used acute /, grave \, and for both ∩ and U, all indicating loudness and softness and sliding of voice from one note to another.[7]

He did not believe that the English language could be governed by the rules for accent devised by the ancients, although he did feel that accent was present in the language and should be considered as stress.

"We have accents in English and syllabic accents too; but there is no change of tone in them; the voice is only raised more, so as to be louder upon one syllable than upon another."[8]

Going a step beyond Rice, Steele saw a relationship of rhythmical pattern to emphasis: "It is the office of *Rhythmus,* aided by the *influence* of this *instructive Poize* to regulate the whole duration of any melody or movement by an exactly equal and periodical pulsation, ... either quicker or slower."[9]

It is evident that Steele was not so much concerned with "poize" as it was applied in the pronunciation of one word, but rather as it was used to shape the rhythm of poetry, and that he considered duration a part of emphasis.

Walker disagreed with Sheridan and those who believed that accent was primarily stress. He held the opinion that accent marked inflection as well as emphasis. To him the "proper slide" was of prime importance because if it were preserved, the other distinctions of the voice were more easily attained.[10] Nevertheless, accent was related to emphasis, according to Walker, and his explanation for this relationship is similar to that of Sheridan in that he does not mention quantity:

Whatever inflection be adopted, the accented syllable is always a little louder than the rest; but if the accent be pronounced with a rising inflection, the accented syllable is higher than the preceding, and lower than the succeeding syllable; and if the accent have the falling inflection, the accented syllable is pronounced higher than any other syllable, either preceding or succeeding. The only exception to this is in the sentence where the accent is on the last syllable of a word which has no emphasis, and is pronounced as forming a cadence at the conclusion of the discourse.

[7] Steele, Joshua. *Prosodia Rationalis.* p. 24.
[8] *Ibid.* p. 117.
[9] *Loc. cit.*
[10] Walker, John. *Elements of Elocution.* preface. p. 9.

"Sooner or later virtue must meet with rewàrd." Here the last syllable, though pronounced louder than the first, is evidently a degree lower.[11]

Walker also explained the differences in the Irish, Scotch, and English speech in terms of accent. Since the word was capable of different inflections—acute, grave, and circumflex—yet able to retain the same emphasis, "accents" were formed by different groups speaking the same language. The following illustrations are given to show the variations:

Scotch—Èxercise and témperance stréngthen the constitútion.
Irish—Èxercise and tèmperance strèngthen the constitùtion.
English—Èxercise and témperance stréngthen the constitùtion.[12]

Not only was Walker the first to emphasize inflection, but he was the first to speak of "harmonic inflection," which later writers called "melody." [13] He considered inflection which was not for the sense but to please the ear a necessary source of variety especially in forming cadences. It might be well to explain that the use of the term "cadence," as far as the writer can discover, referred in the early textbooks only to the pattern of melody at the closing of a line, sentence, or paragraph. Since it will be impossible to give all the rules which Walker devised in his system of teaching, perhaps a few typical examples will suffice. Rule I, for the harmonic inflection is stated in this fashion:

When a series of similar sentences, or members of sentences, form a branch of a subject or paragraph; the last sentence or member must fall gradually into a lower tone, and adopt the harmonick inflection, on such words as form the most agreeable cadence.[14]

The explanation of his Plate II which is reproduced on the following page, reads:

In this table we find the rising and falling inflections very distinguishable in the long words and grow more and more imperceptible in the short ones; they are, however, no less real in one than in the other; as a good ear will easily perceive, by beginning at the long words, and repeating down to the short ones. From No. I to No. IX the contrasted words are rising at the comma, and falling at the note of interrogation; and from No. X to No. XVIII they are falling at the comma, and rising at the period.[15]

Emphasis, to Walker, implied the idea of contradistinction either expressed or understood:

Where the words are in contradistinction to other words, or to some sense implied we may call them emphatick; where they do not denote contradistinction,

[11] *Ibid.* p. 185.
[12] *Ibid.* p. 187.
[13] Fritz, Charles Andrew. "From Sheridan to Rush." *Quarterly Journal of Speech.* 16:75 (1930).
[14] Walker. *op. cit.* p. 248.
[15] *Ibid.* p. 84.

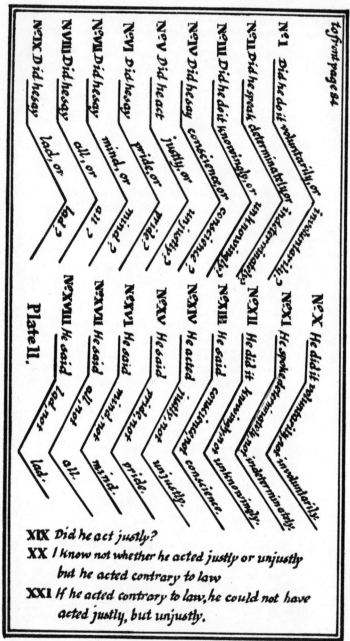

CHART SHOWING INFLECTION
From *The Elements of Elocution*, by John Walker

and yet are more important than the particles, we may call them accented, and the particles and lesser words unaccented or feeble. . . . Whenever the emphatick word points out a particular sense in the exclusion of some other sense, this emphatical word adopts the falling inflection. . . . If the emphasis does not exclude the antithesis, the emphatick word has the rising inflection.[16]

Porter did not agree to this idea and gives a much broader definition:

Emphasis is governed by the laws of sentiment, being inseparably associated with thought and emotion. . . . It is distinctive utterance of words which are especially significant, with such a degree and kind of stress, as conveys their meaning in the best manner.
According to this definition, I would include the whole subject under *emphatic stress and emphatic inflection.*[17]

In comparing the two leaders, we find that while Sheridan used only the grave accent to denote emphasis, Walker used the grave, acute, and circumflex to denote emphasis and inflection, and insisted upon a notation showing all three. Although they disagreed on the subject, they did believe in a relationship between accent and emphasis which had not been considered important before and which still continues to be observed.

PITCH AND MODULATION. The term *pitch* referred to the highness or lowness of the voice, as on the musical scale, and *modulation* had to do with the changes that were made in the pitch while speaking. *Key* was used to denote that pitch which was basic to any particular interpretation. For example, the key for a very happy selection would be higher than for one that was sad and heavy. The same definitions hold today.

There was a general agreement among writers that the natural pitch was the basis of all improvement in speaking, and that one of the chief faults was a confusion of pitch with intensity. The command "Speak louder" should not mean, "Speak in a higher pitch." Many elocutionists suggested that in order to avoid this difficulty, the speaker should begin on a pitch lower than his ordinary speech. Walker suggested that it was easier to regulate the pitch if one were speaking extempore, because if the pitch were too high, he could adopt an emotion which would require a low key, such as hatred, admonition, etc.[18]

This is an interesting example of the Mechanical school's emphasis on technique at the expense of everything else; no matter what the

[16] *Ibid.* p. 199, 206, 208.
[17] Porter, Ebenezer. *The Rhetorical Reader.* p. 39.
[18] Walker, John.   *Elements of Elocution.* p. 301.

subject of the extemporaneous speech should dictate as to delivery, if the pitch had risen to an undesirable height, the speaker had a right to feign hatred or shame to bring it down to normal.

The following quotation from Sheridan's *Lectures on the Art of Reading* gives the other point of view:

> The language of ideas is wholly arbitrary; that is, words which are the signs of our ideas, have no natural connexion with them, but depend purely upon convention, in the different societies of men. . . . But it is not so with regard to the language of emotions. Nature herself has taken care to frame that for the use of man; having annexed to every act and feeling of the mind, its peculiar tone, which spontaneously breaks forth, and excites in the minds of others, tuned invariably by the hand of nature in unison to those notes, analogous emotions.[19]

When this idea is put into a rule for reading, it becomes: "to reflect what tones he would use, and what time he would suspend his voice, were he to speak them as his own immediate sentiments." [20]

Monotony and mechanical variety were, according to Porter, the chief faults in connection with pitch. He suggested that if the student used emphasis properly, these difficulties would be aided. He should also cultivate a discrimination for vocal tones and inflections. In other words, he should work to improve his ear, just as the musician develops an ear for music.[21] To increase the range or compass, so that variety was possible, Walker suggested that the student select exercises which demanded certain notes for their interpretation and, if it were necessary for force and audibility, to practice the whole thing on the same pitch;—to "throw the voice into a monotone" until the pitch was easily attained at will.[22]

They all agreed that modulation was necessary, and Cockin stated that it would not only give pleasure to the ear but that it would be effective in preserving the attention, if properly used.[23] Although the audience-speaker relationship was not discussed, as it is in the books today, the techniques which they suggested were devised with the hearer in mind. In their treatment of pitch and modulation the elocutionists seemed to be extremely sensitive to the faults which are unpleasant to the auditor, such as faulty pitch, lack of variety, and unpleasant speech patterns. They tried to offer as many different kinds of selections as possible, in order to develop flexible voices. In this

---

[19] Sheridan, Thomas. *Lectures on the Art of Reading.* vol. 1. p. 151.
[20] Sheridan, Thomas. *Course of Lectures on Elocution.* p. 102.
[21] Porter, Ebenezer. *The Rhetorical Reader.* p. 47.
[22] Walker. *op. cit.* p. 286.
[23] Cockin, William. *The Art of Delivering Written Language.* p. 77.

connection, it may be interesting to read what John Mason said in 1751 in his essay on elocution:

An irregular or uneven Voice, is a great Fault in reading. That is, when the Voice rises and falls by Fits and Starts, or when it is elevated or depressed unnaturally or unseasonably, without Regard to Sense or Stops; or always beginning a Sentence with a high Voice and concluding it with a low one, or *vice versa*; or always beginning and concluding it with the same key.[24]

Steele, in his preface, presupposed the reader to have knowledge of music since it would be difficult to comprehend his notations without this background.[25] He noted the essential difference between singing and speaking as the sliding up and down of the speaking voice with no graduated distinctions between tones or semitones which can be measured by the ear, whereas, in singing, the voice ascends and descends through a variety of notes, as formally different from each other as the steps of a ladder. He worked out his notation accordingly.

Instead of using round or square heads for the notes to be marked on the scale (as in ordinary music) let us substitute sloping or curving lines such as the expression may require; as **/** or **** or **∩** or **U** ; which lines, when drawn on the foregoing scale will easily show through how many quarter tones the voice is to slide; and these I call the *accents* or *notes of melody.*[26]

In the illustration, the reader will notice that the tails of these notes express the difference of quantity and the markings below the scale indicate the force and emphasis. Other variations were also notated: "Therefore besides the characters which distinguish the variety of sound and of measure of time, there are others required to mark where the forte and piano should be expressed. The modern musicians have no other characters for these than the words themselves. However, they will be better supplied in our scheme by the asper **ʕ** and lenis **ʔ** of the Greeks, the crescendo, rinforzando or swell by ꜱꜱꜱꜱ; and the smorzando or dying away by ꜱꜱꜱꜱ." [27] The pauses or silence are shown by semibrief rest **ı**, minim rest **−**, crotchet rest **ʳ**, quaver rest **ʋ**, and what he termed cadence or emphasis in heavy **Δ** and light **∴** .[28] These last two markings were used by many of the textbooks which followed and the markings of the asper and lenis, the grave, acute, and circumflex may be found in modern textbooks in notations for the study of intonation.[29]

[24] Mason, John. *An Essay on Elocution.* p. 13.
[25] Steele, **Joshua.** *Prosodia Rationalis.* p. xiv.
[26] *Ibid.* p. 4, 7.
[27] *Ibid.* p. 12.
[28] *Ibid.* p. 24.
[29] See 1. Barber, Jonathan. *A Grammar of Elocution* (1830).
       2. Murdoch, James E. *Analytical Elocution.* p. 129 (1884).
       3. Woolbert, Charles H. *The Fundamentals of Speech.* p. 270-1 (1920).
       4. Davis. Estelle H. and Mammen Edward W. *The Spoken Word in Life and Art.* p. 268-81 (1935).

First manner. *Bombaſtic, by an exceſs in the extenſion of acute and grave, and of the piano and forte, and the tones not ſoſtenuto or equally ſupported.*

* *Ordinary walking meaſure.*

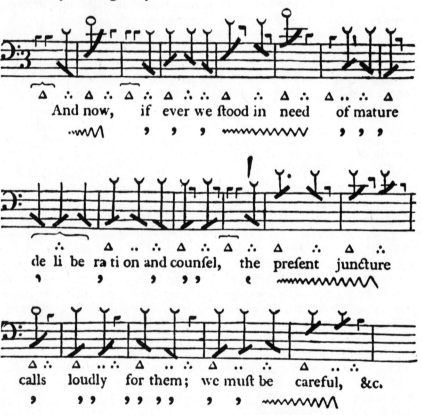

* *Walking meaſure* means, that the duration of the whole quantity of ſyllables and pauſes contained in *one cadence* (that is, as much as are marked between two bars), ſhould be equal to the time of making one ſtep of walking; which admits the varieties of *ſlow, ordinary,* and *quick walking*; the next degree above which, in velocity, is *running meaſure.*

EXAMPLE OF JOSHUA STEELE'S NOTATIONS
From *Prosodia Rationalis*

Joshua Steele was very proud of his contribution. He had not intended to write a textbook, but rather to answer the scholars of the day who were in opposition to him in his ideas concerning the accent and the melody of the English language. He very quaintly claims distinction for himself in the following statement:

In devising a scheme for expressing on paper the musical slides of the voice, in the melody of speech, I chose one which might come as near as possible to the modern notation of music, in order to make it easier to be comprehended by those, whose ideas of sounds and measure are already formed on that plan. I had no intention of imitating the figures of *Greek accents*; and yet by mere accident, in pursuing my own scheme, I found my new invented notes were exactly in the Greek form. From this fortuitous coincidence may we not suspect that we have hit on the true meaning of the Greeks.[20]

The success of Steele's system was dependent upon the natural ability of the reader who used it, and this he recognized. David Garrick, the leading actor of the day, was very much interested in the system and asked concerning the accuracy of imitation of the tone and manner of the original speaker of the one who was using Steele's notation of the speech. Steele replied to his inquiry in the following manner:

Suppose a first rate musician had written down a piece of music, which he had played exquisitely well on an exceeding fine toned violin; another performer with an ordinary fiddle might undoubtedly play every note the same as the great master, though perhaps with less ease and elegance of expression; but, notwithstanding his correctness in the tune and manner, nothing could prevent the audience from perceiving that the natural tone of his instrument was execrable: so, though these rules may enable a master to teach a just application of accent, emphasis, and all the other proper expressions of the voice in speaking, which will go a great way in the improvement of elocution, yet they cannot give a sweet voice where Nature has denied it.[21]

Porter gave two keys for rhetorical notation which he used in marking the selections in his books. Other exercises were given without any marks and the student was supposed to be able to use the keys in marking the selections before he attempted to read them in class. The following description of the classroom procedure from *The Rhetorical Reader* is interesting:

When any portion of the Exercises is about to be committed to memory for declamation, the pupil should first study the sentiment carefully, entering as far as possible, into the spirit of the author; then transcribe it in a fair hand, then mark with pencil, the inflections, emphasis, etc., required on different words; then read it rhetorically to his teacher, changing his pencil marks as the case may require; and then commit to memory perfectly before it is spoken; as any

[20] Steele. *op. cit.* p. 8-9.
[21] *Ibid.* p. 54.

labor of recollection is certainly fatal to freedom, and variety, and force in speaking. In general it were well that the same piece should be subsequently once or more repeated, with a view to adopt the suggestions of the Instructor. For the purpose of improvement in elocution, a piece of four or five minutes is better than one of fifteen; more advance may be made, in managing the voice and countenance, by speaking several times, a short speech, though an old one. . . ."[32]

The following are the keys which he used for inflection and modulation: [33]

KEY OF MODULATION	KEY OF INFLECTION
(°) high	- monotone
(°°) high and loud	/ rising inflection
(₀) low	\ falling inflection
(₀₀) low and loud	U circumflex
.. slow	
≈ quick	
— plaintive	
⅃ rhetorical pause	
⟨ increase	
⟩ decrease	

In his *Rhetorical Reader* he explains the different inflections in terms of their functions. Rising inflection is used for direct question, and falling inflection for the answer to the question. For the word preceding the pause of suspension, for tender emotion, and the last pause but one in a sentence, the rising inflection should be used. The falling inflection is to be used for indirect questions, language of authority, surprise and distress usually, emphatic repetition, and final pause. The circumflex appears when the language is hypothetical or ironical. The examples he chose are chiefly colloquial because he considered the tones of conversation to be the basis of delivery and because they were easily recognized by the ear. "Being conformed to nature they are instinctively right so that scarce a man in a million uses artificial tones in conversation." [34]

Porter was really the only one of the elocutionists in this first period who mentioned quality as a separate aspect of speech. After discussing inflections which he called the absolute modifications of the voice, he states that pitch, quantity, rate and quality are relative modifications. He mentions only two kinds of quality, lively and pathetic. [35]

[32] Porter, Ebenezer. *The Rhetorical Reader.* p. vii.
[33] Porter, Ebenezer. *Analysis of the Principles of Rhetorical Delivery.* preface. p. x.
[34] Porter. *The Rhetorical Reader.* p. 28-38 *passim.*
[35] Porter, Ebenezer. *Analysis of Vocal Inflections used in Reading and Speaking.* p. 8.

In *Analysis of Principles of Rhetorical Delivery,* Porter makes the statement that *modulation* may be considered so generic a term that it includes pitch, and also quantity, rate, rhetorical pause, transition, expression, and representation. This may seem a very radical enlarging of the term, but it shows how these divisions of speech grew in meaning as they were used in teaching the techniques of oral interpretation.[36]

PAUSES AND TIMING. Another problem which had to be considered and properly notated was that of *pausing.* Should pauses follow strictly the punctuation marks; one count for the comma, two for the semicolon, and four for the period? Should additional pauses be added to make the meaning or the grammar clear? What pauses should be observed in reading poetry? These were some of the questions which perplexed the early writers.

Walker offered a theory of rhetorical punctuation in sixteen rules which showed his predilection for grammar and for rules. The pauses were based entirely on grammatical construction and sometimes occurred where there were no punctuation points. He defined different types of sentences according to Campbell's *Philosophy of Rhetoric.* Complex sentences were of two kinds; they were either periods, or sentences of a looser composition for which no name had been devised. The sentence called a *period* had a very close connection between the beginning and the end of the sentence, and the meaning remained suspended until the whole was finished.

The sixteen rules are given below in condensed form:

I. Every direct period consists of two principal constructive parts between which parts the greater pause must be inserted; when these parts commence with conjunctions that correspond with each other, they are sufficiently distinguishable; as in the following sentence:

As we cannot discern the shadow moving along the dial-plate, so advances we make in knowledge are only perceived by the distance gone over.

Here we may observe, that the first constructive part begins with *as,* and the second with *so;* the expectation is excited by the first, and answered by the latter; at that point, therefore, where the expectation begins to be answered, and the sense begins to form, the principal pause is to be used; and, by these means, the two contrasted and correspondent parts are distinctly viewed by the mind.

II. Every inverted period consists of two principal constructive parts, between which parts the greater pause must be inserted; these parts divide at that point, where the latter part of the sentence begins to modify the former;

[36] Porter, Ebenezer. *Analysis of the Principles of Rhetorical Delivery.* p. 20.

in periods of this kind, the latter conjunction only is expressed, as in the example:

Everyone that speaks and reasons is a grammarian, and a logician, though he may be utterly unacquainted with the rules of grammar, or logick, as they are delivered in books and systems.

III. Every loose sentence must consist of a period, either direct or inverted, and an additional member which does not modify it; and consequently, this species of sentence requires a pause between the principal constructive parts of the period, and between the period and the additional member.

Persons of good taste expect to be pleased, at the same time they are informed; and think that the best sense always deserves the best language.

In this sentence an inverted period is constructed at the word *informed*; which requires a pause at *pleased*, because here the former part of the sentence is modified by the latter; and a pause is required at *informed* because another member commences.

IV. When a nominative consists of more than one word, it is necessary to pause after it.

The great and invincible Alexander, wept for the fate of Darius.

Here a pause is necessary between these words, not only that the organs may pronounce the whole with more ease, but that the complex nominative and verb may, by being distinctly exhibited, be more readily and distinctly conceived.

V. Whatever member intervenes between the nominative case and the verb, is of the nature of a parenthesis, and must be separated from both of them by a short pause.

I am told that many virtuous matrons, who formerly have been taught to believe that artificial spotting of the face was unlawful, are now reconciled, by a zeal for their cause, to what they could not be prompted by a concern for their beauty.

VI. Whatever member intervenes between the verb and the accusative case, is of the nature of a parenthesis, and must be separated from both by a short pause.

VII. When two verbs come together and the latter is in the infinitive mood, if any words come between, they must be separated from the latter verb by a pause.

VIII. If there are several subjects belonging in the same manner to one verb, or several verbs, belonging in the same manner to one subject, the subjects and the verbs are still to be accounted equal in number; for every verb must have its subject, and every subject its verb; and every one of the subjects, or verbs, should have its point of distinction and a short pause.

IX. If there are several adjectives belonging in the same manner to one substantive, or several substantives belonging in the same manner to one adjective, the adjective and substantives are still to be accounted equal in number; for every substantive must have its adjective, and every adjective coming after its substantive, and every adjective coming before the substantive except the last, must be separated by a short pause.

X. If there are several adverbs belonging in the same manner to one verb, or several verbs belonging in the same manner to one adverb, the verbs and adverbs are still to be accounted equal in number; and if the adverbs come before the verb, a pause must separate each of them from the last.

XI.   Whatever words are put into the case absolute, commonly called the ablative absolute, must be separated from the rest by a short pause.

XII.   Nouns in apposition, or words in the same case, where the latter is only explanatory of the former have a short pause between them, either if both these nouns consist of many terms, or the latter only.

XIII.   *Who, which,* when in the nominative case, and the pronoun *that* when used for *who,* or *which* require a short pause before them.

XIV.   When *that* is used as a causal conjunction it ought always to be preceded by a short pause.

XV.   Prepositions and conjunctions are more united with the words they precede than with those they follow; and consequently if it be necessary to pause, the preposition and the conjunction ought to be classed with the succeeding words and not with the preceding.

XVI.   When words are placed either in opposition to, or in opposition with each other, the words so placed require to be distinguished by a pause.[37]

The college students were already burdened with rules for Greek, Latin, and Hebrew and to add sixteen more for pausing was not a welcome idea.   Walker apologized for this addition but said that he could, with confidence, affirm that not half of the pauses that appeared in the speech of a good speaker or reader could be found in the printing.   He added that pauses should occur on the average of the fifth or sixth word, and reminded the student that "publick reading" required pausing oftener than private conversation; "as the parts of a picture which is viewed at a distance, must be more distinctly marked, than those of an object which are nearer to the eye, and understood at the first inspection." [38]

Sheridan wanted to be guided entirely by the meaning.   He thought that some of the greatest imperfections in reading were due to the great attention that had been paid to the points, or *titles,* as he called them.   He did, however, work out a notation for pauses which was to be used by the student, and omitted the regular punctuation marks from the exercises to be read in class.   The notation consisted chiefly of inclined lines,—one for shortest pause, three for a full stop, and two horizontal lines for a pause longer than usual stop.   He also marked long and short syllables.[39]

Walker and Sheridan agreed that reading poetry differed from prose and that the final and caesural pauses should be observed.

[37] Walker, John.   *Elements of Elocution.* p. 25-69.
[38] *Ibid.* p. 39-66.
[39] Sheridan, Thomas.   *Lectures on the Art of Reading.* vol. 1. p. 181-2.

Sheridan, however, adjusted his reading to the sense and used what he called a "pause of suspension" at the end of a line where the thought was not completed: "When the voice is only suspended, there is no separation made in the sense, and the subject and attribute in that respect, are as intimately united, as if they had been closely joined in the pronunciation." [40] The caesural pause he used according to sense also, because it sometimes "coincides with the sentential and sometimes has an independent state," therefore making it impossible to place it always in the middle of the verse.[41] In Rules IV and V for the reading of poetry, Walker stated that the caesura in the middle of the line must be carefully observed, but the pause at the end of the line must be a pause "proportional to the intimate or remote connection subsisting between the two lines."

The term "rhetorical pause" was used by Porter. It was closer to Sheridan's ideas than to Walker's sixteen rules and implied a pause which an emotion might dictate in order to intensify its expression. Porter agreed with Sheridan that sense should dictate pauses, and although he did not mark the pauses, he did use symbols for the rate at which different words and phrases should be read.[42]

PRONUNCIATION AND ARTICULATION. The term *pronunciation,* as was mentioned before, during this period sometimes meant the same as *elocution* because of its relationship to the fifth part of rhetoric. *Articulation,* however, meant just what it means now—the making of the several sounds by the articulatory organs. Walker said that elocution in the modern sense of the word seemed to signify that pronunciation which was given to words when they were arranged into sentences and formed into discourse.[43] This definition allows for the variations in pronunciation which are dictated by the meaning and which often produce what teachers now call "strong" and "weak" forms.

It is certain that the pronouns *you* and *my,* when they are contradistinguished from other pronouns, and consequently emphatical, are always pronounced with their full open sound, *you, my.* But it is certain, if we observe the pronunciation of correct conversation that we shall find them sounded *ye* and *me* when they are subordinate words in a sentence and have no emphasis on them.[44]

As mentioned earlier, Sheridan was particularly interested in lexicography and pronunciation. He gave space to the description of the different dialects and commented on the fact that this phase of elocution had never been neglected, since pronunciation had always

[40] *Ibid.* vol. II. p. 257-8.
[41] *Ibid.* vol. II. p. 117, 119.
[42] Porter, Ebenezer. *The Rhetorical Reader.* p. 59-60.
[43] Walker, John. *Elements of Elocution.* p. 17.
[44] Walker, John. *The Rhetorical Grammar.* p. 35.

been a means of labelling men according to their station of life. The only method suggested to improve the pronunciation was to practice saying the difficult words over and over again, and thus to make the correct pronunciation a habit. Since the faults could be corrected only when the person making the mistakes was conscious of them, he suggested that the student prevail upon his intimate friends to tell him every time he made a mistake. He adds this amusing exception; "Tho' this may be easily complied with in private yet as it is contrary to custom to attempt it in mixt company, a private sign agreed on will be sufficient in that case."[45]

The question of accent and its relation to articulation was important to Sheridan as this excerpt from his lectures indicates:

All persons who pronounce English words properly, of course lay the accent right, as that is part of pronunciation; and never fail to do so in conversation. But many, when they come to read or speak in public, transgress the rules of accent. This arises from a mistaken notion in some, that words are rendered more distinct to a large assembly, by dwelling longer upon the syllables which compose them; and in others that it adds to the pomp and solemnity of public declamation, in which they think everything should be different from private discourse. This has been the chief vice of the stage, and has principally given rise to the distinction of what is commonly called Theatrical Declamation in opposition to that of the natural kind. . . .[46]

There was some disagreement as to the number of individual sounds in the language. Sheridan stated that there were twenty-eight—nineteen consonants and nine vowels. The number gradually increased until in the next period Dr. Rush discovered thirty-five elements. Sheridan used the term "pure" for sounds formed entirely by voice and "impure" for those formed of a mixture of voice and breath. He also used the term "vocal" for sounds formed of voice alone as opposed to "aspirated" for those formed of breath. He introduced what he called a scheme for the vowels which was to aid in pronunciation.

SCHEME OF VOWELS [47]

	FIRST	SECOND	THIRD
	1	2	3
a	hat	hate	hall
	1	2	3
e	bet	there	here
	1	2	3
i	fit	bite	field
	1	2	3
o	not	note	prove
	1	2	3
u	cub	bush	cube
	1	2	
y	lively	try	

[45] Sheridan, Thomas. *Course of Lectures on Elocution.* p. 55.
[46] *Ibid.* p. 72.
[47] *Ibid.* p. 11.

Steele's list of vowels consists of seven natural vowels and five diphthongs: [48]

THE VOWELS

a	all, small, or for
a	man, can
e	may, day
i	evil, keen, it
o	open, only, broke
w	fool, two, do
u	tune, supreme

THE DIPHTHONGS

ai	fine, life, I
ae	met, let, get, men (a short sound)
iw	you, use, new, due (a long sound)
aw	unkind, ugly, but
ow	how, bow, hour, town (sounded long)

The present-day reader will notice some resemblances to the International Phonetic symbols for the vowels.

Sheridan divides the consonants into labials, eb, ev, ep, ef; dentals, ed, eth, ez, ezh, et, esh, iss; palatine, eg, ek, el, er; nasal, em, en, ing. The exercises given are first a series of syllables, then lists of words.[49] He insists that the practice follow the natural order—labial, dental, palatine, nasal, rather than the alphabetical order. He warns against falling into any peculiar tone or cant while practicing. "The syllables should be pronounced in neither a higher or lower pitch of voice than they use in common discourse; only they should be delivered with more force, or a greater degree of loudness, which will help to strengthen the voice."[50] Sheridan's list of consonants was not changed until the next period.

There was probably more agreement in the method that was to be used in improving the articulation and pronunciation than in that for cultivating any other phase of the speech. No doubt they would all have agreed with Porter when he stated:

Defective articulation arises from bad organs, or bad habits, or sounds of difficult utterance. Everyone knows how the loss of a tooth, or a contusion on the lip, affect the formation of oral sounds. When there is an essential fault in the structure of the mouth; when the tongue is disproportionate in length or width, or sluggish in its movements; or the palate is too high or too low, or the teeth badly set, or decayed, art may diminish but cannot remove the difficulty. In nine cases out of ten, however, imperfect articulation comes not so much from bad organs, as from the abuse of good ones. . . .

[48] Steele, Sir Joshua. *Prosodia Rationalis.* p. x-xi.
[49] Sheridan, Thomas. *Lectures on the Art of Reading.* vol. 1. p. 13-25.
[50] *Ibid.* p. 70.

After you have ascertained your faults, then make a list of the words and repeat them as a set exercise.[51]

GESTURE. As the methods for teaching gesture are analyzed, a very clear-cut distinction will be evident between the two schools. Sheridan stated that since there was no common standard, each individual either formed a manner peculiar to himself or adopted that of some other that struck his fancy.

Of these two ways, there can be no doubt, which a man should follow. He that forms to himself a manner of his own, will probably acquire such a one as will be most consonant to his own powers and feelings. . . Let him speak entirely from his feelings; and they will find much truer signs to manifest themselves by, than he could find for them.[52]

Here was an allowance for variation in expression from individual to individual. Walker made no such allowance.

In order, therefore, to gain a just idea of suitable action and expression, it will be necessary to observe that every passion, emotion, or sentiment has a particular attitude of body, cast of the eye, and tone of the voice, that particularly belongs to that passion, emotion, or sentiment; these should be carefully studied and practiced before a glass when we are alone; and before a few friends, whose candour and judgment we can rely on.[53]

There were forty-four of these passions which he described in detail:

(Tranquility, cheerfulness), mirth, raillery, sneer, joy, delight, love, pity, hope, (hate, aversion), (anger, rage, fury), revenge, reproach, (fear, terror), sorrow, remorse, despair, (surprise, wonder, amazement, admiration), pride, (confidence, courage, boasting), (perplexity, irresolution, anxiety), (vexation, peevishness), (envy, malice), (suspicion, jealously), (modesty, submission), (shame, gravity), (inquiry, attention), (instruction or teaching), arguing, admonition, (authority, commanding), (forbidding, affirming), (denying, differing), agreeing, (judging, reproving), (acquiting, condemning), pardoning, (dismissing, refusing), (giving, granting), (gratitude, curiosity), (promising, veneration), (respect, desire, commendation), exhorting, (complaining, fatigue), sickness.[54]

Scott described sixty, and Walker had succeeded in cutting that list down considerably. He admitted that it was better to feel the emotion through the lively use of the imagination, but since natural feelings were not always so commanded, the reader, or speaker, should know the tones and gestures so that he would be able to produce them when he was not impassioned. He refers to the *Art of Speaking* as an "ingenious performance" and acknowledges his debt." The example which follows resembles Burgh's description of joy very closely:

When joy arises from ludicrous or fugitive amusements in which others share with us, it is called merriment or mirth. Mirth or laughter, opens the

[51] Porter, Ebenezer. *The Rhetorical Reader.* p. 22, 23.
[52] Sheridan, Thomas. *Course of Lectures on Elocution.* p. 140-1.
[53] Walker, John. *Elements of Elocution.* p. 303-4.
[54] *Ibid.* p. 317.

mouth horizontally, raises the cheeks high, lessens the aperture of the eyes, and, when violent, shakes and convulses the whole frame, fills the eyes with tears, and occasions holding the sides from the pain convulsive laughter gives them.[55]

For exercises, a cutting from Milton's *Comus* and one from *As You Like It* were given. One cannot help wondering how the reader could read, if he put himself into such a strenuous expression of mirth.

Scott mentioned facial expression as the most important of all in conveying the emotions of the mind.

Especially the face being furnished with a variety of muscles does more in expressing the passions of the mind than the whole human frame besides. The change of colour (in white people) shews, by turns, anger by redness, and sometimes by paleness, fear likewise by paleness, and shame by blushing. Every feature contributes its part. The mouth open, shews one state of mind; shut, another; the gnashing of teeth, another.[56]

Walker's directions for stage deportment are quite interesting. He thought that unless reading before a few people, the speaker should stand and hold the book in his left hand. The eyes should be taken from the book as often as possible and directed toward the audience, and the three or four last words of, at least, every paragraph or branch of the subject should be pronounced with the eyes directed to one of the auditors.[57] This last direction is made a little more explicit by Austin when he says:

. . . in the more important and earnest passages, he will look into the very pupils of their eyes. But in the practice of this direction of the eyes, which is of such advantage towards obtaining attention, he will be most cautious not to appear to fix on any particular person as the object of invective, or as the subject and example of the vices he may condemn. . . . In the pulpit it can never be necessary, and is never admissible.[58]

Scott surpassed them all, though, in making his speaker a mechanical man, as the following directions demonstrate:

He should rest the whole weight of his body on the right leg; the other, just touching the ground, at the distance at which it would naturally fall, if lifted up to show that the body does not bear upon it. The knees should be straight, and braced, and the body, though perfectly straight, not perpendicular, but inclining as far to the right as a firm position on the right leg will permit. The right hand must then be held out, with the palm open, the fingers straight and close, the thumb almost as distant from them as it will go; and the flat of the hand neither horizontal nor vertical, but exactly between both. . . . When the pupil has pronounced one sentence, in the position thus described, the hand,

[55] *Ibid.* p. 318.
[56] Scott, William. *Lessons in Elocution.* p. 29.
[57] Walker, John. *Elements of Elocution.* p. 304.
[58] Austin, Gilbert. *Chironomia.* p. 103.

as if lifeless, must drop down to the side, the very moment the last accented word is pronounced; and the body, without altering the place of the feet, poise itself on the left leg, while the left hand raises itself into exactly the same position as the right was before, and continues in this position till the end of the next sentence. . . ."[59]

This use of the left hand is an innovation because most of the books from Bulwer down mentioned the fact that only the right hand was to be used in gestures of importance, and the left only on rare occasions and that, probably, as a rest or variation. Porter mentioned the fact that custom had made the right hand dominant and that it should take precedence over the left.[60]

The best known book on the subject of gesture, and the one most referred to by later writers was Rev. Gilbert Austin's *Chironomia; or a Treatise on Rhetorical Delivery: comprehending many precepts both ancient and modern, for the proper regulation of the Voice, Countenance, and Gesture.* The purpose of the book is stated quite clearly: "To produce a language of symbols so simple and so perfect as to render it possible with facility to represent every action of an orator throughout his speech, or of an actor throughout the whole drama, and to record them for posterity, and for repetition and practice. . . ." [61]

Again we see development of the tendency to work out notations. The following illustrations show the variety of positions possible to the speaker. They are all named according to their position in the imaginary sphere.

The following explanations are given for the figures on page 64:

FIG. 15. If from this position (at rest) either arm be raised as high as it can be, the extremity of the fingers will sweep, in the vertical direction, a semicircle terminating in the zenith, in which are marked five principal points RdheZ, at the interval of about forty-five degrees each. FIG. 16. The center of this is the shoulder, and the radius, a line compounded of both parts of the arm, of the wrist, and of the hand. If in the transverse direction, the arm be extended across the body as far as convenience will permit, and then swept horizontally round and outwards, without turning the back. FIG. 17. In this case also, the extremity of the fingers will describe a curve . . . as a semicircle and in this also are marked five principal points, c f q x b at similar intervals; upon these observations is built the present system of gesture.[62]

This will give the reader some idea of the explicitness of the directions and notations. There are, of course, combined positions

[59] Scott, William. *Lessons in Elocution.* p. 10, 15.
[60] Porter, Ebenezer. *The Rhetorical Reader.* p. 73.
[61] Austin, Gilbert. *Chironomia.* p. 274.
[62] *Ibid.* p. 309.

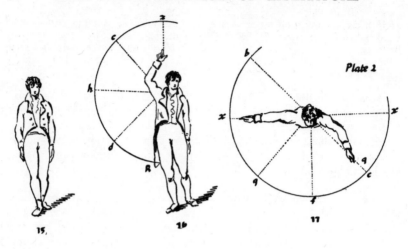

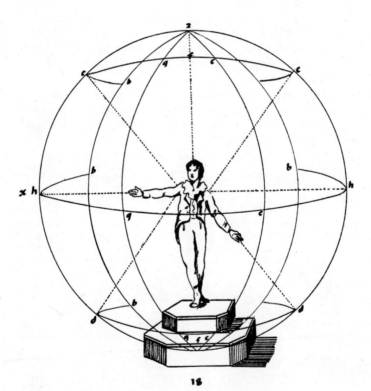

AUSTIN'S SYSTEM OF GESTURE

From *Chironomia*

and these are shown by sets of symbols which always preserve their own place in the succession. In a set such as *phfd*, the first letter relates to the position of the hand, the second to the elevation of the arm, the third to the transverse position of the arm, the fourth to the motion of force of the gesture. Thus, *phfd* reads *prone horizontal forward descending.*[63]

The feet are marked *a* if the person advances, *r* if he retires, *tr* for traverse, *st* for stops, and *sp* for stamps.[64]

In the excerpt from Gray's *Elegy Written in a Country Church Yard*, Austin's notations for gesture are demonstrated. The notations above the words refer to the attitude and gestures, those below give direction for the movement of the feet. (See page 66.) The following explanation is given for *Ls, veq-vhx*:

> In this action the eyes are turned first towards the direction from whence the sound proceeds, and the hand is presented vertical in the same direction; but the eye quickly discovers its own insufficiency, and then the ear, the proper organ, is turned towards the sound, whilst the eyes are bent upon the vacancy, the hand remaining as before. The body leans forward more or less according to the earnestness of the attention. The attitude is expressed by the notation *veq* (vertical elevated oblique)—*vhx* (vertical horizontal extended) which shows the position of both hands.[65]

The small *a* indicates the beginning of the next gesture and —— the completion. The whole notation for the remainder of the first stanza reads, advance both arms and hands, prone, elevated, forward and then downward within forty-five degrees of the nadir. The feet according to the notation below the line advance to the right, two steps. The large letter *F* indicates that the hand should be placed upon the forehead. The letters *phf*, *q* and *x* read that the hand is first prone, the arm horizontal and forward, and then oblique and extended. *B veq* indicate that both hands are vertical extended and oblique; *V* indicates vacancy in the eyes and again both hands are moved forward and then downward until both are at rest, *B R*.[66]

In the second stanza, *R* reads "to the right" and the eyes and head are to begin there and turn toward the other extreme. The hands are first prone and clutched while the arms are horizontal, later oblique, and at the end of the line extended. It is explained that *iec* means that the index finger is elevated and the arm held across the body. "The eye is to follow the object, at which the finger seems to point, a little above the finger and at a small distance; as at a beetle which may be supposed to be seen to fly." [67]

[63] *Ibid.* p. 360.
[64] *Ibid.* p. 365.
[65] *Ibid.* p. 528.
[66] *Loc. cit.*
[67] *Ibid.* p. 530.

AN ELEGY WRITTEN IN A COUNTRY CHURCH YARD.

GRAY.

I.

Ls   veq—vbx   a————B pef————d
The curfew tolls the knell of parting day,
   aR2

F   phf— . . . . . q . . . .
The lowing herd winds slowly o'er the lea,
   rR1

. . . . .—phf————————q   B veq
The ploughman homeward plods his weary way,
   V   B nef————————d————B.R
And leaves the world to darkness and to me.

II.

R   B phc————————————————q————————x
Now fades the glimmering landscape on the sight,
         Bvef————————q
And all the air a solemn stillness holds,
         iec————————————q
Save where the beetle wheels his drony flight,
                    phf p—   R
And drowsy tinklings lull the distant folds;
                    aR2

III.

         —ieq n
Save that from yonder ivy mantl'd tow'r,
   R 1
         —veq   U   —seb
The moping owl does to the moon complain
                    rL1
                    —shq
Of such, as wand'ring near her secret bow'r,
         —veq————p
Molest her ancient solitary reign.

AUSTIN'S USE OF NOTATION FOR GESTURE
From *Chironomia*

The following explanations are made for the third stanza:

In order to vary the gestures, and the better to distribute the objects in the picture, the "tower" is here supposed to be placed on the left side, and the left hand assumes the principal gestures; this is indicated in the notation by the short dash - which precedes the set of letters.[68]

Thus the left index finger is elevated obliquely and is noting the tower. In the next line which mentions the owl, the left hand is elevated obliquely upward and the feet retreat left one step, as the hand supine is elevated backwards. "The eyes," Austin explains, "look upwards at the moon, as if high in the heavens, the hand which was *vertical* in the former gesture, by throwing back the arm becomes *supine.*" [69]

From this example, it seems that great skill in interpreting the symbols would be necessary in order to make them usable. Surely "sight-reading" would be a laborious process and a speaker with any amount of skill would find it difficult to make the gestures anything but very mechanical. However, *Chironomia* was to be the standard treatise on action until the time of Delsarte in the latter part of the nineteenth century.

SUMMARY. From approximately 1760 to 1827, the teaching of *Interpretation* or *Elocution,* as it was called, responded to the two dominant educational trends of the period. The Mechanical school under the leadership of Walker, Burgh, Scott, and Austin developed numerous rules and complicated notations to direct the student in his learning to speak and read. The Natural school, developed under Sheridan, Cockin, Rice, and Porter, believed in a minimum of rules but looked to nature for instruction. The latter school depended upon the individual—his imagination and natural capacity. The Mechanical school made little allowance for any personal element, but felt that a strict adherence to the rules guaranteed uniformly good results.

The leaders were English and the important textbooks used in our colleges and universities were all English until Porter wrote his book in 1827. The English writers were actors, ministers, grammarians, or lexicographers, in the main, and had a very scholarly and academic interest in the study of elocution. Their textbooks seem impractical to the modern teacher, but must be considered in their own particular setting as great contributions. These leaders in Elocution made it possible to include in the study of the oral expression of the language not only Rhetoric, but what is now known as *Oral Interpretation of Literature.*

[68] *Ibid.* p. 531.
[69] *Loc. cit.*

PART II

DR. RUSH AND THE SCIENTIFIC
METHOD: 1827-1870

CHAPTER I

THE PERIOD OF EXPANSION

After the war of 1812, the United States turned away from the Mother country, and as she looked toward the West, she expanded into a nation. She had an adolescent sort of enthusiam and independence which made her determined to develop her own leaders, her writers, her scientists, and her educators. Edward Channing, in his *History of the United States,* explains this rather definite change as the result of a war which not only loosened the minds and broke old associations, but substituted new thoughts and groupings and laid the foundations for a new stage of development. "They exalted the position of the individual in society, burst the bonds of education and religion, and experimented with schemes to better human life." [1]

THE PERIOD OF EXPANSION. Not only were the physical frontiers pushed westward, but the frontiers of the American mind were extended to include many diverse and conflicting ideas. It was stretched to accommodate along with the old puritanism, the tenets of unitarianism and transcendentalism; federalism was forced to admit within the family the republicanism of Jefferson and the democracy of Jackson; industrialism superseded mercantilism; capitalism and socialism were defined, and finally most disturbing of all, evolution was ushered in by the newly found servant, science. There were many problems that were purely domestic, such as a national bank, universal education, purchase of foreign lands, states rights and slavery. These stirred the people to controversy and gave them a national consciousness. If conflict gives motivation to creative power and that in turn means progress, the conditions were admirable for the development of a better life for this new nation.

In an intellectual climate charged with controversy, it is not surprising that oratory had its golden day. It was a period of lectures and lyceums, of famous sermons, political orations, and debates. Public men had to be learned, or appear so, and be able to display their learning in polished rhetoric. Timothy Dwight was known to disapprove of the style of delivery which he termed "too florid," but evidently he represented a minority.[2] Josiah Quincy, in recording his impressions of Daniel Webster's oratory in a court trial in 1821, says that Webster spoke for nearly four hours and held the great assembly

---

[1] Channing, Edward. *A History of the United States.* vol. 5. p. 2-3.
[2] Dwight, Timothy. *Travels in New England and New York.* vol. 1. p. 510.

breathless, and that he gave him the first idea of the electric force which might be wielded by a master of speech.[3]   In *The Flowering of New England,* Van Wyck Brooks finds a parallel between these days and those of Rome in that orators preceded the poets, and chroniclers the dramatists.   Clay, Calhoun, and Daniel Webster, he thinks, did more to make America conscious of her problems during the early part of the century than all of her writers.[4]   Later, the oratory of Wendell Phillips, Henry Ward Beecher, Samuel Chase, Abraham Lincoln, and Stephen Douglas was to set forth in perhaps a little more direct and less verbose fashion the issues of the Civil War.

ROMANTICISM ENTERS.   The swing toward a nationalistic temper has been noted, but it was a romantic one as well, and especially stimulating to the man who expressed his ideas in written form.   Parrington describes the advent of romanticism in the terms of the society which embraced it :

> The half century that lay between these dramatic episodes (the War of 1812 and the Civil War) was a period of extravagant youth, given over to a cult of romanticism that wrought as many marvels as Aaron's rod.   In the South, in New England, and on the western frontier, it laid hold of men's minds, consuming the stubble of eighteenth-century harvests, sweeping away the drab realisms of the cautious past, and offering in their stead more alluring ideals. Revolutions, greater and lesser, trod on each other's heels ; the common adventure led into unexplored paths ; and the final·outcome for which it was all preparing was the emergence of a new middle class that in the succeeding half century was to subdue America to middle-class ends . . . .   It was our first great period of exploitation, and from it emerged, as naturally as the cock from the mother egg, the spirit of romance, gross and tawdry in vulgar minds, dainty and refined in the more cultivated.   But always romance.   The days of realism were past, and it was quietly laid away with the wig and small-clothes of an outgrown generation.[5]

There was a question as to whether this romanticism grew from the doctrine of French equalitarianism as expounded by Jefferson or from Adam Smith's theory of a social utopia, the resultant of economic forces given freedom.   Whatever its root, from it stemmed much that was of great importance in the arts and sciences.

In New England there were three great leaders : Channing in religion, Ticknor in education, and Webster in politics.   According to Parrington, Webster did not keep up with the ideas of the new movement and was derided by the intellectuals of whom Emerson, Thoreau, Channing, Whittier, Lowell, and Margaret Fuller were a

[3] Quincy, Josiah, Jr. *Figures of the Past from the Leaves of Old Journals.* p. 47-8 (1896).
[4] Brooks, Van Wyck. *The Flowering of New England.* p. 117.
[5] Parrington, Vernon Louis. *The Romantic Revolution in America.* introd. p. 3, 5.

substantial part.[6] His failure to identify himself with the anti-slavery movement was the main reason for their condemnation, but no one would gainsay his influence upon the people and his gift for oratory. Emerson says in his journal for February 7, 1843:

> Webster is very dear to the Yankees because he is a person of very commanding understanding with every talent for its adequate expression. . . . His external advantages are very rare and admirable; his noble and majestic frame, his breadth and projection of brows, his coal-black hair, his great cinderous eyes, his perfect self-possession, and the rich and well-modulated thunder of his voice (to which I used to listen, sometimes, abstracting myself from his sense merely for the luxury of such noble explosions of sound) distinguish him above all other men. . . . He has misused the opportunity of making himself the darling of the American world in all coming time by abstaining from putting himself at the head of the Anti-slavery interest by standing for New England and for man against the bullying and barbarism of the South.[7]

ADVANCES IN ART AND SCIENCE. Perhaps the art of oral expression was more used during the early part of the century, but the written word soon proved itself to be an adequate mode of expression and literature had its day—its "flowering" or "renaissance." There were many poets, novelists, essayists, journalists, and historians. Writing became a means of earning a respectable livelihood and printing became an important business during the middle period. Not only were many books published, but magazines increased in popularity. The *North American Review,* 1827, was the first of the magazines which survived for a long time. *Harper's* was first published in 1850 and the *Atlantic Monthly* seven years later. The best-seller of the books was, of course, *Uncle Tom's Cabin,* which ran into a million copies.

A great many of the leaders in literature were indebted to European universities for liberal ideas, but what they produced was colored by their home environment. Most of them came back with the express purpose of being American writers and contributing to a national literature. Channing, the great leader of Unitarianism, was especially sensitive to the possibilities of this new and lusty nation and urged the literary mind to cease its worship of Europe. "A people into whose minds the thoughts of foreigners are poured perpetually, needs an energy within itself to resist, to modify this mighty influence. . . . It were better to have no literature than to form ourselves unresistingly on a foreign one. . . . A country, like an individual, has dignity and power only in proportion as it is self-formed."[8]

[6] Parrington. *op. cit.* p. 314-15.
[7] Perry, Bliss. *The Heart of Emerson's Journals.* p. 194, 195.
[8] Channing, William Ellery. "The Importance and Means of a National Literature," in his *Character of Napoleon and Other Essays.* vol. 1. p. 116.

Noah Webster was one of the first to preach the doctrine of Americanism. His American speller which was published in 1783 was a vernacular word-book based on the common usage of New England. He omitted usage which was distinctly English and insisted upon some simplified spellings, for example, *honor* for *honour* and *theater* instead of *theatre*. The Speller appeared at a time when it was difficult to get English textbooks and became so popular that fifty million copies were sold. However, his interest in the language culminated, as it did for Sheridan and Walker, in a dictionary, published in 1828, the result of twenty-eight years of hard work. It was published in a two-quarto edition of more than one thousand words and more than thirty thousand definitions that had never before been in any dictionary of the English language. It superseded all others and "Webster's" became the standard for English all over the world.[9]

The theater as an institution responded to the spirit of expansion and was to be found following the gold miners to California and the river-boats to New Orleans, but of the many players and plays, the best were foreign. Edwin Forrest and Edwin Booth were the two outstanding American actors who could hold their own and did play with foreign actors especially in Shakespearean plays. Forrest urged native playwrights to write plays about their own country and they did write many but few of them have survived. Scribe's formula for the "well-made" play became too easy and there was a sort of mass production of mechanical pieces that could not live because they had little aesthetic value.

Scientific discoveries were not confined to any one part of the world. The prodigious increase in scientific knowledge was to have a significant influence on the shaping of all our modern institutions. It was as if man had been given a new insight into the workings of nature. Helmholtz is quoted as having said that science was born when men ceased to summon nature to the support of theories already formed, and instead began to question nature for her facts in order that they might discover the laws which these facts revealed.[10]

At the beginning of the century, the interest was mainly in observing and in classifying the observations. Distinct fields such as geology, biology, and physics were delimited. Dalton, Helmholtz, Davy, Pasteur, and Darwin were leaders in research abroad. In the United States, Asa Gray was making his contribution to the science of botany, Bowditch was famous in mathematics, Benjamin Silliman in chemistry and mineralogy, and Benjamin Rush in medicine. The

[9] Channing, Edward. *op. cit.* p. 294-5.
[10] Low, Seth. *The Trend of the Century.* p. 6. (Phi Beta Kappa oration given at Harvard, 1898).

inventors succeeded in improving communication and transportation with such inventions as telegraphy, the Atlantic cable, the rapid development of railroads and the use of steamboats.[11] A new surgery was made possible through the introduction of anesthetics by two American doctors. American scientists were on their toes and were ready for any new theory that might come. Darwin's theory as set forth in *The Origin of the Species,* 1859, was not allowed in the library of Trinity College in Cambridge. It was accorded the most striking reviews, according to the author, by the *North American Review* and the *New York Times.*[12]

The lyceum-lecturing system was begun in 1826 by Josiah Holbrook who went about lecturing on geology and natural history. Courses of lectures were given in privately endowed institutes by the foremost men of letters, art, and science. One of the most notable of these organizations was the Lowell Institute, founded in 1833 in Boston by John Lowell, Jr. According to Channing, Lowell's idea was to give practically free instruction in technical subjects and to provide lectures by leading men in the best thought and practice of the day.[13]

INTRODUCTION OF ELECTIVES. Harvard was destined to take the lead in any liberalizing of higher education during the century. George Ticknor, professor of modern language for so many years, is usually given the credit for persuading the authorities to extend the curriculum to include elective studies. He was a leader among the scholars of the time, had received a great part of his education in Germany, and was very much interested in the liberal ideas concerning education current in that part of the world. Butts in appraising his work says:

Ticknor's efforts for reform at Harvard are exceedingly important, especially in the history of the development of the elective principle, inasmuch as they illustrate some of the causes of the breakdown of the rigidly prescribed curriculum and the substitution of a more flexible course of studies. Paramount among these influences were, first, the demands of a growing capitalistic society that the college offer subjects less literary in emphasis and more useful for making a living; second, the demands of an increasingly democratic society that the aristocratic notion of a liberal education be democratized to include all types of students; third, the necessity of the several colleges to compete for students . . . fourth, the extension of the scope of the studies themselves until the student could not possibly encompass them all in four years.[14]

In the South, Jefferson was preaching a similar doctrine of liberalism in education in his University of Virginia. The two pioneers were in correspondence with each other, even before Ticknor returned

[11] Channing, Edward. *op. cit.* p. 21-34.
[12] Beard, I, 743.
[13] *Ibid.* p. 267-8.
[14] Butts, R. Freeman. *The College Charts Its Course.* p. 106.

from Europe. Ticknor welcomed the idea of a university which might rival Harvard in intellectual liberalism. Their emphasis was slightly different in that Jefferson was interested in the individual being free in any sphere of human endeavor, while Ticknor saw the new curriculum as necessary for the attainment of literary scholarship. Ticknor was not alone in this reform, but became discouraged and resigned in 1835 to be succeeded by Henry Wadsworth Longfellow, another European-trained scholar. President Josiah Quincy, the first president outside the clergy, was successful in adding new professors and new subjects. In 1841 the curriculum showed more elective subjects than ever before.[15]

On the other hand, Yale worked equally hard to retain the old curriculum and its guiding principle of mental discipline. Under President Timothy Dwight (1795-1817), the curriculum had developed in much the same way as the one at Harvard. Yale was the first, in fact, to have a department of science. Benjamin Silliman, a young tutor in Greek, was selected by Dwight for the task of organizing the department. He was sent first to Philadelphia where he listened to Woodhouse and Priestley; the latter having been forced to leave England because his theories were considered too liberal. At the expense of the college, he was then sent to Edinburgh University to be trained. Silliman returned well equipped and in addition to his work as professor of chemistry and mineralogy, he founded *The American Journal of Science* and helped in the organization of the American Geological society.[16] However, when Jeremiah Day became president in 1817, there was enough opposition to expansion that it had to be considered, and the report of Yale University in 1828 declared that the aim of the college was to develop the intellectual powers through mental discipline.[17] Thus the two conflicting ideas of education in the nineteenth century were enunciated by the two leading New England institutions of higher learning.

ORGANIZED COURSES IN SPEECH. As was stated in the first section of this book, declamations, disputations and rhetoric appeared from the very beginning as a part of the college program, but it was not until the early nineteenth century that special chairs were endowed and speech training organized in course form. John Quincy Adams was appointed to the Boylston Chair of Rhetoric and Oratory at Har-

---

[15] *Ibid.* p. 109.
[16] Channing, Edward. *op. cit.* p. 259-60.
[17] *Reports on the Course of Instruction in Yale College by a Committee of the Corporation and the Academical Faculty.* p. 7.

vard in 1806. He was the first to hold such a position. Brooks, in commenting upon the appropriateness of the choice says:

> He (Adams) had heard the greatest orators of the previous age, Fox, Pitt and Burke, as well as their American contemporaries, and Harvard was prepared to hear the doctrine, sanctioned by Cicero and Demosthenes, that, while liberty was the parent of eloquence, eloquence was the stay of liberty. It was a doctrine that Harvard wished to hear, in an age when the art of the pulpit, the art of the forum, the art of the judge and lawyer, soon to be followed by that of the lecture-platform,—all one art, in its several branches,—was the only literary art that performed a vital function.[18]

Coulton found, from a survey of forty-five college catalogs for the period 1835-1840, that 449 semester hours of speech work were required. This work included courses in *Elocution, Declamation,* and *Forensics*; the latter covering *Oratory, Logic,* and *Rhetoric.* An examination of fifty-six catalogs covering the period from 1840-1850 revealed that 448 semester hours of speech were required. During the next ten years, according to the catalogs for seventy colleges, 628 semester hours were offered in speech, while according to the catalogs of ninety-seven colleges during the period 1860-1870, 798 semester hours were required. The colleges were representative of New England, the South, the Middle Atlantic, and after 1850, the Northwest. In addition to this work, there were literary societies, regular college exercises, contests, and commencement orations which required the direction of the professor of rhetoric.[19] Commencement was considered such an important event in Cambridge that a holiday was declared and the banks and custom-houses closed.

There was some confusion as to the nomenclature of the departmental organization; the department of *Moral Science and Belles Lettres* in one college might be as much concerned with speech as the department of *Rhetoric and Oratory* in another college. In the period 1840-1850, *Moral Science and Belles Lettres* had disappeared, and, in some cases, *English and Philosophy, and English Literature* had been added. In the next ten years, *Logic and Rhetoric, Philosophy and English Literature,* and *Rhetoric and English Literature* appeared, and as time went on *English* predominated with such names as *English Language and Literature,* and *Rhetoric and English Literature* as the common name for the department in which courses in reading and speaking were included.[20] The advisability of combining written and spoken English is questioned by the modern teacher of speech

[18] Brooks. *op. cit.* p. 25.
[19] Coulton, Thomas E. *Trends in Speech Education in American Colleges 1835-1935.* p. 42-3.
[20] *Ibid.* p. 42.

and is still a problem to be discussed. Although many separate departments are to be found in our colleges and universities today, the department which combines the two subjects still exists.[21]

There was also some confusion in the classification of the different types of speech work that were taught. Early in his study, Coulton defines the terms which he uses; *Elocution* is reserved for those courses which include training in voice and bodily action; *Declamation* is used for the oral delivery of memorized pieces; and *Oratory*, for the delivery or original addresses, essays, and compositions.[22] However, he admits the absence of a dichotomy between *Elocution* and *Declamation* as used in the early catalogs and indicates that *Oratory* began somewhat later to adopt a historical approach to orators and orations.[23]

Since the present study is confined to the study of *Oral Interpretation of Literature,* it is principally concerned with the courses in *Elocution* and *Declamation,* and only indirectly with *Rhetoric* and *Oratory.* Since it was the custom to describe the courses and the extra-curricular activities rather fully in the college catalog, Coulton was able to uncover interesting facts about the organization of the courses and the related public programs. In line with the addition of electives, he found an elaboration of courses in 1870 as compared with 1840, and a similarity in the work that was being done in all four sections of the country.

In the 1839-1840 catalog, Harvard listed *Declamations* for sophomores, juniors, and seniors, but by 1860 a course in *Elocution* was offered in which the term was generic and included *Lessons in Orthoepy, Lessons in Expression, Lessons in Action,* and *Rhetorical Analysis and Reading.* By 1870, *Mechanism of Speech* given with lectures and lessons on the *Elements, Readings* in *Paradise Lost* and *Shakespeare,* and *Declamations* from *Burke* were added. Yale, true to its more rigid curriculum, did not offer such variety; in the catalogs for 1839-1840 and 1849-1850 the *Professor of Rhetoric* was mentioned as giving lectures and private work. In 1860, *Rhetoric* was offered one term for freshmen, three terms for sophomores, and two terms for juniors and seniors. The sophomore course was described as *Elocution, Declamation,* and *Composition.*[24]

Amherst, in 1842-1843, offered a course entitled *Elements of Orthoepy and Elocution* which was given two semesters to the freshmen, supplemented by a weekly exercise in *Declamation and Composi-*

[21] Weaver, J. C. "A Survey of Speech Curricula." *Quarterly Journal of Speech.* 18: 607-12(1932).
[22] Coulton. *op. cit.* p. 70.
[23] *Ibid.* p. 76.
[24] *Ibid.* p. 70-8 *passim.*

tion. Sophomores and juniors were required to take part in two weekly *Rhetorical Exercises, Declamation, Debates* or *English Composition.* This plan seems to indicate a choice upon the part of the sophomores and juniors. In Bowdoin in 1839, *Elocution* was required of the freshmen for one term and daily exercises were mentioned. In addition, exercises for private declamations were held for the two lower classes and for public declamations given by the juniors and seniors. At Dartmouth during the same year, original declamations were given by the juniors and seniors.

The University of Alabama in 1842-1843 offered a course entitled *Elocution* which included original compositions in Latin and English which were to be given by the freshmen every Wednesday and three times a year by seniors. The University of North Carolina, from the year 1841 until 1871, listed *Declamations* for the three lower classes and *Original Orations* for the seniors. In 1871, the University of Virginia was teaching *Oratory* in the class of *Literature and Rhetoric.*[25]

The University of Pennsylvania, according to the catalogs for 1850 and 1860, required *Declamations* throughout the entire course of speech, while in George Washington University, during the same years, *Declamations* alternating with *Compositions* and *Orations* were delivered before the college once every three months by juniors and seniors. In 1866, half of the "pieces" given by the seniors were original. *Elocution* was given as a freshman course in 1862 at Pennsylvania State College and in 1871, *English Composition* was added and original declamations were required of seniors.[26]

The North Central section offered similar courses as represented by Knox College in Galesburg, Illinois, where in 1865-1866, *English Composition and Declamation* was offered as a course required in all four years. *Lectures on Vocal Culture and Elocution* were offered during the first three years, and *Public Exhibitions in Chapel, Orations,* and *Declamations* were required twice a week in the senior year. This college had the honor of holding one of the Lincoln-Douglas debates on its campus in 1858.[27] Indiana University in 1865 required weekly exercises in *Elocution and Composition* throughout the four years.[28]

Thus an emphasis upon oral expression is seen throughout the country during this period, which has been arbitrarily ended with 1870. Two rather significant changes were made in the teaching of speech. First, written and oral expression became more closely as-

[25] *Ibid.* p. 81.
[26] *Ibid.* p. 79-80.
[27] Sandburg, Carl. *Abraham Lincoln, The Prairie Years.* vol. 2. p. 148-9.
[28] Coulton. *op. cit.* p. 82.

sociated as the period progressed; second, a greater variety of work was offered at the end of the period than at the beginning. These two developments came naturally as a part of the liberalizing of the curriculum of higher education. Teachers of speech recognized that there was a need for trained leaders in the country and that one of their requirements was adequate oral expression of which delivery was a requisite part. They also realized that there must be increased scientific analysis of any subject which claimed to be based upon scientific principles.

Dr. James Rush fitted into this vigorous, scientific, and humanistic period perfectly. Stirred by the interest in scientific research, and stimulated by his study in the University of Edinburgh, he retired from active practice in medicine to write *The Philosophy of the Human Voice* and thereby revolutionize the teaching of elocution. From this book, which was an attempt to treat the subject according to the rules for scientific analysis, a system was developed which influenced the most important teachers and textbook writers of the period. It was the first important original contribution of an American to the field of speech.

Alhough Sheridan, Walker, and Austin continued to exert an influence upon the teaching of Elocution in the United States, and the influence of Blair, Campbell, and Whately on the teaching of rhetoric cannot be questioned, still the day of English dominance had passed. The Rush system stimulated American teachers to write their own books and the next period showed a further development of their self-reliance and independence.

CHAPTER II

DR. JAMES RUSH

It must be explained that the period 1827-1870 is to be discussed in terms of the contribution made by Dr. Rush, not because his system was the most widely used, but because it represented the one significant change in the approach to the teaching of elocution which was offered during the period. Furthermore, in the light of the background of the time, he was sensitive to the new influences and was one of the first American scientists to make a contribution to the field of speech.

"THE PHILOSOPHY OF THE HUMAN VOICE." It is difficult to appraise his work because Rush is unique in the influence he exerted. His one volume on elocution, *The Philosophy of the Human Voice: Embracing its Physiological History; together with a System of Principles by which Criticism in the Art of Elocution may be Rendered Intelligible, and Instruction, Definite and Comprehensive, to which is added a Brief Analysis of Song and Recitative,* published in 1827, seems verbose, needlessly abstruse, and not very scientific to the modern reader. Yet it went through six editions by 1867, was acclaimed the first scientific book on the subject and exerted an unmistakable influence upon the textbooks on elocution which followed it.

The use of the word *philosophy* in the title may be confusing to the reader. According to the New English Dictionary, in its largest sense it means, "The love, study, or pursuit of wisdom, or of knowledge of things and their causes, whether theoretical or practical." In medieval universities it included three branches: natural, moral, and metaphysical philosophy. In this case, Rush is using it to mean natural philosophy which is defined as, "The knowledge or study of nature, or of natural objects and phenomena; 'natural knowledge': now usually called *science.*" [1] It is an attempt to discuss the use of the voice, in speaking, in scientific terms.

There were only five hundred copies published in 1827, and Rush bore the expense himself. In the preface to the second edition (1833), Rush recognizes the fact that the book was criticized because of its being difficult to understand. At this time only two schools used the Rush system—Yale College and Cambridge University, England. Dr. Jonathan Barber was the first to appreciate its value, according to Rush, and it was he who taught the system in both of the aforementioned schools. [2] In the introduction to the third edition published

---

[1] *A New English Dictionary,* ed. by James Murray. vol. 7. p. 781.
[2] Rush, James. *The Philosophy of the Human Voice.* 4th ed. p. xxv, xxvi.

in 1844, it is stated that "upwards of twenty people were teaching its principles,"[3] but in the preface to the fourth edition (1855) Rush acknowledges that his book is known to "a comparatively small number of teachers, to a few inquiring and musical mechanics and a few unmusical members of the Society of Friends." He laments, at some length, the fact that the so-called leaders of the day refused to adopt his principles and thereby failed to "crown the Seventh Muse with Science."[4] Leverton states that although its circulation was small at the time of this fourth edition, it came into more popularity shortly after the Civil War, the Rush system forming the basis of method for that group of teachers who belonged to the objective or "Mechanics School."[5] It was listed in the Brown University catalog as late as 1870-1880.[6]

There were textbooks written during this period which followed the English elocutionists very closely: Mandeville's *The Elements of Reading and Oratory*, 1849, subscribed to Walker without reservation. Samuel Kirkham's *An Essay on Elocution*, published in 1833 did lip-service to the contemporary theories of Dr. Rush, yet the real foundation for the rules was found in the grammatical structure of the sentence and adhered to Walker's ideas of elocution. Some books such as Merritt Caldwell's *A Practical Manual of Elocution*, 1845, acknowledged debt to Austin and to Rush, and William Russell's *The American Elocutionist*, 1844, recognized both Walker and Rush.

His PREPARATION. Dr. James Rush was the son of Dr. Benjamin Rush, the leader in the advancement of medicine in the late eighteenth and early nineteenth centuries. Dr. Benjamin Rush was graduated from the College of New Jersey (Princeton) in 1760, took his M.D. degree from the University of Edinburgh in 1768, and attended medical lectures in London. When he returned to the United States he began his practice in Philadelphia. He was a member of Congress in 1776 and one of the signers of the Declaration of Independence. He was the first medical man in the country to achieve a general literary reputation. His famous work *Medical Inquiries* and *Observations upon the Diseases of the Mind* (1812) showed some appreciation of what would today be known as mental therapy and psychoanalysis. He was very much interested in education and had many plans for improving the organization of higher education, especially those parts concerned with scientific fields.[7]

[3] *Ibid.* p. xvi.
[4] *Ibid.* p. xi.
[5] Leverton, Garrett. *Philosophy of the Human Voice* by James Rush. p. 9.
[6] Coulton, Thomas E. *op. cit.* p. 59.
[7] *Dictionary of American Biography*, ed. by Dumas Malone. vol. 16. p. 227-30.

Although never as well known as his father, James Rush showed similar intellectual interests. After being graduated from the College of New Jersey (Princeton), 1805, he was graduated from the Medical School of the University of Pennsylvania in 1809. He then went to the University of Edinburgh for further training where he was very much influenced by the philosophic thought of the day. He married a very wealthy woman, was relieved of the necessity of earning his living by ordinary practice of medicine, and spent most of his time in writing. He published *The Philosophy of the Human Voice* in 1827. Later he, like his father, became interested in the study of the mind and published *Analysis of the Human Intellect* in 1865. In addition to his writing, he was also Professor of *Theory and Practice of Medicine* in the Jefferson Medical College in Philadelphia.

Rush represented in a way the mid-stage in the modernization of science in which there was a good bit of theorizing about avoiding theory and establishing facts. He objected to inexact descriptions and proceeded to observe, place in categories, and devise new names that would be more explicit than the ones used by previous writers. However, he often found himself falling back on the old adjectives to describe the new categories. He was groping for a system which would develop a science of speech apart from musical systems. His approach, which may truly be said to be scientific, is defined in the following statement: "To know in natural philosophy, we must employ our senses and contrive experiments, on the subject of inquiry, and admit no belief, which may not at any time be made undeniable by demonstration." [8] If the results of his research do not seem as reliable as those of work done today, it is because he did not have at his command the modern techniques.

His Purpose. In the preface to the first edition, Rush stated: "Upon ascertaining some interesting facts in the uses of Speech, I was induced to pursue the investigation and subsequently to attempt a methodical description of the various vocal phenomena with a view to bring the subject within the limits of science, and thereby to assist the purposes of oratorical instruction." [9] Thus his purpose is stated in one of the most direct and simple sentences in his book. He seemed to have had two main objectives: (1) to devise a discriminative nomenclature for the "vocal signs" which he observed and (2) to show how elocution could be taught scientifically. "I propose," he says, "to give, in the course of this essay, an analysis of vocal expres-

[8] Rush. *op. cit.* p. 110.
[9] *Ibid.* p. xxvii.

sion; to point out its modes, forms, and varieties, and to assign a definite nomenclature to them." [10]

In addition to these objectives, there was also the desire to establish a system which would make the art of reading and speaking more permanent. This will be remembered as one of the reasons why the English elocutionists of the Mechanical school worked out their notations for the variations in speech. The following quotation will explain the attitude of Rush toward this problem:

And while in other arts, we can turn to an "Apollo," a "Parthenon" . . . the Rules of the Oratorio, . . . the "Institutes" of Quinctilian, and the Precepts of Horace and of Pope,—let Elocution be able hereafter, not only to bring forward the name of a Roscius, a Garrick, a Siddons, and a Booth, but let it at the same time lay up in the Cabinet of the arts, a history of the available ways and means of their vocal superiority. In short, let the art of speaking well be invested through its descriptive method, with that corporate capacity, by the preservative succession of which, the influence of its highest masters shall never die. [11]

Rush felt that an art must be firmly established upon scientific rules before it could be improved. Music seemed to him to be so established. In explaining this viewpoint, he said that those who did not base their art upon a "language of unchangeable meaning" were not able to discriminate and expressed nothing but their approbation. [12]

In accordance with his purpose, Rush developed a minute classification of the different "modes" of speech and the "vocal signs" by which they were demonstrated and thus he established his system for teaching elocution and for developing reading, acting, and declaiming into reputable and permanent arts.

This so-called scientific approach could not tolerate the natural method which shunned rules and took its cues from nature. Curiously enough the rhetoricians who were most in vogue in the American colleges were representatives of the Natural school. Coulton found that the two texts most used between 1820-1830 were those written by Campbell and Blair, while Whately's ranked first after 1830. [13] They were all English rhetoricians who did not follow Walker's mechanical rules for delivery. To some it seemed that in Rush the *mechanical* method had triumphed and that the rather vague *natural* method was to be superseded. However, this was not true. At the end of the century, "think-the-thought" methods were to

[10] *Ibid.* p. 137.
[11] *Ibid.* p. 513.
[12] *Ibid.* p. xxxvi.
[13] Coulton. *op. cit.* p. 33.

appear. They were reminiscent of Porter and Sheridan but based upon the new psychology, which was clamoring to be considered as a science.

INDEBTEDNESS TO FORMER WRITERS IN THE FIELD. Sheridan, Steele, and Walker are all mentioned by Rush and some credit is given to them as pioneers in the development of elocution. The following quotation from the introduction of the fifth edition lists the debts Rush considered noteworthy:

> In a general view of its amount it appears:—That the number, the kinds and the organic causes of the Alphabetic Elements have long since been recorded with accurate detail.—That Quantity, or the Time of syllabic utterance, together with the subject of Pause had been distinguished only by a few indefinite terms, until Mr. Steele, with much discriminative perception applied to speech some of the principles and symbols of musical notation.—That accent or the means of distinguishing a syllable by stress or intensity of voice, has been definitely described in English orthoepy, both as to its places and degrees.—That this syllabic stress, though attentively regarded in the grammatical institute of the Greeks, is yet in their records, so confounded with some indistinct idea of the sliding rise, fall, and circumflex turn of the voice, that we are left together in doubt as to their systematic and separate use of these different functions.— That Emphasis, when restricted to the purpose of making one or more words conspicuous by intensity of voice, has long been a subject of rhetorical attention; Mr. Walker being the first among modern philologists, who attempted, under the terms upward and downward slide to connect any formal idea of Intonation with it.—And finally that the Analysis of Intonation has not been extended much beyond the recorded knowledge of the ancients.[14]

According to James Murdoch, one of his most faithful followers, Rush was the first writer to use the term *intonation* in the discussion of the sounds of speech although it had been used by writers on music for at least a century before to denote the precise recognition of the intervals.[15]

Fritz asserts that Dr. Rush was the first writer to make any mention of the quality of the voice or to claim that the tone of the voice could be improved.[16] Porter mentioned quality earlier, in *Analysis of Vocal Inflections Used in Reading and Speaking,* but used only two divisions—lively and pathetic—and considered it a relative modification, whereas inflection was an absolute modification of the voice.[17] And so it is in the treatment of quality and intonation that Dr. Rush seems to make his most important contribution. At

[14] **Rush**. *op. cit.* p. xxxiv.
[15] Murdoch, James. *A Plea for Spoken Language,* p. 70.
[16] Fritz, Charles A. *The Content of the Teaching of Speech in the American College before 1850.* p. 44.
[17] Porter, Ebenezer. *Analysis of Vocal Inflections Used in Reading and Speaking.* p. 8.

least, his nomenclatures for these phases of speech are the ones most used by his successors.

Since this book is concerned with methods of teaching, we shall consider *The Philosophy of the Human Voice* in terms of its effect upon teachers and textbooks. It will not be criticized as a scientific study but as a system which exerted a great influence upon the teaching of oral interpretation of literature.

HIS DEFINITION OF SPEECH. Dr. Rush's definition of speech was not a new one,—every state of mind has its corresponding vocal signs in some of the varied forms of pitch, force, time, and quality. In his explanation, however, it becomes involved:

> Speech is employed to declare the States and Purposes of the Mind. These are first known to us as Ideas; and ideas are divided into thoughts and Passions. According to this view, the design of speech is to declare our thoughts and passions.

* * *

> The first state or condition of the mind is its simple perception of things, their actions, and relationships, with no reference to the exciting interests of human life. We apply to this state of plain idea, or thought, and to the vocal sign that denotes it, the term, *Thoughtive*. Its vocal sign consists in the simple rise and fall and shorter wave of the interval of the *Second*; of an unobtrusive Quality; with a moderate degree of Force; and short syllabic Time or Quantity.

> The second, or intermediate condition has that relation to human life, which excites moderately self-interesting reflections in the mind; and embraces dignity, pathos, awe, admiration, reverence, a serious sentiment, and other states congenial in character and degree with these. We call this condition of the mind, and its vocal signs, the *Inter-thoughtive*, but preferably the *Sentimentive* or *Reverentive*. Its signs are variously the interval of the semitone, the second, occasionally the third and fifth, with their waves; an extended time; a full orotund quality; and with a moderate and dignified force.

> The third condition. . . . Its signs are the semitone and wider rising and falling intervals, with their waves; either a short or an extended time, a striking variety of quantity, abruptness; with high degrees, and impressive forms of force. We call this state of mind and the signs which denote it the *Passionate*.[18]

In his attempt to be truly scientific, Rush finds himself confronted with the problem of explaining why this relationship between the mind and speech exists. He falls back on the word "nature" in what seems to be a rather reluctant fashion and explains:

> As I profess, in this work, to draw the history of the human voice, altogether from observation by the ear, and experiment with the tongue, it will be convenient, and even necessary, from the constant reference to the combined agencies that make up the system of speech, to have some brief term to

[18] Rush. 5th ed. p. 161-4.

designate what we imagine to be the directive principle or general agent over these subordinate and perceptible agencies. I have, therefore, in the text adopted an abstract sign for all these agencies, and their effects, in the word Nature; a word often taken in error, and in vain, but not yet obsolete. This term, this Nature, I use every where and always with the same meaning when personified as the representative of an all-sufficient, and everpresent system of causes; which in the broad wisdom of its ordination, and universal consistency of its effects, is the bright and unchanging example of truth, and right, and goodness, and beauty; and worthy of increasing study and imitation, for beginning, without delusive hopes, the intellectual, the political, the moral, and esthetic refinement of man.[19]

This explanation is a good example of his laborious style of writing and his struggle to be exact and not use words, especially descriptive adjectives, that have been used in a rather loose fashion by the writers who preceded him.

It is necessary now to explain and describe these vocal signs which accompany the different states of mind and are constitutents of the different bases of speech.

THE MODES OF SPEECH. Rush divides vocal expression into five modes: Pitch, Force, Abruptness, Quality, and Time, in which are to be found all the vocal signs.[20] *Abruptness* is really a part of *Force,* but such an important part that Rush accords it a place by itself. In comparison with the divisions made in the first section, those made by Rush are more extensive. *Accent* is not discussed separately. *Quality* and *Abruptness* are the two new divisions added as a result of research. *Articulation* and *Pronunciation* do not concern Rush except indirectly, and *Gesture* is omitted entirely.

HIS ANALYSIS OF THE MODES. (a) *Pitch.* Rush maintains that there are four scales of pitch. The terms used are musical if the functions are identical for singing and speaking. First, there is the *Concrete* scale in which from beginning to end the voice is either rising or falling and there is no appreciable interval or interruption or continuity. This can be demonstrated on the violin when the finger is moved along the string and makes what is called a *slide.* The *Diatonic* scale is made up of discrete tones that "skip" rather than slide, and the transitions are made principally by whole tones. The *Chromatic* scale consists of a discrete succession of half-steps or semitones. The *Tremulous* scale consists of momentary impulses separated from each other by very minute intervals. This is not to be confused with the *tremolo* which uses a tremor on a straight line. The extent to which

[19] *loc. cit.*
[20] Rush. 4th ed. p. 49.

the voice is used in any one of these scales within the limits of distinct articulation is called the *Compass of Speech*.[21] Although the scales are represented separately in the discussion, in actual practice they are used variously and in combination. However, the *Concrete* is always used and is the chief distinguishing characteristic between singing and speaking. In fact, in the *Concrete*, Rush finds the peculiarity in the human voice which is not copied by musical instruments— "The equable gliding, the lessening volume and the soft extinction of the yet inimitable radical and vanishing movement."[22] He explains his choice of names for these two parts in the following way: "I have called the first part of the concrete, or that of 'a'. . . (a—e) the Radical movement; because, with a full beginning or opening, the following portion of the concrete proceeds from it as from a base or root. I have called the last part, or that of it, 'e' in the example, the Vanishing Movement, from its becoming gradually weaker as it rises, finally dying away in the upper extreme of tone." When an alphabetic sound is pronounced with smoothness and without emotion, it commences full and somewhat abruptly and gradually decreases its upward movement until it becomes inaudible. This form Rush names the *Equable Concrete*. If the radical is prolonged too long it is a *Protracted Radical;* the ending also may be prolonged into a *Protracted Vanish*. These forms are to be heard in song and recitative and are not good for speech.[23] Rush proceeded to investigate the syllables and the individual sounds to see how many of them showed this phenomenon and devised symbols to illustrate the radical. (See page 89)

The thirty-five elements of sounds he divides into three general groups: (1) tonics, (2) subtonics, (3) atonics. The first division, the *tonics*, embraces sounds with the radical and vanish in most nearly perfect form. The sounds are illustrated by the following words: *all, art, an, ale, our, isle, old, eel, ooze, err, end,* and *in*. They are all described as being produced by the joint function of the larynx and parts of the internal and external mouth. "The tonics," Rush comments, "are of a more tuneable nature than the other elements. They are capable of infinite prolongation; admit of the concrete and tremulous rise and fall, through all the intervals of pitch, may be uttered more forcibly than the other elements as well as with more abruptness: and while these two last characteristics are appropriate to the natural fullness and stress of the radical, the power of prolongation upon their pure and controllable quality, is finely accommodated

[21] *Ibid.* p. 61-2.
[22] *Ibid.* p. 71.
[23] *Ibid.* p. 70.

I have not given symbols for the concrete and discrete minor third, and semitone, since their representation on the staff may be easily imagined.

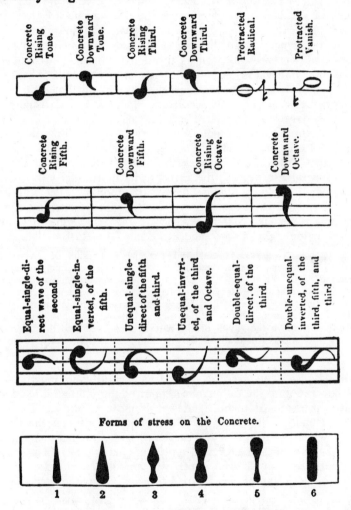

Forms of stress on the Concrete.

In the above notation, there is no meaning in the curve of the vanish, nor in the circular enlargement of the radical.

NOTATIONS USED BY DR. RUSH
Reproduced from *The Philosophy of the Human Voice*

to the delicate structure of the vanishing movement." The second group, the *Subtonics,* have vocality but in some of them it is combined with aspiration. The following words illustrate the sounds; *bow, dare, give, vile, zone, ye, woo, then, azure, sing, love, may, not roe; b, d, g, ng, l, m, n, r,* have unmixed vocality while *v, z, y, th,* and *zh* have a mixture of vocality with aspiration. The third group are the *Atonics* or the Mutes; *up, out, ark, if, yes, he, wheat, thin* and *push.*[24]

Both the concrete and discrete scales move through syllables and phrases and sentences, as well as through the individual sounds and the choice of interval is determined by the state of mind. The interval of the sound or of one whole tone expresses plain thought. The interval of the semitone expresses some emotion and is usually combined with larger intervals. The intervals of the Third, Fifth, or Octave, if rising are interrogatory in character. If falling, they denote positiveness and command. In all states where the vocal signs are the Third, Fifth, or the Octave; the Third will represent the mind in the least intense degree; the Fifth, in its more intense degree, and the Octave in its most intense degree of emotion. The interval of the octave indicates the movement of the voice from any assumed radical place through superior parts of the scale, until it ends or vanishes in the eighth degree above the radical. Rush explains:

> This concrete interval is employed for the expression of interrogation; and for astonishment, wonder, and admiration, when they imply some slight sentiment of doubt or inquiry. It is further used for the emphatic distinction of words. Nor is it limited to phrases having the common grammatical construction of a question; for even declaratory sentences are made interrogative by the use of this interval. Although the voice in interrogation and emphasis, may sometimes rise above the eighth of the natural voice, and into the falsette; the octave is the widest interval of the speaking scale, technically regarded in this work.[25]

The *Wave* of the voice is defined as a continuous moving of the rising concrete into the falling concrete or of the falling into the rising. As an expression of mental states it is most effective. The Wave of the Second, or the rising of one whole tone, enforces the Diatonic Melody which is inexpressive. It adds dignity to this melody. The Wave of the Semitone, however, represents many different states; sorrow, grief, vexation, chagrin, contrition, condolence, pity, love, fatigue, or pain. The Wave of the Third, Fifth and Octave is used to denote

---

[24] *Ibid.* p. 81-3. The later phoneticians added ten or eleven sounds to this list and grouped the consonants into voiced or voiceless divisions. The modern school allows only three nasals in English; *m, n, ng,* whereas Dr. Rush included three more; *b, d, g.* These are now called plosives and labeled according to the articulatory organs which work to produce the sounds. *b* is bi-labial, *d* is lingua-dental, and *g* lingua-velar. cf. Jones, Daniel. *Outline of English Phonetics.*
[25] *Ibid.* p. 206.

earnestness and emphatic distinction. The use of the wave of these intervals is largely in combination with other vocal signs.[26]

The *Tremor* of the voice is a trembling of the uttered tone. The tremor of the concrete semitone denotes grief, tenderness, and suffering, while the tremor of the larger intervals, the second, third, fifth or octave denote mirth, exultation, derision, and contempt.[27]

The melody of speech involves the perception of the radical and vanishing movements of successive syllables. This melody may be subdivided into *Current Melody* which is the succession of sounds that prevail in the general sentence, and the *Melody of the Cadence* which is present at the end of the sentence. A further distinction is called the *Phrases* of melody which break up the *Current Melody* into distinctive parts.[28]

(b) *Force.* There are two main degrees of force which may, according to the Rush system, be characterized as *Piano* and *Forte.* *Piano* characterizes the weak voice and is indicative of such emotions as humility, modesty, shame, doubt, irresolution, apathy, caution, repose, fatigue, and prostration from disease. The *Forte* of the voice has to do with loudness and is associated with states of mind which denote muscular energy and vivid degrees of passion, such as joy or fear. Rush explains the two types in relation to the states of the mind when he says: "All sentiments, unbecoming or disgraceful, smother the voice to its softer degrees, in the desire to conceal even the voluntary utterance of them. Joy is loud in calling for companionship through the overflowing charity of its satisfaction. Bodily pain, fear, and terror are also strong in their expression; with the double intention of summoning relief, and repelling the offending cause when it is a sentient being." [29]

There is no particular disagreement with former writers on this subject of force in terms of accent and emphasis, although previously it seemed to be viewed as the only means of emphatic distinction, while the Rush system gives it "an influential but not an overbearing agency among the modes of the voice." [30]

In line with his emphasis on the *Concrete* in the study of *Pitch,* Rush develops his discussion of *Force* primarily in terms of stress applied to different parts of the concrete syllable itself. The different stresses are distinguished by names according to the part of the concrete syllable which receives the stress. Thus, there is *Radical stress*

[26] *Ibid.* p. 413.
[27] *Ibid.* p. 415-16.
[28] *Ibid.* p. 145-7.
[29] *Ibid.* p. 321.
[30] *Ibid.* p. 414-15

at the beginning, *Median stress* during the syllable, and *Vanishing stress* at the end. In addition, there is a *Compound stress* which falls both at the beginning and at the end, and a *Thorough stress* which applies the stress equally throughout the syllable. These last two, however, are to be avoided because they tend to give a rude or vulgar effect.[31]

(c) *Abruptness.* From the discussion of *Radical stress* develops the mode *Abruptness.* The scope of the character and occasion for Abruptness is limited. Rush says: ". . . it has no varied forms and but slight difference in degree. It might indeed be arranged under the term abrupt-radical stress; since it is at the opening, alone, of the concrete, that its effect as a peculiar function and as an independent Mode of Speech is recognized.[32] He explains the manner in which this abruptness is accomplished in the following way:

> The Radical stress consists in an Abrupt and forcible utterance at the beginning of the concrete movement. . . . A single impulse of coughing is not in all points exactly like the abrupt voice or syllable; for the single impulse is a forcing out of almost all the breath which is not the case in syllabic utterance; yet if the tonic element *"Awe"* be employed as the vocality of coughing, its abrupt opening will truly represent the function of radical stress, when used in discourse. The clear and energetic radical stress must be preceded by an interruption of the voice. There seems to be a momentary occlusion in the larynx, or, somewhere, to speak with caution, by which the breath is barred and accumulated for the purpose of a full and sudden discharge. This occlusion is more under command and the explosion is more powerful, on syllables beginning with a tonic element; or with an abrupt one preceding a tonic, for in this last instance, the articulative, if there is any difference in the bases, is combined with the vocal occlusion.[33]

Although Rush describes the breath as being exploded, he does not use the terms, *explosive, effusive,* and *expulsive* which are often attributed to him. Since *The Philosophy of the Human Voice* was written as a scientific treatise and was too cumbersome and involved for the ordinary student, a number of teachers who followed the Rush principles wrote books which attempted to simplify and make the system usable. Murdoch and Russell wrote such a book in 1845. They use the above-mentioned terms in their explanation of the orotund quality. They say:

> "Orotund" quality may, in one of its aspects, be regarded as the maximum of "pure tone" united with the intensest force. Like pure tone, however, it

[31] *loc. cit.* cf. Woolbert, Charles. *The Fundamentals of Speech.* p. 239-41. It is interesting to note that Woolbert uses these same divisions in his discussion of stress in *The Fundamentals of Speech,* published in 1927, with one additional division called *Intermittent stress* where force is applied in waves across the whole sound.
[32] *Ibid.* p. 355.
[33] *Ibid.* p. 323.

admits of degrees; and we find it existing according to the greater or less intensity of the emotion, in the different forms of "effusive," "expulsive," and "explosive" force.[34]

Abruptness, according to Rush, is a supplement of *Force.* It may be added to force to make it more emphatic just as force may be added to passionate intonation to enhance its expression. This mode is peculiar also, in that it is found in only two places: at the opening of the radical, and in the vocule at the end of the subtonic.[35]

(d) *Quality.* A good quality of voice seems so important to the teacher of Oral Interpretation today, that it seems incredible that the writers before Rush were not interested in its explanation and in methods of improving it. Rush considers it extremely important and says of it: "Quality is, as it were the material of speech; and many of its forms are employed for the purpose of expression.[36] The principal forms according to the system which he has devised are: the *Whispering,* the *Natural,* the *Falsette,* the *Orotund,* and the *Guttural.*

There are many states of mind which are instinctively associated with the appropriate quality. The *Whisper* denotes secrecy, the *Falsette* is used for the scream of fear, pain or surprise, the *Natural* for ordinary conversation and "familiar" reading, while the *Orotund* is used for deliberation and for dignity. Few people have the last quality, the *Orotund,* by nature and are forced to spend much time in practice in order to acquire it.[37]

Since Rush believes this quality is the most desirable one, much space is given to a discussion of its origin and its functions in expression of the mind. Perhaps it will be well to let Rush define his own term:

On the basis of the Latin phrase, I have constructed the term Orotund, to designate both adjectively and substantively, that assemblage of eminent qualities which constitutes the highest character of the speaking voice.

By the Orotund voice, I mean a natural, or improved manner of uttering the elements with a fullness, clearness, strength, smoothness, and if I may make a word, a sub-sonorous quality, rarely heard in ordinary speech; and never found in its highest excellence, except through long and careful cultivation.

By fullness of voice, I mean a grave and hollow volume, resembling the hoarseness of a common cold.

By Clearness, a freedom from nasal murmur and aspiration.

By Strength, a satisfactory loudness or audibility.

By Smoothness, a freedom from all reedy or guttural harshness.

[34] Murdoch, James E. and Russell, William. *Orthophony or Vocal Culture.* p. 101.
[35] *Ibid.* p. 203.
[36] *Ibid.* p. 162.
[37] *Loc. cit.*

By Sub-sonorous quality, its muffled resemblance to the resonance of certain musical instruments.[38]

The method of achieving the Orotund is a little difficult to understand, but it seems to depend upon interrupted expiration. "The frequent occurrence of exaggerated sentiments in the drama, joined to the effort required by the dimensions of the Theatre, produces the habit of interjective expiration, which exerted through a wide extension of the mouth, leads the speaker to the attainment of the Orotund, if his voice is capable of it." [39]   The orotund was, according to Rush, more tuneable, fuller in volume and the only voice appropriate for epic and dramatic reading.[40]

Rush did not wish to go too deeply into the physiology of the mechanism because he was not quite sure of some of the descriptions given by previous writers. Although he admitted that a knowledge of the mechanism would be helpful, he thought that an observation of its function always preceded the knowledge of the anatomical structure. As a result, Rush says that he is not sure whether the natural voice is produced by the vibration of the cords of the glottis, neither is he quite sure what the differences between falsette, natural, and guttural voices imply as to the origin and resonance of the sound. "It has been supposed that the falsette is produced at the 'upper' orifice of the larynx formed by the summits of the arytenoid cartilages and the epiglottis; and the difficulty of joining the falsette with the natural voice, which is thought to be made by the inferior ligaments of the glottis is ascribed to the change of mechanism in transition." [41] His statement concerning the guttural voice is a little more positive; "There is a harsh quality called guttural; produced by the vibratory current of the air between the sides of the pharynx and the base of the tongue, when apparently brought into contact above the glottis." [42]

It is interesting to refer to modern textbooks in which these qualities of the voice are listed. Orotund, Pectoral (chest resonance), Oral (cheek resonance), Falsetto, Guttural, Whispering, and Nasal (nose resonance) are terms still in use.[43]

(e) *Time*. The discussion of time adds little that is original or new. A syllable is said to have a long or short time, or *Quantity*. This is dependent, of course, upon the state of mind. To quote Rush:

[38] *Ibid.* p. 123-4.
[39] *Ibid.* p. 129-30.
[40] *Ibid.* p. 129-31.
[41] *Ibid.* p. 81-3 *passim.*
[42] *Ibid.* p. 153.
[43] cf. Woolbert, Charles. *op. cit.* p. 202-6. Davis, Estelle H. and Mammen, Edward W. *The Spoken Word in Life and Art.* p. 315-20.

"Sentiments of dignity, deliberation, doubt, and grief affect slow time; those of gaiety, anger, and eager argument, together with parenthetic phrases, assume the quick time in utterance." [44]

In elaboration of this mode, the syllables are divided into three classes: (1) Those very short terminated by an abrupt element, and containing a tonic, or an additional sub-tonic, or the further addition of an atonic, such as *at, ap, ek, hap*less, *pit*fall, ac*cep*tance; (2) Those limited to a quantity somewhat greater than that of the first, terminated by an abrupt element, and containing one or more sub-tonics or atonics, with a short tonic as *yet, what, tip, grat*itude, des*truc*tion; (3) Those long syllables which are capable of different quantities terminated by a tonic, or a sub-tonic, except *b, d,* and *g* as in syllables *go, thee, till,* de*lay,* ex*treme.*[45]

The power of giving indefinite prolongation to syllables for the purpose of expression is not one that is common to speakers, according to Rush. "A reader who has not by practice, a facility in executing the prolonged quantity of speech, will be liable, in extending his syllables, to fall into the protracted radical or protracted vanish."[46]

Phrasing is important to good reading and is dependent upon proper pauses. The question of the relationship to punctuation marks is disposed of in the following manner: "All the parts of a connected discourse, should both in subject and in structure bear some relation to each other. But these relations being severally, nearer and more remote, grammatical Points were invented to mark their varying degrees. The common points, however, very indefinitely effect their purposes, in the art of reading. They are described in books of elementary instruction, principally with reference to the *time* of pausing; and are addressed to the eye, as indications of grammatical structure."[47]

Rush acknowledges Walker to be correct in his idea that points should consist in directing appropriate intonation at pauses as well as the duration of the pause. Rush was himself so anxious to be exact in use of points that he added a symbol of punctuation in his fifth edition, the double comma ', which was to indicate a pause between the length of the comma and the semicolon.

Murdoch tells us that Rush obtained a great part of his knowledge from observing the great English actress, Mrs. Siddons. Rush mentions her especially in connection with accurate timing.

While listening to the intonations of this surpassing Actress, I first felt a want of that elementary knowledge which would have enabled me to trace

[44] Rush. 4th ed. p. 166.
[45] *Ibid.* p. 166-7.
[46] *Ibid.* p. 169.
[47] *Ibid.* p. 191.

the ways of all her excellence. I could not, however, avoid learning from her instinctive example, what the appointed elders over my education should have taught me; that one of the most important means of expressive intonation consists in the extended time of syllabic utterance.[48]

The use of the pause is, then, for sense and for sentiment. The rate, the quantity, and the pauses may affect any unit of speech from a syllable to a full sentence.

(f) *Summary of the Analysis.* There are three states of mind that are commonly revealed by speech: the Thoughtive, the Reverentive, and the Passionate. There are some states which do not have vocal signs and these have to depend upon the choice of words for expression.

The divisions of speech are Pitch, Force, Abruptness, Quality, and Time. These have their own peculiar vocal signs which work together in communicating the meaning to the hearer. There are thirty-five elemental sounds in our language and these demonstrate the radical and vanishing point in their formation according to the kind of sound the element happens to be. The three divisions are: Tonics, Sub-tonics, and Atonics. The Tonics show the equable concrete to the best advantage; also the mode, Abruptness.

The scales are the Diatonic, the Chromatic, Concrete, and Tremulous. These may be combined in speech and the intervals may vary, for either concrete or discrete sounds, from a semitone to the octave. The perception of the radical and vanish in successive syllables gives the melody of speech. Force may be either soft or weak and may be applied to different units from the integral parts of the syllable to the sentence. Time may be found in varying duration within the element, syllable, or word. The quantity given to the syllable is especially important to the expressive intonation of the word. Phrasing is important to the proper expression of a sequence of thoughts and although sometimes coincident with the punctuation points does not depend entirely upon them.

The qualities of the voice are: Whispering, Natural, Falsetto, Orotund, and Guttural. The orotund is the most difficult to attain and the most desirable.

METHODS OF TEACHING. Rush is convinced that the art of speaking well can be taught by rules developed from his analysis. He discounts the belief that elocution cannot be taught because it is the work of genius or "as a kind of sleight: the ways and means of which are unknown and immeasureable." [49] Genius is, to him, merely an apti-

[48] *Ibid.* p. 180.
[49] *Ibid.* p. 515.

tude for the intelligent and exclusive attention which perceives and accomplishes more than is done without it. He admits, however, that in the course of instruction, "genius is oftenest the pupil of itself." [50]

Although he recognizes some imitation as necessary and hopes that a better speech may be handed down from the parents to the children, yet he feels the need of a uniform system, since there will be many different idols that will be followed blindly if it is lacking, and there will be no basis for criticism. ". . . an art must be set up with the consent of all: and that consent can be drawn only from a common source of instruction and knowledge. . . ." [51]

The practice of rules must be accompanied by careful thought. The rules for practice are all based upon the alphabetical elements and the plan justified because of a similarity between the teaching of speech and of grammar.

> Language was long ago resolved into its alphabetic elements, and its Parts of speech. Wherever that analysis is known, the art of grammar is with the best success, conducted upon the rudimental method. Now, if the *expressive* uses of the voice should be taught by a similar analysis, the advantage would be no less than that resulting from the *alphabetic* and *grammatical* resolution. In this way we teach the child the elements and their combinations in speech; surely then, there is no reason why a clear perception of the varieties of stress, of time, and of intonation, and the power of consciously employing them in current utterance, should not be acquired in a similar elementary manner. [52]

Rush designs a didactic system for the student which is similar to the exercises which he practiced while analyzing speech and from which he learned all that "the well-read critic may find to be new, in this work." [53] He suggests eleven different forms of practice that will be useful in developing the art of elegant reading. [54]

1. *Practice on the Alphabetic Elements.* It is important to practice each individual vocal sound, rather than the syllables, because many are found to be neglected in actual practice and the audience finds thoughts and passions obscure simply because the sounds are not all intelligible. In addition to improvement in intelligibility to the audience, exercises which give the student command over each alphabetic sound will contribute to the musical quality of speech and to the elegance of reading.

2. *Practice on the Time of the Elements.* It is necessary to practice the elements as a kind of "time table" on which the student is to

[50] *Ibid.* p. 516.
[51] *Ibid.* p. 423.
[52] *Ibid.* p. 424.
[53] *Loc. cit.*
[54] *Ibid.* p. 424-36.

learn all their varieties of quantity. It is of no value to practice the prolongation of the atonics but such practice on the tonics and the sub-tonics will give him command over them so that he may give any quantity that the syllable may demand to convey a particular idea or emotion. There are a few sounds which allow slight variation; among these are *b, g, d,* and *s.* "The element *s,* when alone and prolonged, is a sign of contempt. In syllabic combination it is offensive if much extended in quantity. Under its shortest time it does its part in speech and loses much of its character of the hiss. Let the pupil therefore practice the shortest quantity on this element, by abruptly terminating the breath, or by separating the teeth at the moment its sound is heard; for this at once cuts it short." [55]

3. *Practice on Vanishing Movement.* In the elementary intonation of the equable concrete, the most difficult part is the vanishing movement. The student should practice until he is able to give such a delicate expiration that its limits are almost imperceptible.

4. *Practice on Force.* It is not necessary to practice force in connection with each element since the other constituents of expressive speech are brought under command when force is effected. It is better, then, to practice reading or speaking sentences and larger units in order to test the varieties of force and their effect upon the thought. It should always be considered in practice for the orotund voice, since it is an important means of acquiring that quality.

5. *Practice on Stress.* Even though radical stress is made with emphatic stress on the tonics, the subtonics must not be neglected entirely since they carry other stresses. "The full power of radical abruptness in tonics is acquired, by opening the elements into utterance, with a sort of coughing explosion. The pupil cannot be too strongly urged to a long and careful practice, in exploding the radical stress." [56] There is particular direction necessary for median stress since it is usually employed in the wave and its practice is included in exercises for pitch. The vanishing stress may be practiced in an effort which is something like a hiccough for the wider intervals of the scale and something like sobbing for the minor third and semitone. Compound stress and the loud concrete should be practiced so that the student may execute them, if necessary. However, in ordinary speech they are not used, and neither is the minor third, but it is well to practice them so that they will be familiar to the ear.

[55] *Ibid.* p. 429.
[56] *Ibid.* p. 431.

6. *Practice on Pitch.* It is well to begin practice with the piano until every interval is familiar. If a piano is not available, the student may discover the intervals through the meaning conveyed by the sentence. The following direction for finding the interval of the second is an interesting example of a negative approach in giving directions. How effective or exact it is might be questioned.

> I must negatively describe the effect of the simple and uncolored interval of the second, by saying,—it is not the semitone, with its plaintive character; nor the rising third, or fifth, or octave, also well known as the sign of interrogation; nor the downward movements of positive declaration and command; nor the wave, with its admiration, surprise, mockery, or sneer. If then, in syllabic utterance, we produce none of these effects, we may conclude we have passed through the simple second of the diatonic melody.[57]

The student is urged to practice this interval on all tonics and subtonics until he has mastered it. He will then have no difficulty with the larger intervals. The rising intervals should be compared with the falling intervals and thus the difference between the intonation of a question and of a command will be made very plain. After practicing the rising and falling intervals, he should practice the wave in which they combine.

7. *Practice on Melody.* The student must be able to perceive the radical changes in the second in the progression of the current melody. If he has a musical ear, he will find it easy to vary the several phases that have been mentioned earlier in the discussion of melody. If he does not have a nice perception of sound or an ingenuity in experiment, he must learn the diatonic progression from the voice of a master. It is absolutely necessary to use variety in melody, and the practice must be on successive syllables as in current discourse. The student should keep in mind the diatonic progression of a portion of discourse and utter the tonic sound on each syllable. Thus the rise and fall of pitch will be more apparent and monotony more easily avoided.

8. *Practice on Cadence.* The student must practice all the different forms of cadence with attention to their construction and effect. If he has command of this form of intonation, he will have an ample supply of endings to fit any meaning which is to be conveyed and will be able to give variety when it is necessary.

9. *Practice on Tremor.* An accuracy should be acquired in using tremor on the individual elements. The practice of laughing and crying offers a wide field of practice on this vocal sign, but it is difficult to make the tremor seem unaffected. If the tremulous

[57] *Ibid.* p. 432.

expression is employed to affect an audience, "it should be governed in its taste. . . ." [58]   An analysis is therefore necessary in order to give the student command over this form, and the practice should be confined to the alphabetic elements.

10. *Practice on Quality.* This practice may be either on the elementary sounds or on current discourse, but since it is most perceptible on the tonic sound of a syllable, it is perhaps more effective if the exercises emphasize these sounds. Since the orotund is the most desirable quality and the hardest to cultivate, it should be practiced most conscientiously.

"It might seem sufficient," Dr. Rush says, "for a teacher of elocution to exemplify the orotund, that his pupil might imitate it. Vocalists in their lessons on Pure Tone do little more. But singing has long been an Art; and its many votaries have rendered the public familiar with its leading principles, and accustomed the ear to the peculiarities of its practice. . . . In describing, therefore, without the opportunity of illustrating, it becomes necessary to address the pupil as if he had no principles to help his understanding, nor exemplified sounds to satisfy his ear. For this purpose, it is necessary to make him teach himself, by referring to functions of the voice, familiar to him both by nature and name." [59]

11. *Practice in Rapidity of Speech.* Extreme rapidity of speech may be employed as a means for obtaining a command over the voice. It is recommended that the student select some material that is very familiar and that he read it or speak it with the "utmost possible precipitancy of utterance" taking care to articulate every separate sound properly.[60]

According to Rush, the three faults which may defeat this system are: defects of the mind, of the ear, or of the industry. "Speech is intended to be the sign of every variety of thought and feeling. If therefore, the mind of a scholar be not raised to that generality of condition, which can assume all the characters of expression, he will in vain aspire to great eminence in the art." [61] This is, of course, a defect that may well be called a misfortune. The musical ear will always give superiority to a speaker. However, the ability to detect fine shadings and variations of the vocal signs may be greatly improved through practice. The last mentioned fault, that of lack of industry, is the most deplored by Rush, and seems to him to be the worst fault which students demonstrate.

[58] *Ibid.* p. 434.
[59] *Ibid.* p. 125-6.
[60] *Ibid.* p. 436.
[61] *Ibid.* p. 464.

He mentions specifically many common faults such as: stress on the wrong word or overstress on all words; use of the chromatic or any other melody instead of the diatonic melody when it is required; not keeping cadence within the limit of distinct articulation; using the singing melody; speaking in monotone; using improper intonation at the pauses so that the listener does not know whether the thought is to be continued or not; faults in pausing which destroy the thought group; the faults of mimicry or of ranting, or of affectation or of mouthing. All of these along with any harsh or unpleasant quality of the voice are to be avoided.[62]

Not only did Rush think that his book would be the basis for the study of all English speech through his analytical study of the human voice, but he hoped that it would be useful for the elocutionist of any nation in the development of a didactic system for his native language. He hoped that the rules of speech might be as universal as those of music. This task Rush felt he had ably completed and it was a great disappointment to him when his book was not well received. It took time for the book to be recognized, but eventually there were faithful disciples of the Rush system who wrote books and taught in the colleges and universities. James Murdoch, the actor, was one of the most enthusiastic. In his book, *A Plea for the Spoken Language,* he observed that fifty years after the first publication, a very different opinion prevailed concerning the importance of *The Philosophy of the Human Voice.* It was then considered a great contribution to the scientific study of spoken language and was recognized abroad as well as at home. The French Academy of Sciences indorsed it as "an exposition of the vocal organs and their peculiar functions in the production of those elevations and depressions of the voice, technically known as pitch." [63]

The outstanding textbooks written by men who followed the Rush system extended from Dr. Jonathan Barber's *Grammar of Elocution,* published in 1830, to J. H. McIlvaine's *Elocution,* published in 1870, and included those written by Comstock, Bronson, North, Caldwell, Russell, Day, and Murdoch. The influence of Rush did not die with McIlvaine's *Elocution* but it competed with other systems such as that of Delsarte. Leverton, in his study of Rush, found influences of the Rush system in all the schools of speech functioning in 1925.[64] Anthony F. Blanks cites *The Technic of the Speaking Voice* by John

[62] *Ibid.* p. 465-510.
[63] Murdoch, *op. cit.* p. 93.
[64] Leverton. *op. cit.* p. 38.

R. Scott published in 1915 as the most recent book to follow Rush closely throughout.[65]

Not only were mechanical methods of elocution used in the college teaching of speech but also in the work done in reading in the public schools. Many *readers* and *speakers* were written during this period and they invariably included some instruction in elocution. McGuffey's readers were the most famous. The first two were published in 1836; in 1844 three more were added; by 1851 there was a series of six which was revised five times. The last revision was copyrighted in 1901 and the books were still being sold in 1927. Although McGuffey's acknowledged only Walker and his followers, some mentioned Dr. Rush. *The Practical Elocutionist* by Henry B. Maglachlin, 1850, followed Rush in the fifteen pages devoted to elocution, and also mentioned many of his followers: Murdoch, Russell, Bronson, Caldwell, and Day. Lucius Osgood's *Progressive Fourth,* 1856, followed Rush's terminology for quality and included some of the tongue-twisters which have appeared in many later books; for example, "Theophilus Thistle" and "Amidst the wildest, fiercest blasts, he thrusts his fists against the posts." In the same year, Salem Town and Nelson Holbrook published *The Progressive Fifth or Elocutionary Reader; in which the Principles of Elocution are Illustrated by Reading Exercises in Connection with Rules for the Use of Schools and Academies.* Epes Sargent published *The Intermediate Standard Speaker* in 1857 which preceded the famous *Standard Speaker* that went into its sixtieth edition two decades later. The interest in speaking "pieces" was evidently widespread and did not confine itself to higher education.

[65] Blanks, Anthony F. *An Introductory Study in the History of the Teaching of Public Speaking in the United States.* p. 258.

CHAPTER III

IMPORTANT TEACHERS OF THE PERIOD

A number of teachers wrote textbooks during this period. Some of the books were based entirely upon Rush; others acknowledged earlier writers as well. A few made unique contributions to the development of the teaching of oral interpretation.

DR. JONATHAN BARBER. Dr. Barber was a physician from the Royal College of Surgeons in London who came to this country, became interested in Rush, and incorporated the ideas he found useful in teaching into a book, entitled *A Grammar of Elocution; containing the Principles of the Arts of Reading and Speaking; illustrated by appropriate Exercises and Examples, adapted to colleges, schools, and private instruction; the whole arranged in the order in which it is taught in Yale College.* Barber modestly stated that he did not present his book as a discovery and that it was based on two books which preceded it: Steele's *Prosodia Rationalis,* and Rush's *The Philosophy of the Human Voice.* He praised Dr. Rush for writing "the first work that ever presented a true and comprehensive record of the vocal functions," and stated that his own book was the fruit gathered from the vine planted by Rush.[1]

The terminology is practically the same as that used by Rush, but the explanations are simpler. The same five modes are the basis of the exercises and discussion. The discussion of quality varies the most, but the *orotund* voice is extolled. The following excerpt will explain his concept of this vocal characteristic:

The quality of the voice, no doubt, depends partly, on unknown circumstances in the structure and action of the organs of speech; as the same tune played upon two organs or piano-fortes will differ in quality of tone, because one instrument differs from another in its peculiar power of modifying sound, owing to its physical properties as an instrument. . . . Its most important properties are *gravity,* or depth of tone; *fullness,* or volume of sound; *smoothness, sweetness,* and *strength*; by which latter property is meant the power of rendering syllables audible through an extensive space.[2]

The exercises which are given first are based on the elementary sounds—the vowels and consonants. These sounds, forty-six in number, since all the short vowels are included, are arranged in a table with illustrative words. All sounds except mutes are to be sounded individually first and then in combination. If no teacher is

[1] Barber, Jonathan. *A Grammar of Elocution.* p. 1.
[2] *Ibid.* p. 56, 172.

at hand to demonstrate the sounds of the elements, the student is to pronounce them in a slow and drawling manner and to notice carefully the positions of the organs of speech. He is to repeat the element over and over until it is clearly distinguished from the rest of the word. The elements are to be sounded with such energy as to make them full and forceful.[3]

Abruptness and the *radical* are important to Barber. "Let the voice open upon the element," he directs, "with some degree of fullness and abruptness,—let it gradually and equably diminish in volume of sound as it progresses, ending in a feeble vanish of sound into silence. This full opening and final vanish are essential to the preservation of pure speech." [4]

Articulation is rendered distinct and impressive by a prolongation of certain vowel elements as well as by giving them percussive force. If the student makes proper use of his voice, he will be able to utter every sound "with the suddenness of the report of fire-arms, without any apparent effort preceding the explosion, with a very high degree of percussive force, and with strength and fullness of tone. We should perhaps add, that we greatly doubt whether persons in general will ever gain strength of voice, in any other way, . . ." [5] The explosion, he says, is to consist of a short and single act of coughing forcibly made upon each vowel element.[6] This exercise demonstrates explosive stress, but care must be taken that the sound is purely vocal and not a mixture of tone with aspiration.

The technique used in class consists in asking each individual to sound the vocal element individually, then to ask the class to sound it in concert. The teacher must watch carefully that there be no deviation from the correct sound and that all are sounding the element with the proper degree of force.[7]

Selections are given for reading after these preliminary exercises are mastered. Attention must be given to the intonation, the cadences, the proper use of intervals, and so on. One of the faults that distressed Dr. Barber the most is the lack of rhythm in reading poetry. This attention to measure goes back to Steele and the notations used are the same, although only those for time and stress are used by Barber. (See p. 51) Exercises using the notations are recommended:

By the use of the exercises, it will soon be perceived that most persons are deficient in rhythm. By an exact observation of it, two consequences will

[3] *Ibid.* p. 22-3.
[4] *Ibid.* p. 32.
[5] *Ibid.* p. 30.
[6] *Loc. cit.*
[7] *Ibid.* p. 24.

follow; reading will cease to be laborious, and the sense will be rendered perfectly clear, as far as it is dependent on the capital point of the distribution of time, or measure. Lastly, the progress of the voice is to be distinct from the accented to the unaccented syllable, or from heavy to light, and not from light to heavy.[8]

Bad transitions are considered to be serious defects in reading. Barber asserts that, "nothing relieves the ear more agreeably than a well regulated transition, and suggests four ways of showing clearly that the speaker is entering upon a new train of thought. They are: by change of pitch, by alteration of rate, by an abatement of the previous force, and by a change in the phrases of melody. The other frequently considered faults are monotonous or inappropriate pitch and intonation; harsh, thin, nasal or mincing quality; the misuse of quantity and pauses which lead to bad rhythm; force unevenly applied according to demands of the thought; and beginning the sentence on a high forceful note and concluding on a low feeble note. The student is urged to avoid these faults and to work hard to gain complete control of his voice since it is "more improvable than any of our powers." [9]

Dr. Barber was not a popular teacher at Yale, although Wendell Phillips testifies in a letter to James Murdoch that he had the good fortune to be in Barber's class at Harvard where the values of his system were fully appreciated. Phillips goes further and testifies:

Whatever I have ever acquired in the art of improving and managing my voice, I owe to Dr. Barber's system, suggestions and lessons. No volume or treatise on the voice except those of Rush and Barber has ever been of any practical value to me. . . . His teachings tended to make good readers and speakers, not readers and speakers modeled on Barber.[10]

The young men at Yale, according to Murdoch, another student of Barber, were not willing to endure the long period of practice on the elementary exercises because they felt that they had passed beyond the alphabetic stage of their language. Barber himself says: "I have never yet pronounced the vocal elements of our language in one of my public lectures without exciting the mirthful wonder of the audience. Perpetually using or often misusing these elements, persons in general are ignorant of their existence as single, specific sounds." [11] Evidently the mirthful wonder turned into ridicule and Dr. Barber was forced to resign his position. After his resignation from Yale, he went to Harvard. Fritz found in his examination of

[8] *Ibid.* p. 197.
[9] *Ibid.* p. 96.
[10] Murdoch. *op. cit.* p. 101-2.
[11] *Loc. cit.*

college catalogs that Barber's book was used in Harvard from 1835 to 1840.[12]

Even though his course did not seem practical to all of his students, the purpose of teaching elocution in the colleges as he saw it was exceedingly practical, and in keeping with the new demands of the community upon the curriculum of the institution which prepared the leaders of the day.

> Oratorical pre-eminence can be the aim of few only, but a correct and impressive elocution is desirable by all; by all, at least, among the educated classes of society. . . . Great numbers of young men are daily entering our colleges, who are to become ministers of the gospel, or lawyers. In this country, too, no freeman is excluded from the state and national councils; on the contrary, talent, when combined with an emulous spirit, is naturally invited to participate in their administration; to say nothing of the frequency of public meetings for municipal or beneficent purposes. . . .
>
> Hereafter, young gentlemen of America, some of you will deeply regret your neglect of the art of delivery; when you are obliged to do that indifferently, which you might have learnt to do well; when, on some interesting occasion, (and such occasions will come,) you find you cannot fix the attention of your audience. . . .[13]

ANDREW COMSTOCK. Andrew Comstock's *A System of Elocution* was published in 1841. Although no record has been found of the book being used in a college, it is interesting because it is one of the first of the texts designed for special schools, which increased as the century progressed. Mr. Comstock owned and operated his own private school of elocution and perhaps was forced to over-advertise in order to make a living. Elocution was offered as a panacea for all speech defects and many bodily ailments. Good readers were supposed to be developed in thirty-six lessons in elocutionary training which consisted of vocal gymnastics and gesture. The system was based upon Rush and Austin. Comstock recommended the use of the metronome to mark time. His exercises were divided into measures, for example, ba ba ba ba / bi bi / bo bo bo / bu bu bu / bou.[14] This innovation in method is an interesting one in the use of the "elements" in training the voice. Other vocal techniques are traceable to earlier writers.

His emphasis upon gymnastics is new and significant. It marks the beginning of a trend in teaching speech which emphasized the interaction of the body and the mind. Physical exercises to develop a strong body became important to speech and in turn speech was

---

[12] Fritz. *op. cit.* p. 34.
[13] Barber. *op. cit.* p. 5.
[14] Comstock, Andrew. An earlier book, *Practical Elocution* was published Philadelphia, U. Hunt, 1930.

advertised as a curative for bodily ills. *A System of Elocution* states that its principles are based upon the science of the voice, and that the training consists in rapidity, precision and effect. Remarkable results are promised:

> . . . . Such healthful measures should be adopted as are calculated to invigorate the pulmonary apparatus, and enable it to maintain its integrity . . . were we to exercise our voices a few minutes, every day, according to just principles, the number of deaths from pulmonary affections, especially consumption, I have no doubt, would be greatly diminished.
>
> While vocal gymnastics give a keenness to appetite, they are a powerful means of promoting digestion. A young clergyman entered my vocal gymnasium, for the purpose of improving his elocution, as well as his health. He laboured under dyspepsia which was attended with a loss of appetite, general debility, languor, and dejection of spirits. But in twelve days after he commenced the exercises, there was a radical change in his mental and physical condition; he had become very cheerful; and, to use his own words, his appetite was *ravenous.*[16]

DR. C. P. BRONSON. According to testimonials printed in the appendix of the book, *Elocution; or Mental and Vocal Philosophy; involving the Principles of Reading and Speaking; and designed for the development of Both Body and Mind, in Accordance with the Nature and Uses, and Destiny of Man,* published in 1845, Dr. C. P. Bronson taught five classes in the academic department and three in the theological department of Yale College, and had taught elocution in Princeton College and in Marietta College, Marietta, Ohio.

He followed Comstock in recommending vocal exercises for their therapeutic value and was particularly concerned with deep breathing. His statement at the beginning of the book in the form of a testimonial gives his theories:

> Some years ago, the author was extensively engaged as a Public Speaker and, in consequence of the habit of speaking, principally, with the muscles of the throat and breast, he finally broke down, falling senseless, after speaking about an hour and a half; that was followed by a protracted illness; during which, he providentially discovered the *Causes,* and also the *Remedies* of the difficulties under which he had labored; and now, for months in succession, by the aid of these principles, he often speaks from six to ten hours a day, without the least inconvenience: the principal cause of which is, that the effort is made from the dorsal and abdominal region. Few are aware of the comprehensive nature of the principles here partially unfolded; and probably the Authors would now be in a similar state, had it not been for the teachings afforded by children and Indians. To secure a perfectly healthy distribution of the vital fluids throughout the body, and a free and powerful activity of the mind, there must be a full and synchronous action in the *brain,* the *lungs,* and the

[16] *Ibid.* p. 13.

viscera of the abdomen; the soul operating, naturally, on the dorsal and abdominal muscles, and thus setting in motion the whole body.

That he was the first to teach the specific use of those muscles, for a healthy breathing, and the exercise of the vocal organs, as well as blowing on wind instruments for hours together, without injury, he has not the least doubt; and, if any person will produce evidence to the contrary, from any medical writer, or teacher of elocution, previous to 1830, he shall be handsomely rewarded.[16]

Scott, in the preceding period, discussed the importance of deep breathing, but did not use physiological terminology or offer detailed exercises.[17]

Bronson illustrates his discussion of the physiological bases for speech with pictures of larynx, lungs, and ribs. He includes the picture of a young lady's thorax which showed the effects of having worn a corset too tightly laced. He describes the bad effects of improper dresses and admonishes, "cease to do evil and learn to do well." He gives the following directions for posture: "Sit or stand erect with the shoulders thrown back, so as to expand the chest, prevent the body from bending, and facilitate full deep breathing." [18] When practicing exercises for the vowels, this posture was to be taken and the mouth opened wide enough to admit two fingers sidewise; if this was difficult a piece of hardwood or ivory an inch and a half long with a notch in each end should be placed between the teeth.[19]

The relationship of speech to music is stressed in *Elocution*. In the vowel sound, according to Bronson, are involved all the elements of music. The eight vowels when naturally sounded, follow the notes of the scale: *oo* in ooze, is sounded on the A note, *o* as in old, on the G note, *a* as in at, on the F note, *a* as in ale, on the E note, *a* as in are, on the D note, *a* as in all, on the C note, *e* as in eel, on the C note, half tone, and *i* as in isle, on the B note.[20]

The book contains, "Two or three hundred choice anecdotes, three thousand oratorical and poetical readings, and five thousand proverbs, maxims, and laconics, and several hundred elegant engravings." It follows the earlier writers in working out gestures according to the emotions and is a queer mixture of the old ideas with the new emphasis upon physiology. It cannot truly be said to follow Rush, except chronologically. It is important because of its emphasis on breathing exercises.

[16] Bronson, C. P. *Elocution* (advertisement in book). 5th edition.
[17] Scott, William. *Lessons in Elocution*. p. 47.
[18] Bronson. *op. cit*. p. 17.
[19] See *Life*. March 11, 1940. p. 86. Shows pictures of Northwestern University students using same kind of gadget.
[20] Bronson. *op. cit*. p. 34.

Dr. Erasmus Darwin North. Dr. North was a physician, who like Dr. Rush and Dr. Bronson, became interested in the vocal organs and their functions. In his textbook, *Practical Speaking as Taught at Yale College*, published in 1846, he states that every complete work on physiology treats of voice, gesture, and of the alphabetic elements, and that Elocution is properly a branch of this science and no more connected with rhetoric than with any of the arts. He acknowledges Rush and Porter as contributing to his system, but condemns Austin as too mechanical.

His outline for the first lesson in acquiring a commanding and expressive voice follows his theory of elocution very logically. First, to stand in an attitude for speaking, then "heave up the chest by taking a very deep breath," and to take another before that one is completely used in speaking. The vocal effort should be assisted by talking in a state of strong and excited emotion, and the natural action of the breast should be aided with strong gestures of appeal with the right arm or with both arms.[21] Dr. North recalls the preachments of the Natural School, when he speaks about good delivery resulting from the natural impulses, and deplores the schools which follow Austin and teach gestures that are ungraceful and unnatural. The student must acquire those "unfettered bodily habits, in consequence of which attitude and gesture become as varied and graceful as the impulses from which they spring." [22]

To speak in public, the voice must have greater compass, depth, and flexibility than is developed in conversation, and this will depend partly upon the control of the breath.

In fact the peculiar open state of the fauces, the more tense the contraction of the vocal muscles, and the more sudden and complete emission of the breath which produce the tone of speaking, are natural indeed, but natural only in that sort of excitement of mind which leads a person to speak rather than to talk, and which is not needed in ordinary life. . . . Boys and young men never exhibit it except after considerable practice; when once however it is established, from that time they find no difficulty in speaking whenever they wish to do so. . . . It is indeed a kind of muscular action, which like that of swimming or of skating, is perhaps attained after a long continuance of repeated efforts, but when in fact mastered, is often gained suddenly and at once.[23]

The desired quality of the voice is discussed in terms of pure tone, and the pitch in keys lower, middle, and upper. Articulation depends somewhat upon the strata of society in which the student belongs and the best way of improving it is to be found in a "vigorous and con-

[21] North, Erasmus Darwin. *Practical Speaking as Taught at Yale College.* p. 52.
[22] *Ibid.* p. 10.
[23] *Ibid.* p. 13.

centrated effort of the mind, *to explain or set forth to the auditors, the* IDEA *conveyed by the word. . . ."* [24] Pronunciation should never attract attention. Pauses should always be placed between groups of words which give complete thoughts.

The techniques used in teaching do not include exercises based on the elementary sounds but seem to emphasize giving memorized original selections before the teacher for correction and approval. Much more leeway seems to be given to the student than in the other systems discussed. The three lower classes in Yale were given instruction throughout the year and the seniors were given private instruction as often as they wished. North mentions that in the past they had been taught the philosophy of English phonology, orthoepy, the structure and rhythm of English meters, and reading of poetry, but these, to his way of thinking, were not practical and so only the speaking of the students' own written or extemporaneous ideas was included in his course.[25] The appointments for practice before the instructor were five minutes in length. The instructor made a practice of telling the student when he was right rather than when he was wrong, and of making positive suggestions as to what he should do. "It is intended never to interrupt or make a criticism, without at the same time giving a direction that shall at once unfetter the speaker from the embarrassment of some practical difficulty which he is at the time experiencing, in regard to executing his own intentions." [26]
The accidental and occasional presence of a classmate for these private lessons is recommended as helping to give steadiness and self-possession to the student.

North felt that a "good delivery" was not absolutely essential to success in life but that there was an obligation resting upon educated persons to acquire this accomplishment if the opportunity was given to attend a class in practical speaking. According to him, it was one of the most powerful of all instruments for the purpose of communicating ideas and was capable of freeing the mind and body and thus giving the student a pleasant feeling of freedom and power. He did not claim therapeutic values for the lungs or the digestion, but did feel that it would counteract some of the injurious effects of a rather confining college life.[27]

Throughout the book the approach seems to be one of adapting the system to the student and his needs. This is a significant innovation because in textbooks of this period, which have been examined, certain

[24] *Ibid.* p. 76.
[25] *Ibid.* p. 17.
[26] *Ibid.* p. 401.
[27] *Ibid.* p. 26, 28.

rules have been laid down as inflexible limits for the instruction. Dr. North sets down his principles of teaching as three:

First, at no time to require of the learner, that which it is not reasonably natural and easy for him to do.

* * *

Secondly, Faults that experience has shown to be liable to occur in speaking, are as far as possible to be anticipated and prevented. But when faults actually occur, the learner is not to be expected to improve by simply endeavoring to avoid them, but on the contrary is to have set before him some method of practice which cultivates a mode of delivery exactly the opposite of the faults.

* * *

Thirdly, In all instruction and practice, to keep in mind the distinction between a mere exhibition of adherence to rules of elocution, and a genuine living eloquence. The one is to be so managed as to assist rather than obstruct the other. . . . In delivery, as in composition, the most interesting things will be original and not derived from a teacher.[28]

His theory of teaching seems reasonably modern. In fact, he sounds very much like a "progressive educator" when he defines the function of the teacher.

Those who feel their own deficiencies in reading or speaking, have a conception more or less perfect of what they ought to exhibit, but find on trial that their delivery is in fact strangely inferior to the ideal standard in their minds. In this state of disappointment, an elocutionist at his elbow, should be able at once to inform such a one—in the first place what tones he is using, and in what they differ from those of nature and cultivated power; and in the next place to explain the reason why his voice proceeds differently from what he wishes. This last is the most important service required of the teacher of elocution.[29]

MERRITT CALDWELL. *A Practical Manual of Elocution: embracing Voice and Gesture Designed for Schools, Academies and Colleges as well as for Private Learners* was published in 1845, and, according to its author, made Rush and Austin practical. Caldwell was a professor of Metaphysics, Political Economy, and Elocution in Dickinson College. He says that he rarely deviates from Rush in his description of the vocal phenomena and really offers little that is original. He gives eight pages of tables of sounds in combination, such as *ba ba ba bi bo bu* for articulation practice, and sentences which are made up of words which repeat the combinations.

He presents the "expression of the passions" not in terms of gesture and facial expression but according to the vocal signs. For example, —Dignity, Solemnity, Gravity, etc. are most fully expressed by the orotund voice, the partial drift of the monotone, slow time, and long

[28] *Ibid.* p. 30.
[29] *Ibid.* p. 8.

quantity combined with the single equal wave of the second, both direct and inverted and with median stress.   Mirth and Raillery require quick time and short quantity, loudness, and the concrete rise of the second, combined with the radical stress.   If these sentiments are to be exaggerated, the falsetto is used in either a concrete rise or the octave or by the direct wave of the same interval, and the tremor may also be added to heighten the effect.[30]

WILLIAM RUSSELL.   *The American Elocutionist* was published in 1844.   The author, William Russell, is listed on the title page as being instructor in elocution at Abbot Female Academy, Phillips Academy and the Theological Seminary, Andover, Massachusetts.   During the same year, the *School of Practical Rhetoric and Oratory* was opened in Boston "under the care of William Russell and James E. Murdoch." In 1845 *Orthophony or Vocal Culture* was written by these two men. In 1888 this book was re-edited in the 80th edition by William Russell and his son, the Rev. Francis Russell, who was professor of oratory at Trinity College and at Hobart College.   Another and probably the last edition appeared ten years later and was dedicated to Murdoch.

According to the prospectus for the *School of Practical Rhetoric and Oratory,* the exercises for elocution were all founded upon *The Philosophy of the Human Voice* and comprised a "systematic course of Vocal Culture designed to impart vigor and pliancy to the organs of speech, together with Fullness and Purity of Tone."   There was a gymnasium in connection with the school and physical exercises were a part of the training.

The athletic training embraces all the forms of invigorating and exhilarating exercise, adapted to the full and perfect Development of the Muscular System, to the acquisition of firm and easy Attitude, united with forcible, chaste and graceful Action,—and to the command of a clear and full-toned utterance. . . . Separate rooms are provided for the practice of Rhetorical, Elocutionary, and Calisthenic exercises, adapted to Young Ladies.[31]

There was also a preparatory department for children.   The school seems to have flourished until the superintendent of the high school ruled its students out of oratorical and declamatory contests because he said they had an advantage over other contestants.   As a consequence the attendance decreased and the school was discontinued.

Russell's theory of teaching is clearly explained and faithful to the Rush system.   He begins with elementary exercises and proceeds to words and sentences.   Finally, he discusses reading poetry, and in this connection, he advocates analyzing the poem with the student so

[30] Caldwell, Merritt. *A Practical Manual of Elocution.* p. 128-33.
[31] Prospectus for the School of Practical Rhetoric and Oratory. p. 4.

that he may thoroughly understand the meaning and feel the emotion. He divides his book into *Lessons in Enunciation, Exercises in Elocution, and Rudiments of Gesture.* A compromise between the Natural and Mechanical methods is attempted:

> If we regard enunciation and pronunciation as the *mechanical* part of elocution; inflection, emphasis, and pausing, may be designated as the *intellectual* part. The former regards, chiefly, the *ear,* as cognizant of *audible* expression; the latter regards the *understanding,* as addressed by *intelligible* utterance, and requiring the exercise of *judgment,* in consecutive and rational communication. . . . A third department of elocution, embraces the consideration of tone, as adapted to the utterance of *passion,* or the strongest forms of emotion, and is designated by the technical name of *Modulation.*

In his discussion of gesture Russell insists that the glow of an earnest speech will always bring action and that it is instinctive. The student and teacher must work together to trace those principles which suit the action to the word and to embody these in practical rules and disciplined habits.[32]

The faults that are most obvious in the reading of poetry are, according to *The American Elocutionist*: too rapid utterance by which the effect of the verse is lost to the ear, a plain and dry articulation without emotion or rhythm, a want of true time, a chanting or mouthing tone, the mechanical observance of the final and caesural pauses without regard to meaning, and reading literally and uniformly to rhythm. "Poetry should be read *more slowly than prose,*—with a *moderate prolongation* of vowel and liquid sounds,—with a *slight degree of musical utterance,*—in *exact time,* as prescribed by the emotion expressed in given passages, and by the nature of the verse. The *utterance should indicate the metre,* but should *never render it prominent*; and, in rhyming lines, the rising inflection should generally terminate the first; the falling being carefully avoided, unless when indispensable to force of emotion, or to the completion of sense not connected with subsequent expression." [33]

General suggestions given for pulpit elocution summarize rather well the author's idea of a speaker's needs. First, the minister is warned that he must maintain a "healthy condition of the bodily frame," since eloquence depends upon the vigor and flexibility of the muscular system. He must in addition to an active body add an active mind and a powerfully active imagination. The attitude of the mind is most important and is mentioned in many connections. The teacher is urged to use conversation and illustrative anecdotes to bring the

[32] Russell, William. *The American Elocutionist.* 5th ed. p. 6.
[33] *Ibid.* p. 193.

student's mind into the proper mood before asking him to read. The approach of the book approximates that of the modern book on interpretation of literature.

HENRY N. DAY. Dr. Day's *The Art of Elocution* was first published in 1859, and later revised in 1867. It was one of the popular textbooks, according to Coulton. The popularity is not surprising when it is compared with the others of this same decade. It was written as a textbook and succeeded very well in simplifying and organizing the Rush theories into usable form. It includes only two general divisions: *Orthoepy,* or the pronunciation of words, and *Elocution Proper,* or the expression of thought and feeling by means of the voice. Each of the minor divisions within the chapters which deal with the functions of the voice is numbered, explained in a rather precise, clear style, and followed by exercises. Often there is a short paragraph to elucidate further, printed in small type, and labelled either, "remarks" or "observations."

Day mentions the fact that he found it necessary to differ with Dr. Rush on a few of his observations. For example, he adds the fourth interval as a useful variation in the slides and the skips of the semitone and as the movement often used in the transitions in pitch from one member of a sentence to another. The most noticeable difference, however, is in the form in which the material is presented. One is a scientific study; the other, a textbook.

The method of vocal training is set down plainly in the introduction:

In training the voice, there are three things which need to be distinctly regarded. They are, first, the acquisition of a ready command over the respective organs employed in speech; secondly, the increase of the strength of the organs; and thirdly, the promotion of flexibility in the organs.

While these respective ends should be regarded, each at its own time and in its own degree, they are to be attained by the same general means—by habitual and systematic exercise. It will be found, however, that some of the succeeding exercises are more directly adapted to promote one of these ends than another. Practice on the slides and waves, for instance, and on difficult combinations of elements, will conduce more especially to rendering the organs flexible; while the explosion of the vowel elements and some of the exercises on pitch will tend more directly to impart vigor and strength to the voice. The ready command of the organs will be promoted, farther, by exercises in the expression of the passions.[34]

Definite ends to be attained from the practice of the exercises used in training the different organs of speech are also outlined at the beginning. The respiratory organs must be trained to inspire a sufficient

[34] Day, Henry N. *The Art of Elocution.* 2nd ed. p. 17.

quantity of breath and to use it economically. The articulatory organs must aim to secure flexibility, distinctness, and readiness of expression through frequent practice of the alphabetic elements. The vocal organs, properly so-called, should be exercised to obtain control of force, compass, clearness, smoothness, and readiness in commanding quality of voice.[35]

The four functions of speech: pitch, quality, time, and force are analyzed as means of expressing thought and feeling. There is a noticeable emphasis upon the training necessary for the proper use of changes in pitch. Vocal training in elocution involves, according to Day, a mastery of the various discrete and concrete movements of the voice in speech, in the skips and slides through the musical intervals and in the combination of slides in the wave. This makes necessary the classification, description, and exemplification of all the slides, skips, and waves. The following excerpt is an example:

Imperative words in a sentence, as they imply positiveness, readily take the falling slide.

Go, then, ye defenders of your country.
Proceed, I am attentive.

Remark. In this case, as well as also in the exercise of the following section, a slight increase of positiveness in the expression will lead to the use of the downward third, instead of the second.[36]

In order to be able to use these variations in pitch accurately, the student must be familiar with the intervals: the major and minor seconds, the major and minor thirds, the fourth, the major and minor fifths, and the octave. These intervals should not only be familiar to the ear, but familiar enough to the vocal organs that they can be used at will. Day suggests that the teacher should either demonstrate the different intervals or use a musical instrument in training the student's ear. He should practice the scales himself to improve his own production of these variations in pitch. Singing sounds may be used, if necessary in this latter practice, but the tones of speech on the letters or the numerals are preferred.[37]

Quality is treated rather briefly; everyone has his own natural voice and should be able to make it pleasant and flexible through practice. Only three kinds of quality are mentioned as necessary variations in expressing different emotions: *orotund, guttural,* and *aspirate.*[38]

Force is discussed in terms of volume, abruptness, and syllabic stress and adds nothing particularly original. In the same way, time

[35] *Ibid.* p. 18.
[36] *Ibid.* p. 66.
[37] *Ibid.* p. 58-9.
[38] *Ibid.* p. 98-9.

is discussed, as it often has been treated before, in terms of quantity and pause. Emphasis is discussed separately and divided into two types: logical, and passionate. The passionate derives from the logical, since feeling is always contained in some thought. Variations and combinations of the four modes of speech are used to emphasize thoughts and emotions. As it is explained in *The Art of Elocution,* emphasis is "the distinctive expression of thought or feeling, and may vary indefinitely in degree, as it follows that it may be expressed by any variation of the voice that shall indicate distinction, . . ." [39]

Grouping of Speech is defined as "the vocal designation of the relations of thought both grammatical and logical, in discourse." Instead of considering the pause alone as a means of grouping, Day includes force and pitch also. He observes that in grouping by pitch, a relatively less important thought is often distinguished from the rest by being depressed, sometimes even by being elevated in pitch above the others. The monotone, the rising and falling skip of the second, also separate in different degrees the parts of a sentence. The following sentence is given as an example: "Mr. Fox had a captivating earnestness of tone and manner; Mr. Pitt was more dignified than earnest." [40] Grouping by force or stress is to be effected either by stress on the close of the first of two phrases to be connected, which would not otherwise receive any emphasis, or by abatement of force on the intervening clause. [41]

The mode of delivery, Day explains, should be determined by the occasion, and by the character of the material:

> The *occasion* on which the piece is to be delivered, will determine the loudness and abruptness of the utterance, or the degree of force, and, also, to some extent, the melody and quantity. . . . The *character of the piece* will affect the determination in regard to all the various functions of the voice to be employed. The kind and degree of passion should be ascertained first. This will generally determine the melody to be adopted. . . . The *thought* should then be carefully analyzed, in order to determine, first, the relative prominence of the ideas to be expressed; and secondly, the relations between the different phrases. Finally, the structure of the piece as to verbal expression should be studied, in order to determine the emphatic words, whether emphatic on their own account, or as representatives for a phrase; and, also, the degree of prominence to be given them. [42]

Over half the book is given over to selections to be used in general exercises. It is interesting that no form of notation is used in these exercises. It seems reasonable to believe that the student was

[39] *Ibid.* p. 146.
[40] *Ibid.* p. 161.
[41] *Ibid.* p. 162.
[42] *Ibid.* p. 164-5.

given some freedom in interpretation after the preliminary training was accomplished.

JAMES E. MURDOCH.   James E. Murdoch was an actor of some reputation in the United States and England, a public reader who gave readings for the benefit of the soldiers during the Civil War, and a teacher of elocution in Boston and Philadelphia.   He was a most enthusiastic Rush devotee, as the following quotation from a speech delivered before the visiting committee and pupils of the Murdoch School of Vocal Culture in 1869 will show:

> The system to which I have devoted my life, and in the interests of which I hope, under God's Providence to end it, is that that founded by Dr. James Rush, a physician of Philadelphia.   Though not a teacher of his science, Dr. Rush instructed me while I was yet a mere youth in the principles of his philosophy, and by these principles I have stood unswervingly throughout all these years.[43]

Murdoch wrote one textbook, *Analytic Elocution,* published in 1884, which added nothing new and was really a re-hashing of *Orthophony* written in conjunction with Russell, when they were teaching together in Boston.

Orthophony puts the emphasis upon the physiological bases of elocution and recommends training as a curative for impaired health. All the organs of the speech mechanism are illustrated and the descriptions are very clear.   For example, the following description is given of the vocal chords.

> The vocal chords, which extend across the upper part of the larynx, and form the lips of the glottis, and by their vibration, together with the action of the current of air expelled through the trachea and larynx, produce the phenomena of vocal sound or voice and by their tension or remission, the effect of high or low pitch.[44]

There are many exercises for deep breathing, either *effusive* or tranquil, *expulsive* or forcible, *explosive* or abrupt, sighing, sobbing, gasping, and pouting.   The directions for effusive breathing are as follows:

> Draw in a very full breath, and send it forth in the prolonged sound of the letter *h.*   In the act of inspiration, take in as much breath as you can contain. In that·of expiration, retain all you can, and give out as little as possible, merely sufficient to keep the sound *h* audible.   But keep it going on, as long as you can sustain it.[45]

Quality is discussed at length and the "orotund" extolled as the only good quality for cultivated utterance.   It is to be produced by

[43] Murdoch. *op. cit.* p. 9.
[44] Murdoch, James E. and Russell, William. *Orthophony, or Vocal Culture.* p. 18.
[45] *Ibid.* p. 24.

a free and wide opening of the mouth and pharynx, deep inspiration and expiration "in order to assist in opening all the resonant chambers of the chest, throat, and head." The chief security against the nasal quality consists in this habit of opening the mouth "not only in the front, but in the back part, by raising the veil of the palate, as is mechanically done in the act of coughing, in consequence of which the voice escapes in the proper direction, instead of being allowed to drift with force against the nasal passages while they remain shut." [46]   The elements which impair purity of tone are: a hollow pectoral quality, aspirated quality, guttural tone issuing from an obstructed throat, nasal tone, and the oral or slightly indifferent tone.

J. H. McILVAINE.   The last book to be discussed in this period is *Elocution,* by J. H. McIlvaine, published in 1870.   It holds very closely to the Rush principles, gives similar exercises to those mentioned before but differs in that it develops a definitely psychological approach.   It is better organized and more comprehensive than the other textbooks of the period.

The definition given for elocution establishes it as an art:

> The most general definition of art, is knowledge applied to production. Elocution conforms to this definition; for it applies the knowledge of vocal sounds to the production of oral discourse. . . . *The art of speaking is essentially an imitative art, the rudiments of which are actually taught and learned in childhood.* . . .   The process is the same; and that is no sound training in elocution, which does not aim to develop in the student the same habits of close observation and vocal imitation by which he learned to speak at first.[47]

Because it is an art, elocution has great educative powers.   "Almost everything in the common curriculum of a liberal education, except the arts of rhetoric and elocution, belongs to science.   Now science terminates in mere knowing, whilst art applies knowledge to the production of what did not before exist; that is to say, science is simply determinative, whilst art is creative." [48]   As the art of reading, elocution brings the student into the closest communion with great minds. He is required to store his memory with the finest passages of eloquence and poetry and the influence is cultural and esthetic.

The inherent difficulties of the art lie in the numerous mental operations which must be carried on simultaneously, some of them sub-processes.   McIlvaine lists some of these processes as: "those of invention and style, of memory, or of reading."   The student must be able to keep steadily in view: the object for which he is aiming in

[46] *Ibid.* p. 42-7.
[47] McIlvaine, Joshua H. *Elocution.* p. 18, 19, 20.
[48] *Ibid.* p. 38.

respect to the effect upon the audience, the perception and feeling for the meaning of each word in itself and its grammatical relations and connections at the very moment of speaking it, and the necessity of holding the audience in the full consciousness that he is speaking directly to their minds. Many of these mental operations have to be carried on almost unconsciously and must be suppressed entirely from the oral expression. These mental processes that must be suppressed are called *sub-processes.*[49]

The audience is given more consideration in this book than in any of the previous ones. The means of engaging attention include: having something to say that is worthy of attention and sympathy, a simple earnest and respectful manner, fixing the eye on the audience, and using power without showing any irritation. "Therefore, with unruffled temper, and perfect good nature, by his eye, countenance, tones and whole manner, he should seem to say, My friends, I am here to speak to you, and I am going to do it; you are here to listen, and you have got to do it—the sooner you begin, the better it will be for us both." [50]

McIlvaine acknowledges his indebtedness to Rush for the discussion of the modes of the voice and the exercises that accompany the descriptions, but he feels that it has been necessary to go beyond the plan laid down by Rush. Rush's system, he says, embraces only the treatment of the "elements," excluding entirely the preceding sources of power, from which the very life and spirit of delivery must be derived.

SUMMARY.

Dr. James Rush, in his *Philosophy of the Human Voice,* published in 1827, introduced science into the teaching of elocution. Although his book was not a textbook, it succeeded in analyzing the functions of the voice in such a minute fashion that it became the basis for most of the books written during this period. At first, physiology was the branch of science most emphasized and the training in elocution became not only a means of developing a useful and necessary skill, but in some cases was prescribed as therapy for bodily ailments. By 1870, however, the trend had changed and a psychological emphasis became evident which made the interpretation of literature primarily an intellectual process, much less mechanical than before and much more of a "liberal art."

[49] *Ibid.* p. 24.
[50] *Ibid.* p. 114.

PART III

PSYCHOLOGY AND ORAL INTERPRETATION:

1870-1915

CHAPTER I

NEW CONCEPTS OF AMERICAN CULTURE

An American Plutocracy. This period, which began with what Mark Twain dubbed "The Gilded Age," instituted a plutocracy which was to displace the aristocracy of the Southern planter and the New England philosopher and orator. New standards for thought and conduct based upon materialistic values touched every phase of American life. It took time to adjust to new wealth, to develop controls for the excesses that accompany a social philosophy which seemed to consist in "preemption, exploitation, and progress." It was a period of transition with all the advantages of a new freedom and the disadvantages of an extremism which lacked stability and good taste.

Parrington explains this gilded age in terms of the causes which produced it:

> Science and the machine were twin instruments for creating a new civilization of which the technologist and the industrialist were the high priests. The transcendental theologian was soon to be as extinct as the passenger pigeon.
>
> * * *
>
> With the substitution of the captain of industry for the plantation master as the custodian of society, the age of aristocracy was at an end and the age of the middle class was established. A new culture, created by the machine and answering the needs of capitalism, was to dispose the old culture with its lingering concern for distinction and its love of standards—a culture that should eventually suffice the needs of a brisk city world of machine activities. But that would take time. In the meanwhile—in the confused interregnum between reigns—America would be little more than a welter of crude energy, a raw unlovely society where the strife of competition with its prodigal waste testified to the shortcomings of an age in process of transition.[1]

Because the country in which the American plutocracy flourished was new, there were few controls, especially over taste. In *The Rise of American Civilization,* Beard notes the fact that the bourgeoise who found themselves in power were not curbed in matters of restraint and taste by the members of the older order.

> Except for a few select segments on the Atlantic seaboard, the new age of American culture was without form and void; the young plutocracy had yet to acquire canons of propriety and aesthetics. Unchecked by classical traditions, unhampered by the contempt of strong upper classes, and not yet disciplined into culture by generations of leisure, it attacked its problems of living unusually free from customary repressions—emancipated from the inferiority complexes of European peasants and merchants.[2]

---

[1] Parrington, Vernon Louis. *Main Currents in American Thought.* vol. 3. p. 4, 9.
[2] Beard, Charles A. and Mary. *The Rise of American Civilization.* p. 384.

However, this American plutocracy was typical in one respect of the *nouveaux riches* the world over—they loved display and glitter. Their architecture revealed this trait most plainly, and unfortunately in a very permanent manner. It is described in *The Growth of the American Republic* as follows:

> Victorian Gothic was like much of the oratory of the period, florid, vain and empty; characterized by over-decoration, over-ornamentation and ostentation. . . . Sullivan, indeed, more clearly than any architect of his time, realized the connection between architecture and society, . . . "What the people are within," said Sullivan, "the buildings express without. . . . " This interpretation of the functional character of architecture in the Gilded Age was not a flattering one, and Sullivan observed somewhat acrimoniously that "the unhappy, irrational, heedless, pessimistic, unlovely, distracted, and decadent structures, which make up the great bulk of our contemporaneous architecture, point with infallible accuracy to qualities in the heart and mind and soul of the American people."[3]

The same clutter and lack of taste was within the house, and the excrescences of functionless and extravagant objects that supposedly fed an artistic taste have created a problem of disposal for most moderns.

This desire for ornamentation showed itself in the elocution of the time. Delsarte, a French music teacher, designed an extravagant system of bodily expression which was welcomed with great enthusiasm by schools of "vocal and physical culture." Although he did not write a book, his system as interpreted by his students exerted a great influence.

As far as the word "culture" was concerned, it was more used than ever before. There was a great demand for organizations which would uplift and polish the great mass of common people who had entered the purchasing class for "the better things of life." The wash was thin but it must of necessity be applied to larger and larger areas. The frontiers were far distant from New England and culture had to be taken to the provinces by means of books, magazines and newspapers, religious revivals, lyceums, and chautauquas. The lack was not of interest but of discrimination. It was a gaudy and vulgar age but this was not generally known or recognized and the energy and ambition of the adolescent urged it on. Everyone wanted more of everything which he had, but some had very little intellectual taste to begin with. Thus, it was impossible to develop quickly an indigenous culture that could meet European standards. It was the day of the self-made man.

By going down the list of the prominent figures of the day in America it could be seen that four out of five had achieved success without the assistance

[3] Morison, Samuel E. and Commager, Henry S. *The Growth of the American Republic*. p. 295, 298.

of a college education. From the time when the government had been established, when many of the men of state had been graduates of distinguished European schools, we had passed to a time when there was something near to deification of those who had wrung fortune from the wilderness by early rising and the calloused hand, who had done this with a "common school education" and who were in name, as in effect, "self-made." [4]

THE CHURCH. In spite of the impact of science which resulted eventually in a decided weakening of the authority of the church, religion was very much alive. There was a remarkable growth in the Catholic church due to a steady influx of immigrants from Catholic sections of Europe. A new religion, Christian Science, arose under the leadership of Mary Baker Eddy in 1866 and built up rich congregations all the way from Boston, the mother church, to San Francisco. There were famous Protestant preachers, chief among them: T. Dewitt Talmadge, Dwight L. Moody, Henry Ward Beecher, and later Billy Sunday. These men presented in revival meetings and on chautauqua platforms a simplified and emotional creed for salvation. Religion became less aristocratic and more sentimentalized.

This spectacular growth of Catholicism, though it amazed some defenders of the inherited order, was really welcome to many Americans of colonial descent who were now recoiling before the advance of radical and scientific thinking. Priests of the Catholic denomination were found in practice to have as a rule, a moderating influence on strikers and labor agitators; and often a Protestant capitalist, such for example as James J. Hill, looked to the Catholic hierarchy for support in the maintenance of law and order.

Moreover the large right wing of the Protestant clergy, engaged in sustaining the accepted dogmas of their respective denominations, were happy to reckon the Catholic clergy among their allies in throwing up bulwarks for the faith.[5]

The church had been touched by the same liberating influences as had every other institution. It reacted by being more emotional and sentimental in its message and by shunning an intellectual approach, partly as a reaction and partly, perhaps, because it feared it could not cope with the intellectual forces of science if it spoke the same language. Perhaps the whole reaction was a natural pagan reaction to puritanical repressions as Parrington believes:

Liberalism was passing from the political to the social—a free welling-up of repressed desires, a vast expansiveness. Too long had the natural human emotions been under the ban of asceticism; too long had a God of wrath dispossessed a God of love. Life is good in the measure that it is lived fully, and to live fully is to live in the flesh as well as in the spirit. Emerson the prophet of the earlier decade had suffered from an extreme unfleshiness;

[4] Oberholtzer, Ellis Paxson. *A History of the United States Since the Civil War.* vol. 3. p. 450.
[5] Beard. *op. cit.* p. 409.

Whitman the prophet of the fifties would recover the balance. As the current of emotionalism gathered force a frank *joie de vivre* submerged the old reticences; candor, frankness, a very lust of self-expression, was the new law for free men and women—a glorification of the physical that put to rout the traditional Hebraisms. A riotous sentimentalism ran about the land until it seemed to timid souls as if liberty were quite running away with decency.

It was not alone Walt Whitman who threw down the gage to the Comstockian watchmen in the gates. The apostle of the new freedom, the high priest of emotional liberalism, was Henry Ward Beecher, lately come out of the West, who from the pulpit of Plymouth Church swept his thousands of idolizing followers along the path of Utopian emotionalism.[6]

The amusement business catered to the same desire for emotional outlet and succeeded in offering a variety of lively and gaudy entertainment especially designed for the urban working population.

Vaudeville shows, prize fights, circuses, dime museums, and cheap theatres, like the spectacles of ancient Rome, kept countless millions happy in penury, not at public expense, as in Caesar's day, but at the expense of those who enjoyed them and to the advantage of those who owned them. Indeed, tickling the urban masses—creating popular tastes and standards of culture—now became one of the large and highly lucrative branches of Capitalistic enterprise.[7]

Two of the famous contributors to this game of amusing the multitude were P. T. Barnum, who launched his "Greatest Show on Earth" in 1871 and "Buffalo Bill," Colonel Cody, who startled the country with his wild west shows in 1883.[8]

THE CHAUTAUQUA AND THE LYCEUM. It was in the small towns of the country from New York state westward that there was a great demand for adult education along with amusement, and it was here that the Chautauqua really grew into an institution with an influence that can scarcely be measured. Bishop Vincent, who had experience in camp meetings where people gathered under the trees for days or weeks to praise the Lord, realized that they were more than a religious gathering—a sort of community get-together where people enjoyed themselves as a by-product of religious experience. In 1874 on the camp-meeting grounds at Fair Point, Chautauqua Lake, New York, he established the Sunday School Teachers Assembly which became the original Chautauqua.

Gay McLaren describes the Chautauqua movement very vividly, in terms of her own experience as a "dramatic reader," in *Morally*

---

[6] Parrington. *op. cit.* p. 74-5.
[7] Beard. *op. cit.* p. 397.
[8] *Ibid.* p. 398.

We Roll Along. The title is most apt, since the Chautauqua was an "uplift" organization from the first.

While the original purpose was the study of the Bible, the fame of the institution grew and its patronage increased when the course of study was expanded to include secular subjects. Lectures, music, and readings were added to furnish "pure, wholesome entertainment" for the Bible students. Boating, bathing, and outdoor games were provided to encourage healthful exercise. Thus the Assembly developed a uniquely American blending of religion, education, and recreation. . . .

An intense, almost fanatical interest in education took possession of the Chautauqua devotees. Heretofore the pursuit of knowledge had been confined to the four walls of the schoolroom. Adult education was almost unknown. But with the establishment of the Assembly at Lake Chautauqua, pupils from eighteen to eighty began to enroll. Men and women who, like Dr. Vincent, had been denied the advantages of a college education flocked to the great resort where they could pursue their studies with dignity and at the same time take a vacation. . . .

Chautauquas now began to spring up all over the country in groves of trees and by lakesides. The original idea of combined studying and entertainment with the health-making influences of trees and water seemed the keynote of Chautauqua's appeal, because when the idea was tried in cities it was almost always a failure.[9]

The lyceum was established much earlier than the Chautauqua and for much the same purpose. Josiah Holbrook, a traveling lecturer on geology and mineralogy, began the first lyceum in 1826 in Millbury, Massachusetts. In the beginning it was made up almost entirely of lectures and was often called the "lecture course." But the first Lyceum Bureau was founded by James Redpath about 1868. Charles Dickens is said to have complained because of the difficulties encountered in arranging his lectures in the United States, and Redpath, a crusading journalist, seeing the need for a central booking agency, opened the Boston Lyceum Bureau. On Redpath's list were such names as Horace Greeley, Wendell Phillips, Ralph Waldo Emerson, and Mark Twain. Gradually, readers, musicians, and other types of entertainment were added to the lectures on the lyceum course. When the Chautauqua began, it turned to the Redpath agency for "talent." Later, Redpath developed a circuit Chautauqua which relieved the local committee of making contracts with individual lecturers and entertainers. A new and successful business had been launched.[10]

The lecture was the logical background of the Chautauqua. Here was fertile ground for the politician, for the religious leader, for anyone who espoused a cause. A large and attentive audience was

[9] McLaren, Gay. *Morally We Roll Along.* p. 74-7.
[10] Nevins, Allan. *The Emergence of Modern America 1865-1878.* p. 238.

assured, and there were few of the leaders of the day who did not make Chautauqua or lyceum appearances. The following names will give some idea of the variety and importance of the speakers: Beecher, Talmadge, Mark Twain, Hays, Garfield, Grant, McKinley, Bryan, Carrie Nation, Maud Ballington Booth, and Jane Addams. Russell H. Conwell delivered his famous lecture "Acres of Diamonds" five thousand times before Chautauqua audiences and earned four million dollars.[11]

The Chautauqua was recognized as an institution by the *New York Times* in 1880 and credited with being a sign that some of the American people at least could "pursue purely intellectual questions having no relation to dollars and cents." Some people must have questioned its particular brand of condensed culture, but it was undoubtedly one of the most cherished of middle class ventures in improvement. Beard gives a good appraisal of it when he says:

> It was after lecturing to comfortable and excellent people at Chautauqua that William James heaved an immense sigh of relief as he escaped into the freight yards at Buffalo where the noise, grime, and jar of reality broke the monotony of moderation, purity, and median lines of thought. Nevertheless, it was this respectable middle class that in the main sustained the churches, filled the colleges with sons and daughters, supported the "clean" press, kept alive foreign and domestic missions, supplied the sinews for the anti-saloon movement, backed the Women's Christian Temperance Union, and, according to Matthew Arnold, carried the burden of American civilization in the gilded age.[12]

As the Chautauqua program became more varied, public reading became an essential part. The word "reader" was an outgrowth of the term "elocutionist" and was first applied only to one who read a play or book in monologue form. Later, according to McLaren, it might designate a performer who either read or recited poems, stories or plays. There was an excellent reason for this new profession of the reader; acted plays were taboo.

> In the early days of Chautauqua "Culture," the audiences were made up, almost exclusively, of church people who were violently opposed to the theatre and everything connected with it. . . .
> The only way that Chautauqua patrons could hear the plays of Shakespeare or other dramatic literature was in a "reading." . . . The "reading" referred to as "platform art" was exclusively a product of the Chautauqua and Lyceum and was little known outside of these institutions.[13]

Until later years when plays were admitted to the Chautauqua, one or two readings were included on every program. One of the earliest of the readers was Katherine Ridgeway who usually gave a

[11] *Ibid.* p. 167-74 *passim.*
[12] Beard. *op. cit.* p. 401.
[13] McLaren. *op. cit.* p. 134.

program of short numbers. Later on, Margaret Stahl, Maude Willis, Janette Kling, Adrian Newens, Phidelah Rice, and Edwin Whitney read plays. There were some professional actors who gave readings from plays in which they had acted on Broadway. Among them were: Mr. and Mrs. Coburn, Edith Wynne Matthison, and Charles Rann Kennedy. Emerson Brooks, Edmund Vance Cooke, Lew Sarett, and Carl Sandburg read their poetry.[14]

PROFESSIONAL SCHOOLS OF ELOCUTION. The demand of the Chautauqua and lyceum for professional readers gave impetus, without doubt, to the increase and the popularity of special schools of elocution which were distinct from the colleges and universities. They were really professional schools that were attempting to offer more specialized and adult training than the college could offer. It was a relatively new business, as was Redpath's business of managing lectures, and, in keeping with the times, occasionally displayed traces of charlatanism.

The National School of Elocution and Oratory was established in Philadelphia in 1866, and in 1875 the principal J. W. Shoemaker made the following claims of priority for his school: "We are not aware that previous to the organization of the National School of Elocution and Oratory, any institution has ever existed with the distinctive object, the culture of human speech." [15] However, two earlier schools have been mentioned in this study. Russell and Murdoch had established their *School of Practical Rhetoric and Oratory* in Boston in 1844 and gave daily practice in the Rush "elements." Comstock was principal of *The Vocal and Polyglot Gymnasium* in Boston, which the advertisement in the back of his text, published in 1851, called a "lyceum for the promotion of health, the cure of stammering and the improvement in reading and speaking." [16]

One of the most famous and most important of the professional schools of the period being studied was *The School of Expression* in Boston. The following history shows that it developed from a college course which was evidently not adequate:

> The School of Expression was organized from private classes in the spring of the year 1885 by the now Professor of Elocution and Oratory, Boston University, with the permission of the trustees to carry on the work of the University School of Oratory, discontinued in 1879 at the death of the lamented Dean Monroe. The work of the school has so grown that it has been incorporated as a school entirely separate from the University." [17]

[14] *Ibid.* p. 136, 138.
[15] *Catalogue* of the National School of Elocution and Oratory. p. 13 (1875).
[16] Comstock, Andrew. *A System of Elocution.* 3rd ed.
[17] School of Expression. *Fourth Annual Catalog.* 1888.

Dr. Samuel S. Curry took over the classes in Boston University in 1879 and was head of the school until his death in 1921. The school continues to give professional training today. In its sixtieth year, 1939, it was given the degree-granting privilege by the Legislature of Massachusetts and now gives degrees in the Science of Oratory.[18]

Other famous schools in Boston were: Emerson College of Oratory founded by Charles Wesley Emerson in 1891, and Leland Powers School founded in 1904. In Chicago, there were three well-known schools. Robert McLain Cumnock founded a school in connection with Northwestern University in 1878. It is now the School of Speech and holds the same rank in the University as any other professional school. The Phillips School of Oratory was organized by Arthur Edward Phillips some time around the beginning of the century and the Columbia School of Expression was operating in 1899 in Chicago with a staff of four women and one man. The advertisement for the latter in *Werner's Magazine* stated that it gave special courses in Bible reading and one class especially for the W. C. T. U.[19] The Byron King School of Oratory, established in 1888, gave professional training in Pittsburgh. There were no doubt many more schools of the same type but these were outstanding and, with the exception of the Phillips School of Oratory, all exist today.

There were some schools which specialized in Delsartian training. Important teachers in these schools were: Steele Mackaye, Lewis B. Monroe, Moses True Brown, Genevieve Stebbins, Anna Diehl, and Emily Bishop. Much of the training was primarily gymnastic in form. Gay McLaren in her description of the Manning College of Music, Oratory and Dramatic Art in Minneapolis gives an idea of the technique used:

> Greek posing, or "poses plastique," as it was called, was an important part of our course of study, and was supposed to correct our posture and help us to attain proper platform carriage. The posing was done to music. Arrayed in white cotton robes, we stood a few feet apart and changed slowly from one pose to another with Delsarte movements to the count of ten.[20]

These methods seem more absurd than any of those of the preceding period and did not persist in elocutionary training. However, they had a wide appeal then. Nevins mentions the posture called the "grecian bend" as being cultivated by women in general.[21] *Werner's Magazine* shows many illustrations of pantomimes, in which women dressed in Grecian costumes are interpreting literature, usually poetry.

[18] Curry College. *Catalogue.* 1939-40. p. 10, 18.
[19] *Werner's Magazine* 1899. p. 83.
[20] McLaren. *op. cit.* p. 44.
[21] Nevins. *op. cit.* p. 209.

In the December issue, 1895, there are pictures of pantomimes of Tennyson's *Lotus Eaters* and one of *Jesus Lover of My Soul.* No doubt, these Delsartian techniques were consonant with the "chromo civilization" of the last part of the nineteenth century.

There were, of course those who saw the ridiculous aspect of Delsartian training. The following excerpt from a popular song written by Joseph Newman quite plainly makes fun of it:

> Since Birdie commenced her Delsarte:
> Her right hand goes this way, her left one goes that,
> And she flings them high into the air,
> To show her improvement she gives the "wave" movement
> And impersonates Hate and Despair.
> ....
> There's lots of sleep-walking, also dumb talking,
> Since Birdie's commenced her Delsarte.[22]

THE EFFECT OF THE NEW PSYCHOLOGY UPON HIGHER EDUCATION. Higher education found that it was forced to change radically during this period. Not only did it have to accommodate its curriculum to meet the practical needs of an increasingly heterogeneous group of students, but it had to absorb the new theories of evolution and pragmatism and adapt its methods to the new psychology. This was a logical development, as Morison and Commager explain:

> Between transcendentalism as expounded by Kant and Coleridge and Emerson, and the new doctrine of organic evolution as expounded by Darwin and Huxley and John Fiske, there could be no logical compromise. . . . It was clearly necessary to formulate a new philosophy, one which would harmonize with science and yet avoid the pitfalls of materialism. This task was undertaken and concluded by a brilliant group of philosophers who came to maturity in the last third of the nineteenth century: Charles Pierce, William James, and John Dewey. Pragmatism is the name of the philosophy which they formulated; although European philosophers cried out with one voice that the demand that truth must "work" and "pay" was just a piece of American sordidness, it may yet be admitted that pragmatism was one of the really important novelties in the history of thought through the ages.[23]

Since this is a study of methods, the developments in the field of psychology are particularly significant. The two dominant sources of present day scientific psychology, according to Joseph Jastrow, are the experimental method and the principle of evolution. The nucleus of investigation became the physiology of the senses. Wilhelm Wundt established the first experimental laboratory in Leipzig in 1879, but America was soon to feel the "wave of laboratory founding." The

[22] Sullivan, Mark. *Our Times.* p. 97.
[23] Morison and Commager. *op. cit.* p. 270.

American students who studied with Wundt came home to start laboratories and to develop theories which progressed far beyond those of their teacher. William James, Titchener, and Hall were among these students. James undoubtedly exerted the greatest influence of them all in the development of American psychology.

The movement away from structuralism has come to be known as functionalism; it leads directly to an adjustment psychology—which is a more cogent name for finding what the mind is in what it does. This pragmatic view characterizes the American movement in psychology. It was above all William James' *Principles of Psychology* (2 vols., New York 1890) with its sweep and power and vivid vitality of presentation, which spread the doctrine of the mind as an active moving power. . . . Dewey and Angell by precept and practise gave the functional view currency, and substantially all current psychology is functional in scope and purpose.[24]

James' *The Principles of Psychology* is one of the most popular expositions of modern psychology. It is unusually readable, lucid, and human. It is easy to see why teachers became interested in developing methods which made use of their knowledge of James' psychology. His emphasis upon the emotional side of man's life made the whole thing seem less detached from practical experience and more usable in pedagogy. In 1899, *Talks to Teachers* was published; it was republished in 1900 and in 1939. These talks were originally lectures given to Cambridge teachers in 1892. John Dewey and William H. Kilpatrick, who have written the introduction to the last edition, make clear the pertinence for teachers of today.

Perhaps a short excerpt from the evaluation of James' psychology in *Seven Psychologies* by Heidbreder will help to epitomize his theories and make clearer their inevitable influence upon the teachers of elocution:

It was his general speculative bent, of course, that made him turn from the speculative contemplation of the mind to the direct observation of immediate experience and its conditions; but it was his specific biological interest that made him see mental processes as activities of living creatures maintaining themselves in the world of nature—as activities, indeed, presumably useful to the creatures practising them. . . .

Closely related to his attitude toward mental life in general is the emphasis James places on the non-rational side of human nature. Throughout the entire book, he never permits the reader to forget that the creature he is discussing is a creature of emotion and action as well as of cognition and reason. . . . He states with the utmost clearness, notably in his chapters on habit and association, his conviction that the intellect operates under definite physiological conditions. And he goes farther. Belief, he insists is determined by emotional and volitional

[24] Jastrow, Joseph. "Psychology." *Encyclopedia of Social Sciences.* vol. 12. p. 591-3.

factors; conception and reasoning, arising under the influence of particular wants and needs, occur for the sake of action.[25]

The doctrines of modern speech teachers concerning the necessary integration of mind and body for effective speaking evolve from this theory. Dualism is no longer accepted.

Now that the psychologist had become a naturalist his findings had much more practical importance and became more pervasive in the field of education. It was really the effect of Darwin's principles of evolution which was far reaching.

> . . . The psychologist was not whole-heartedly a naturalist until the insight of Darwin established the principle of evolution and the wide implications of that enlightening principle had become a common possession. Within a remarkably short period all the sciences of life were recast in a biologico-genetic mold, particularly psychology. . . *The Expression of the Emotions in Man and Animals* (London 1872) represents an evolutionist's solution of an intrinsically psychological problem. . . . From then on the biological criterion and reference claim consideration in every problem, even though the actual investigation is experimental or sociological.
>
> The biological emphasis centered upon function through the leading idea that behavior, like endowment, is an expression of the adjustment of organism to environment in which the better adjusted survive.[26]

The current theories concerning behavior put a new complexion upon the study of emotions or "passions" as they were called by earlier teachers. The expression of the emotions was always a problem to the teacher of elocution. The study of gesture and bodily action had to be based upon the available knowledge concerning the natural expression of the primary emotions. In the first section of this study such books as Bulwer's *Chirologia* . . . *Chironomia,* Burgh's *The Art of Speaking,* and Austin's *Chironomia* were discussed. In each one, an attempt was made from personal observation to catalog the different emotions. Burgh probably listed the largest number. There was nothing scientific about these books. The men interested in this field seemed to be somewhat hazy about the relationship of the mind to the body, which was usually considered one of dualism, and had little information concerning individual differences. Although the psychological findings of the nineteenth century eventually affected the methods of teaching oral expression, it took time. Delsarte showed some contact with current scientific thought, but he did not understand it thoroughly enough to use it intelligently. Bacon's *Manual of Gesture,* published in 1872, harked back to Austin and paid no attention to newer theories.

[25] Heidbreder, Edna. *Seven Psychologies.* p. 198.
[26] Jastrow. *op. cit.* p. 593.

However, Darwin's contribution to the study of emotions could not be ignored. An appraisal of his contribution is given by Flügel.

> . . . In the *Expression of the Emotions in Man and Animals* (1872) he suggested an evolutionary interpretation of the changes of feature and of posture that are characteristic of the major emotions. These changes, he endeavored to show are either themselves of biological utility, are associated with or are remnants of movements possessing utility (e.g., the showing of the teeth in anger), or are the results of social tradition (as in clasping the hands in supplication, which Darwin looks upon as a mute offer to let the hands be bound). Although many of Darwin's individual interpretations still remain matters of speculation, the book is a monument both of bold suggestiveness and patient inquiry, and remains to this day by far the most important single contribution to its subject.[27]

Other psychologists were interested in the same problem. In the introduction to *Expression of the Emotions in Man and Animals,* Darwin referred to work that French scientists had done in the same field; among them, Duchenne's *Mécanisme de la Physionome* (1862), and Gratiolet's *De la Physionomie et des Mouvements d'Expression* published in 1865. He used pictures taken by Duchenne in addition to observations of his own of infants, of the insane, and of different races, as basis for his conclusions.[28]

Undoubtedly Delsarte was in contact with the new psychological thought in France and was influenced by it. The artists as a group had been interested for a long time in the subject of the expression of the emotions; LeBrun the painter, published *Conférences sur l'Expression des différent Caractères des Passions* in 1667 which was republished by Moreau in 1820. Delsarte's use of the words *genus* and *species* in working out his charts relating emotion to action shows an influence of contemporary thought. The basis of his system, however, was a transcendental theology which did not allow a very extensive or exact application of the new scientific theories. Only his belief in a unity of mind, soul, and body seemed in line with the new trend of thought.

In the conclusion to *The Expression of the Emotions in Man and Animals,* Darwin suggested the theory which is well known to present-day teachers as the James-Lange theory of emotions. This theory asserts that the action often induces the emotion:

> The free expression by outward signs of an emotion intensifies it. On the other hand, the repression, as far as this is possible, of all outward signs softens our emotions. He who gives way to violent gestures will increase his rage; he who does not control the signs of fear will experience fear in a greater

[27] Flügel, John Carl. *A Hundred Years of Psychology, 1833-1933.* p. 113-14.
[28] Darwin, Charles. *The Expression of the Emotions in Man and Animals.* p. 4-6, 18.

degree; and he who remains passive when overwhelmed with grief loses his best chance of recovering elasticity of mind. These results follow partly from the intimate relation which exists between almost all the emotions and their outward manifestations; and partly from the direct influence of exertion on the heart, and consequently on the brain. Even the simulation of an emotion tends to arouse it in our minds.[29]

From Darwin's principles of evolution—one of which was human variation—developed the study of individual differences. The results of these studies dealt severe blows to pedagogical ideas of mental discipline and human perfectibility, and a new curriculum was the logical outcome. However, the elective system had been introduced before Cattell's physical and mental measurements were made of the freshmen and senior students of Columbia University in 1894.[30] President Eliot had succeeded in abolishing at Harvard all required subjects for seniors in 1872, for juniors in 1879, and for sophomores in 1884. Requirements for freshmen were reduced, until in 1894, the only requirements were English and a modern language.[31]

The elective principle went hand in hand with the idea that education should be useful and that the classical curriculum should be remodeled to fit the needs of the day. This proposition provoked a bitter controversy among educators. The classics had been enthroned in higher education because they were thought to contain that body of revealed truth which the process of education passed on from one generation to another. There was religious authority for this concept of higher education which was challenged by Darwin's theory of evolution, and the traditional classical education would not die without struggle. Butts enumerates the arguments for the old curriculum:

The conservatives quickly rallied to the fight and defended with all the power at their command the traditional meaning of a liberal education. The favorite defenses centered around three or four main types that viewed the traditional classical education as the "best expression of the eternal spirit of man" and as the best way to elevate man "to the highest and best ideals of human life". . . .

A second type of argument emphasized that the true liberal education was sought for its own sake and would be destroyed if utilitarian values were inserted into it. . . .

A third phase of the argument stated that a liberally educated man should be acquainted with all of the principal fields of thought before being allowed to specialize. . . .

A fourth type of expression commonly found in support of the traditional liberal education was the argument that the meaning of a liberal education and the integrity of the bachelor of arts degree must be maintained by keeping out of the course of study any practical or utilitarian studies.[32]

[29] Darwin. *op. cit.* p. 366.
[30] Murphy, Gardner. *An Historical Introduction to Modern Psychology.* p. 177.
[31] Butts, R. Freeman. *The College Charts Its Course.* p. 176.
[32] *Ibid.* p. 216-17.

The elective principle won the argument though, and the new century was to see an approval of science which almost amounted to a deification of that subject. The idea of culture had to change. Butts explains this change as reflected in an enlarged curriculum as follows:

> Numerous articles and books began to portray the advancements being made in such newer fields of study as the modern languages, English, biology, physical sciences, history, economics, political science, sociology, and anthropology. This growing amount of literature in the younger fields of knowledge indicated that they were coming to maturity in the organization of subject matter and in methods of teaching. . . . They were consequently challenging the classics on all of the grounds upon which the classics had ever been justified; they were asserting that they could discipline the mind and provide just as much "culture" as the classics could.

> Moreover, the modern subjects were insisting that they were even more adequate than the classics, because they dealt with more recent materials and embodied the "best that had been thought and said" within the last hundred years. They were therefore appealing to students on all the familiar grounds and were adding for good measure the arguments that they were up-to-date, practical, and interesting. Thus, the newer subjects continued to shoulder their way into the liberal arts curriculum and to make more impossible than ever before the continuance of a prescribed curriculum.[33]

Since Rhetoric had a classical background, it was natural that it should suffer when the curriculum was extended to take in all the new subjects. It was probably considered old-fashioned. At any rate, there was a noticeable decline in the teaching of Rhetoric in the colleges after 1870. According to Hayworth, the higher institutions that had used Blair, Campbell, or Whately gradually replaced them with Hill, Genung, and other rhetorics which dealt chiefly with written composition. The requirements dealing with the delivery of orations and declamations before the student body were dropped, and by 1890 required courses were taken out rather generally. Nevertheless, some elective courses and more extra-curricular work in speech were to be found.[34]

Coulton found in his study of speech education that when Whately lost his outstanding position, Russell's *Elocution,* Cohen's *Throat and Voice,* and Bacon's *Manual of Gesture* took his place. It is rather difficult to get exact information concerning the names of the textbooks used in this period because some of the college catalogs no longer listed the names of the textbooks as they had done in previous years. For the decade 1850-1860, seventy institutions mentioned seventy-two textbooks which were in use in courses pertaining to

[33] *Ibid.* p. 221.
[34] Hayworth, Donald. "The Development of the Training of Public Speakers in America." *Quarterly Journal of Speech.* 14:501 (1928).

speech work, while in the decade from 1880 to 1890, only forty-nine were mentioned in the catalogs for a total of one hundred and eleven institutions. However, the ones that were mentioned give some idea of the popular textbooks. Austin, Delsarte, and Curry were mentioned more often than any other in the period 1890-1900; Trueblood, Sammis and Palmer, Emerson, Bacon and Shurter were added to the trio in the next decade; after 1910, Delsarte and Austin were no longer mentioned.[35]

Evidently, the demand for some kind of speech training was not lacking in the colleges and universities of this period. Sometimes, itinerant teachers were employed to give lessons in expression or oratory outside the regular curriculum. Thomas C. Trueblood was an early itinerant teacher before he became the head of the speech department of Michigan University. An excerpt from his article, "A Chapter on the Organization of Courses in Public Speaking," gives a description of the itinerant teacher's work and explains the necessity for it.

> Speech training in the seventies was largely in the hands of special schools of oratory which did not live up to the name, for most of them taught but one phase of the subject—delivery, declamation and dramatic reading. Most of them paid no attention to speech construction, to the content of the speech and to methods of gathering material. Their small libraries were made up largely of books on elocution, and choice selections for public entertainment.
>
> Even before the seventies, itinerant teachers of public speaking began to come to the colleges. They gave short courses without credit and received tuition directly from the students rather than through the college administration. Notable among the teachers and readers of that time were James E. Murdoch, the distinguished actor, and author of several works on speech and the stage, and S. S. Hamill, one of his pupils. . . .[36]

When public speaking finally crept back into the curriculum it was known by many different names. According to Coulton's study, from 1890 to 1910 the organization of speech work began within the English departments. An English course in which speech was the main offering was often called *Oral English*.

> . . . At Brigham Young University, at Columbia University, Fisk University, and the University of Tennessee there was given a course in "English" with the description of "Oral and Written Composition" while the State University of Montana offered "English and Oral Composition" and "Oral English" was offered by Marquette University in Wisconsin. Thus was indicated a growing dichotomy between oral and written composition which was viewed with varying degrees of approbation or condemnation by those interested in speech education.[37]

[35] Coulton, Thomas E. *Trends in Speech Education in American Colleges, 1835-1935*. p. 63, 84.
[36] Trueblood, Thomas C. *Quarterly Journal of Speech Education*. 12:1-2 (1926).
[37] Coulton. *op. cit.* p. 48, 88.

According to the same authority, *Declamation* as a course title largely disappeared during the decade from 1890-1900. Four new course titles: *Voice, Gesture, Interpretation,* and *Public Speaking* are added to Coulton's tabulation of courses for 1900-1910.

THE NATIONAL ASSOCIATION OF ACADEMIC TEACHERS OF PUBLIC SPEAKING. In 1914, the teachers who were interested in oral rather than written English, withdrew from the National Council of Teachers of English and organized The National Association of Academic Teachers of Public Speaking, which later became The National Association of Teachers of Speech. This marked a new period in the development of the teaching of Speech.[38] A questionnaire sent out during this same year to thirty-six representative universities showed that twenty-three of them had a department of Public Speaking distinct from the department of English.[39] Here was a nucleus of able teachers who were determined to bring the subject back to the curriculum and to restore it to an important place in higher education. Some of the leaders in the organization of the academic group were: O'Neill, Sarett, Hardy, Rarig, Winans, and Bassett.[40]

The National Speech Arts Association, formerly The National Association of Elocutionists, held a meeting in San Francisco in 1915. This group represented primarily the professional schools. A report of their meeting shows the emphasis upon delivery and professional reading which Trueblood mentioned above and also the effect of the Curry School of Expression upon terminology used.

The day programs this year attempted a unified and organic discussion of the subject of expression. The first day provided for discussion of expression as an instinct, and the transition from instinctive to conscious expression; the second day, the technique of expression, voice, bodily expression, and the spoken word were considered; the third day, the interpretative side of expression, including the speaker in relation to himself, the speaker in relation to literature, and the speaker in relation to his audience were taken up; the fourth day artistic forms, platform reading, public speaking, and acting were on the program.[41]

Although professional-school elocution was criticized by the academic teachers, there was a great overlapping of the two associations as far as membership was concerned, and the Speech Arts Association was gradually absorbed by the new organization. Another group which cooperated was the Eastern Conference group. The first East-

[38] *Quarterly Journal of Public Speaking.* 1:55-8 (1915).
[39] Lyon, Clarence E. "The English-Public Speaking Situation." *Quarterly Journal of Public Speaking.* 1:44-50 (1915).
[40] *Quarterly Journal of Public Speaking.* 1:55-8 (1915).
[41] *Loc. cit.* 1:320 (1915).

ern Public Speaking Conference had been held in 1910 at Swarthmore College with Erastus Palmer as the first president. The official organ, *The Public Speaking Review,* was published until the *Quarterly Journal of Public Speaking* began in 1915. The Eastern Public Speaking Conference, an academic group, was interested primarily in rhetoric as the articles in the review testify, but many of its members were looking forward to the day when all the different phases of speech could be coordinated in a strong department.

James A. Winans, the president of the Eastern Public Speaking Conference in 1914, gave a prognosis of the work to be done in the field of speech which was remarkably correct as the study of the next period will reveal. The following quotation is taken from the president's report in the *Public Speaking Review*:

> As regards tendencies of our work, the President expressed his belief that less attention will be paid in the future to expression as a means of entertainment, and more to the practical public speech, using the word practical, broadly. Oral interpretation will continue to be taught, both because of its high cultural value and as a means of developing power in public speakers. Voice training will receive much and will be better, because guesswork will give way to science. No speaker can afford to overlook the importance of a well trained voice. But the stress will be upon public speech as a means of expounding, convincing, and persuading. In using the term practical public speaking there is no intention of suggesting a crude, unfinished type. Demosthenes and Webster were practical public speakers. But we shall work for a simpler form of speech than "college oratory." And much of our work will have to be very simple indeed, and probably rather crude; for a strong demand is coming from our technical students, who can, or think they can, give us but little time. . . . We must meet these technical and other students on their own ground, putting aside our preconceptions, and, after study, give them what they need. . . . We must fit into and serve the communities in which we are placed, rather than offer work better adapted to special schools of expression.[42]

In the same report, the subject of the relation of public speaking to the English department was discussed. Winans was of the opinion that public speaking would never fare well in the English department unless the teacher of public speaking were the head of the department as at Hamilton and Colgate colleges. The need for a separate department and for the broadening of the field of speech beyond that of the professional school was felt. The organization of academic teachers of public speaking was not only an indication of this need, but a prediction of the next period which established speech in all its forms firmly and honorably in the college curriculum.

[42] Winans, James A. "Report of the Eastern Public Speaking Conference." *Public Speaking Review.* 4:12 (1914).

SUMMARY. The professional schools undoubtedly exerted a great influence upon the teaching of interpretation during the period from 1870-1915. The textbooks used were, for the most part, written by the heads of these schools. A national organization of teachers was sponsored by them and the itinerant teachers who went out to the colleges and universities, where no adequate training was available, were supplied by these same schools. Their methods seem artificial and sometimes ludicrous to the modern teacher, but they were compatible with the background of the period and dictated by its needs. The professional schools are to be commended for carrying a great part of the responsibility for teaching this subject of speech when the colleges and universities would not give it adequate attention.

It is unwise to condemn this period of transition. It contributed much that was praiseworthy; such as, the new psychology, new ventures in adult education, and the great liberalizing and modernizing of the college curriculum. As for the general culture of the nation, it made respectable progress toward an indigenous literature and art. Nevins says of it:

A post-war era which, amidst boodling, scandal and money grubbing, could produce *Scribner's* and the *Nation, Life on the Mississippi* and *Old Creole Days,* Edwin Booth in "Hamlet" and the Boston Museum of Fine Arts, was an epoch full of healthy and irrepressible growth in every cultural field. They represented achievements of enduring value, and indicated powerful and promising currents flowing *beneath* the surface of the life of the new nation.[48]

The most important single influence upon the methods used in teaching Elocution was that exerted by the new psychology; emphasis is now upon mental processes rather than the physiology of speech. The great interest in the mind and in the outward manifestations of its activities diverted the attention of the teachers of speech from the emphasis established by the preceding period on physiology and the mechanism of the voice. In fact, the influence of the pragmatic philosophy which activated the new psychology influenced all higher education. The curriculum was liberalized and the purpose was defined in much less aristocratic terms than it had been in the preceding period. There was a definite swing away from the classical tradition.

Comparing the period 1870-1915, with the previous periods which have been discussed, it does not seem to present two clearly defined schools of method in the teaching of Oral Interpretation of Literature. There is more variety than before, and eclecticism has become a more common guiding principle. The problem was more complex because of the diversity of student needs and the multiplicity of demands for

[48] Nevins. *op. cit.* p. 263.

public entertainment. But although oral interpretation received more professional emphasis than it ever had before, the courses which emerged at the end of the period were designed primarily to teach students to appreciate literature and to read it acceptably rather than to train them to be public performers.

CHAPTER II

THE DELSARTE SYSTEM

The Delsarte system was the most important innovation of this period. The Walker-Austin-Rush tradition was carried on by such men as Alexander Melville Bell, E. P. Trueblood, and Erastus Palmer. The Natural school took new life from the current psychological emphasis and made progress under the leadership of S. S. Curry. However, the two schools were not as clearly defined as before and part of the variation was due to the influence of Delsarte. His system was unique, in perfect harmony with the exaggerations and absurdities of the late nineteenth century, and destined to affect the majority of teachers of elocution and many of the teachers of physical education until the next century was well under way.

FRANCOIS DELSARTE. François Delsarte taught music and acting in Paris from 1839 to 1871. He is said to have lost his voice because of faulty teaching methods used in the conservatory in which he was enrolled, and as a result to have devised his own system which was accounted scientific by his followers. However, he did not base his methods or theory on scientific experiments but rather upon the belief that theology holds the key to all knowledge. He held a kind of transcendental philosophy which he used as a basis for his theories of expression. He believed that every part of nature could be resolved into its fundamental three parts, even as the supernatural power was divided into the Holy Trinity. Shaver has analyzed Delsarte's system through a study of the notes of one of his most famous students, Steele Mackaye. He explains it as follows:

According to the theory everything in nature is triune. Man is, however, the highest form of nature representing a duality. Man is at one and the same time, a physical being and an incorporated spirit. In his spirit-being man was created in the image of God. In his physical being he was created to resemble God. Man thus belongs to two worlds. . . The spiritual being is called the immanent being; the physical being is called the organic being.

Each of the two natures of man, the spiritual being and the organic being is composed of a trinity . . . the trinity of the immanent is life, mind, and soul, and the corresponding trinity of the physical or organic being is feeling, thought, and love; feeling produces the perceptual state of memory; thought produces the intellectual state of understanding; love produces the moral state of will. Thus memory corresponds to life; understanding corresponds to mind; will corresponds to soul.[1]

[1] Shaver, Claude L. *The Delsarte System of Expression As Seen Through the Notes of Steele Mackaye.* p. 41-4.

The love of classifying data, of devising rules, and of developing a complicated explanation for natural phenomena was shared by many during the nineteenth century. Complicated mechanical theories were often accounted scientific. Rush's system is a good example of this trend in speech. His system, although not based on faultless inductive reasoning, was derived from the sciences of physiology and physics and had a better right to be called scientific than Delsarte's which derived from theology. The Delsarte System was of necessity mechanical and meretricious. The careful division of every part of expression into a pattern of three or nine made it inflexible and unnatural. It was by nature speculative and non-scientific.

The belief in a very close relationship between the two natures of man had something in common with the new psychology which was monistic. The name given by Delsarte to this interaction of the immanent and organic beings was *circumcession*. Shaver comments upon this principle in the following manner:

> The principle of circumcession would lead to the conclusion that the controlling influences of movement are so interwoven that any bodily expression is not only under control of major influences but also is operated upon by all the influences at work on the body. Thus each movement is made through a totality of control. Inversely every part of the body probably exerts influence on every other part of the body through its major control. Perhaps this theory has had some influence upon the premise of modern speech, that speech is a totality of bodily action.[2]

In addition, Delsarte analyzed the different parts of the whole and assigned functions to each. Shaver also explains this part of Delsarte's theories:

> Life, with its immanent acts of sensation, instinct, and sympathy, is expressed by the vocal mechanism; mind, with its accompanying immanances, judgment, induction, and conscience is expressed by the buccal mechanism; soul, with its immanances of sentiment, intuition, and contemplation, is expressed by the dynamic mechanism.
> Each of these mechanisms is also triple in its composition. The vocal mechanism is composed of the lungs, the back of the mouth, and the larynx. The buccal mechanism is composed of the velum, the lips, and the tongue. The dynamic mechanism is composed of the head, the body, and the face. The limbs serve as accessories in expressing the three parts of the body. Each of these mechanisms produces its own peculiar form of expression. The vocal mechanism produces inflection; the buccal mechanism produces the word; the dynamic mechanism produces gesture. These three products produce as the result of successive activity, three languages. These are the language of music resulting from inflection; the language of logic, resulting from the word; the language of mimicry, resulting from gesture.[3]

[2] *Ibid*. p. 113.
[3] *Ibid*. p. 51.

According to the principles of circumcession, the soul is produced by the common inspiration of life and mind and is considered, by Delsarte, the highest of the three, just as the Father is basic to the Divine Trinity. Since gesture expresses the soul, it is considered the highest form of expression. Delaumosne, a student of Delsarte in Paris, clearly minimizes speech and stresses gesture in keeping with this principle. "Speech," he says, "is inferior to gesture, because it corresponds to the phenomena of mind; gesture is the agent of the heart, it is the persuasive agent. . . . So much the better if the speaking is good, but gesture is the all-important thing." [4]

All the followers of Delsarte classify gestures according to the zones of the body affected and according to the kind of movement. The zones are three: the torso, the *vital* zone; the head, the *intellectual* zone; and the face, the *moral* zone. As an example, a gesture of the hand toward the head is termed a mental gesture. Movement is also fitted into a trinity; movement about the center is *normal*; away from the center is *eccentric*; toward the center is *concentric*. A reciprocal influence of life and mind and soul is traced in both trinities. The vital zone indicates life, and so also do normal movements which are circular or spiral. The mental zone is, of course, the mind which is indicated by eccentric movement away from the body. Those toward the body are the concentric and correspond to the soul. Shaver illustrates the application of these forms of movement from Mackaye's notes on the action of the feet.

> . . . These states may be illustrated by the position of the feet. In the normal state, the feet are parallel and close together and the weight is evenly distributed on both legs; in the concentric state, one leg is drawn back and the weight of the body is shifted onto the rear leg while the front leg is comparatively free; in the eccentric state one leg is advanced and the weight of the body is shifted onto the forward leg leaving the rear leg comparatively free. [5]

The chart on p. 145 appears in textbooks based upon the Delsarte system. Any action may be labeled according to it. The explanation given by Delaumosne is indicative of the importance which was placed upon the chart as a sort of formula:

> The normal form, either in the genus or the species, we place in the middle column, because it serves as a bond of union beween the two others, as the moral state is the connecting link between the intellectual and vital states. . . . This is a universal algebraic formula, by which we can solve all organic problems.

[4] Delaumosne, L'Abbé. "The Delsarte System" in *The Delsarte System of Oratory.* p. 48, 49.
[5] Shaver. *op. cit.* p. 60.

We apply it to the hand, to the shoulder, to the eyes, to the voice—in a word, to all the agents of oratorical language.[6]

The illustration, Criterion of the Legs (see p. 146), shows the application which was made and perhaps indicates why Delsarte's theories in practice may well be called a system. Similar illustrations were given for the action of hand, head, eye, nose, etc.

	SPECIES		
GENUS	1	3	2
II. Concentric	II-1 Eccentric-Concentric	II-3 Normal-Concentric	II-2 Concentric-Concentric
III. Normal	III-1 Eccentric-Normal	III-3 Normal-Normal	III-2 Concentric-Normal
I. Eccentric	I-1 Eccentric-Eccentric	I-3 Normal-Eccentric	I-2 Concentric-Eccentric

Although gesture was considered of prime importance, Mackaye's notes do mention the voice and divide the vocal apparatus as another trinity. Three agents are mentioned: the inciting agent, the lungs, the vital part of sound; the resonating agent, the mouth, the mental part of sound; the vibrating agent, the larynx, the moral part of sound. All vocal effects arising from these fundamental agents express the life, mind, and soul of the organism.[7]

Delaumosne probably gave the voice more consideration than the other Delsartians. Of course, it is impossible to know how many original ideas were added by the followers of Delsarte in their books purporting to set forth his theories. Delaumosne notes the three dimensions of the voice: height, which may also be called diapason or tonality; depth, also called intensity or timbre; and breadth, also called duration or succession. He says that there are three kinds of voices: the chest-voice, the medium voice, and the head-voice. These follow the vital, mental, and moral classification and the cultivation of each one is stressed as necessary for expression. The medium voice is con-

[6] Delaumosne. op. cit. p. 5-7. Note the use of the words *species* and *genus* in this pseudo-scientific chart which is called by Delaumosne "a universal algebraic formula."
[7] Shaver. op. cit. p. 109.

sidered the basic voice and the following method is suggested for developing it:

The articulation of the three syllables *la, mo* and *po,* is a very useful exercise in habituating one to the medium voice. Besides reproducing the tone of this voice, these are the musical consonants *par excellence.* They give charm and development to the voice. . . . It is only a hap-hazard sort of orator who does not know how to attain, at the outset, what is called the white voice. . . . The coloring of the larynx corresponds to the movements of the hand or brows.[8]

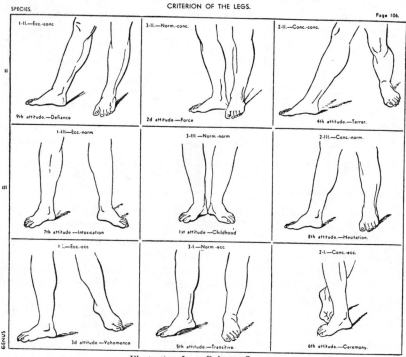

Illustration from *Delsarte System*

This method indicates a coordination of gesture with speech which would be a necessary part of the methods used by any teacher of elocution who followed Delsarte.

THE EFFECT OF DELSARTE UPON PHYSICAL EDUCATION. As might be predicted, the emphasis upon bodily action made Delsarte an influence in the field of Physical Education as well as in the field of

[8] Delaumosne. *op. cit.* p. 15-19 *passim.*

Oral Expression. Emmett Rice, in his *History of Physical Education,* appraises the contribution of Delsarte to this particular field. He states:

> During the early nineties the so-called Delsarte System of Physical Culture received much notoriety, and great numbers, especially women, were converted to its theories. François Delsarte, a French vocal and dramatic teacher, found the ideal poses and gestures necessary to effective dramatics and singing could best be taught through certain physical exercises. However, he did not have in mind the founding of a new system of gymnastics. In America many teachers of the art of elocution accepted his methods and with the addition of their own ideas there was evolved a system of exercises which claimed to produce poise, grace, beauty of face and figure, and health. These claims gave the Delsarte System a universal appeal entirely aside from its connection with the vocal and dramatic arts.
>
>   *   *   *
>
> Genevieve Stebbins, who wrote "Society Gymnastics," introduced the Delsarte principles into the "fashionable" schools of New York City. She also gave matinee exhibitions in Madison Square Garden. Emily Bishop, author of "Americanized Delsarte Culture," taught in the Delsarte Department of the School of Physical Education at Chautauqua Assembly, Chautauqua, N. Y.
>
> The fad of Delsartianism barely outlived the nineties. It left almost no trace in either art or education; however, through its influence a great number, who could have been reached no other way, became interested in their physical well-being and in the cause of physical education in general.[9]

There were three laws which the physical exercises based upon Delsarte followed: The law of correspondence, the law of opposition, and the law of equilibrium. Henry Davenport Northrop explains these in *The Delsarte Speaker*:

> One of the fundamental principles of Delsarte's philosophy is the law of correspondence, which was discovered by Swedenborg, who held that the material world corresponds to the spiritual world and is the manifestation of man's mental being. In other words, that the spiritual world is symbolized in the physical world. . . . Delsarte held that in gesture or movement of the body, the parts should move in opposition. . . . Parallelism offends our idea of fitness and grace. . . . Fundamentally, underlying the law of opposition, is the law of equilibrium. To maintain equilibrium of parts there must be opposition.[10]

Since Greek Art was considered a good example of the last two laws, many exercises and pantomimes were based on it. Stebbins in her book, *Delsarte System of Expression,* uses thirty-two illustrations of famous statues as a basis for the exercises called *statue-posing.* The report of the National Convention which met on June 29, 1897, records a controversy over Miss Stebbins' paper entitled *The Relation of*

---

[9] Rice, Emmett A. *A Brief History of Physical Education.* p. 181-3.
[10] Northrop, Henry Davenport. *The Delsarte Speaker.* p. 22-3.

Physical Culture to Expression: A Plea for Statue Posing with Delsarte Fundamentals. Some teachers objected to statue-posing because they thought it was exhibition rather than expression.

Emily Bishop demonstrates the fact that she subscribed to the same laws in the gymnastic exercises. The following is an example:

Exercise 1. Hold some thought of proportion.
Standing on both feet, the knees straight, the arms relaxed, bend the body slowly forward. Note the movement of the hips; they recede as the torso goes forward. Keeping the hips as nearly stationary as possible, raise the torso to an upright position and push the crown of the head upward. . . .[11]

Perhaps the most valuable part of the physical exercises devised by these disciples of Delsarte was the relaxation or devitalization which Stebbins called "decomposing" exercises. The following directions are given as an example:

Exercise 1. Let fingers fall from the knuckles as if dead; in that condition shake them. Vital force should stop at the knuckles.
Exercise 2. Let hand fall from the wrist as if dead; shake it in that condition forward and back, up and down sideways, rotary shake. . . .[12]

The same technique follows through for the arm, head, foot, torso, leg, eyelids, etc. The necessity for relaxation exercises to relieve tension and to get the best results in voice production and in bodily action is still recognized by teachers of speech, although they are described in a little different manner.

MOSES TRUE BROWN. Moses True Brown published *The Synthetic Philosophy of Expression as applied to the Arts of Reading, Oratory, and Personation* in 1886. In this work he attempted to do justice to Delsarte's system and also to apply the principles of Darwin and Mantegazza. Brown was a student of William Russell and a great admirer of Austin, so traces of the influence of *Orthophony* and of *Chironomia* may be seen too. The result is a book so laden with rules and philosophic discussion that its practical use as a textbook in speech is to be questioned. However, Brown was principal of the Boston School of Oratory and professor of Oratory at Tufts College and probably used it as a basis for his teaching.

From Darwin's *The Expression of Emotion in Man and Animals,* Brown takes the three principles: the principle of serviceable associated habits; the principle of antithesis; and the principle of direct action of the nervous system on the body. He recognizes Mantegazza's *La Physionomie et l'Expression des Sentiment* (1885) as an extension

[11] Bishop, Emily M. *Americanized Delsarte Culture.* p. 42.
[12] Stebbins, Genevieve. *Delsarte System of Dramatic Expression.* p. 12.

of Darwin's theories. From Delsarte, he takes his nomenclature, with a few changes. *Emotive* is substituted for *moral* and *poise* for *normal* because Brown felt that the terms used were not exact. He makes a statement in the preface that he feels that there has been no adequate treatment of the theories of Delsarte and mentions voice and articulate speech as being neglected by those who have applied his principles to expression. However, Brown devotes fifteen chapters to gesture and the last two to speech. His chief interest seems to be in the transcendental theory of mind related to the universe and he reiterates the importance of the Law of Correspondence throughout the book. He says:

There are two subsistences of whose reality man is conscious, and whose recorded phenomena, and deductions therefrom, make the sum of that knowledge which he calls science. These subsistences are (1) Matter; (2) Spirit, Mind, or Soul. . . . These words are the Universe, and God. The Universe is matter in form, occupying Space, existing in Time, held by law. . . . God is Spirit; and is sustaining Cause, animating Centre, and pervading Soul of the Universe. . . .

. . . It is unthinkable that Matter can exist and be active without Soul; or that Soul can manifest its existence without Body. . . . Man as we find him on this earth is a union of matter and Soul. Let us call this mysterious union of matter and Soul in form, The Organism. And we may say, Man is a Soul served by organs.

The Philosophy of Expression, then is the Philosophy of Manifestation. In its broadest sense it is the Philosophy of the Infinite, as revealed in the Universe. In its restricted sense it is the Philosophy of Man, as revealed through the Organism.[13]

The Triad or Trinity of Restriction was considered very important since voice, gesture, and articulate speech were all affected by it:

1. *Soul can manifest itself, both in the Universe and in man, only through matter.*
2. *All manifestations of Soul—both in the Universe and in Man—must declare themselves in relation to, and correspondence with, Space, Time, and Motion.*
3. *Whatever successively appears in Time is simultaneously extended to Space.*[14]

According to Brown, man is a psychic being; the term *psychic being* is defined as an energy centered in the organism and controlling its action. He uses the term as generic and as covering the three specific terms: Life, Mind, and Soul. His development from that point through zones to special organs of expression is identical with Delsarte's System. The laws of motion, though, are discussed at length

[13] Brown, Moses True. *The Synthetic Philosophy of Expression.* p. 1-4, 40.
[14] *Ibid.* p. 6.

and with originality beyond that shown in other textbooks based on Delsarte.

The proposition which he states for the Law of Opposition is as follows: "The greater the number of agents that unite in balanced and harmonious opposition, the higher the form of Expression." [15] He falls back on Herbert Spencer for his explanation of the beginnings of this principle and quotes him as saying that the process of life is the continuous adjustment of internal relations to external relations, or as Delsarte interpreted it, the opposition of forces as an *instinct* of the soul.

The Law of Reaction is defined as the return of force; every emotion when it becomes extreme produces action. The following are corollaries to the law devised by Brown:

1. *Every extreme of Emotion tends to react to its opposite. Concentric states tend to explosion, and explosion tends to prostration.*
2. *The only passion that does not tend to its own destruction is that which is poised, or is in equilibrium.*
3. *The soul in its highest moods translates itself by poising its agents. Poise the Soul and the whole muscular system is in action to poise the body. Here we state the Law of Climax:—*
   Law: There should be but one strong climax in a perfect work of Art. The artist should work steadily toward that climax. [16]

The Law of Radiation is simply stated: "Animal Radiations are downwards. Human Radiations are upwards and outwards." The three gravitations are:

Man gravitates to the Earth through his feet.
To humanity through the torso.
To the Universe through the eye.

*   *   *

Thus man is conscious that he stands at the centre of the Universe, and projects radial lines from where he stands into the infinite spaces.

In his littleness, he is a finite speck of matter crawling upon the face of a cosmic sphere; in his greatness, he is a Soul who creates anew the orderly procedure, unfolding, and continuance of the Kosmos. [17]

The influence of Austin's *Chironomia* is evident in the concept of man's position. Brown visualizes each human being at the centre of a visible, objective sphere, and all objects which are related to him are either within this sphere or outlined against its periphery. The brain is another sphere and its subjective images correspond to the visible objects. [18]

[15] *Ibid.* p. 77.
[16] *Ibid.* p. 63-4.
[17] *Ibid.* p. 104, 106, 238.
[18] *Ibid.* p. 150.

Brown attempted to harmonize many ideas that were interesting to him as the title of the book, *The Synthetic Philosophy of Expression*, suggests. As was stated previously, it was an impossible task to reconcile transcendentalism and the new science. Therefore, Brown succeeded not in improving the Delsarte system but in making it more elaborate. The philosophy was more clearly defined; the so-called science may have used a more exact nomenclature, but was only classificatory and certainly not experimental in its method or dependable in its conclusions. However, the concept of man as an integral part of his environment and possessing a unity of mind and body is clearly stated:

> It will be seen that in its broadest application such a Philosophy must embrace all the phenomena resulting from the mysterious union of soul and body.
> It must recognize the action of the environment—near and remote—upon the soul, as also the modes of reaction of the soul upon its environment.
> It should trace—if it were pushed to ultimate grounds—the manifestations of the simplest life upon the earth, up to imperial man, whose expressions would epitomize and reveal the Kosmos.
> It must embrace, also, all the complex phenomena which arise from the necessity man feels, while in the presence of Nature, to embody, and thereby attempt to realize his worship of the True, the Good, and the Beautiful. Hence a complete Philosophy of Expression would embrace the philosophy of the Fine Arts, plastic, graphic, and dramatic—the Arts of the eye and ear.[19]

Although Brown was familiar with Darwin and Mantegazza and was intensely interested in making expression scientific, he could not succeed in his task, because he rested too heavily upon Delsarte. Some of the terminology was changed and explanations made that were sometimes clearer and often more elaborate than ones made previously, but he could not surmount the contradiction of making scientific theories which were based upon theology.

SUMMARY. Although it is impossible to know how many ideas which the Delsartian teachers held stemmed directly from the original teacher, it is possible to summarize the basic principles upon which the Delsarte System operated. (1) Everything in nature is triune. (2) Man is made up of two beings: the immanent or spiritual, and the organic, which are interwoven. (3) The spiritual being is composed of soul, mind, and life. (4) The organic being is composed of love, thought, and feeling. (5) The body of man contains three mechanisms for the expression of mind, soul, and life, and their correspondents, love, thought, and feeling: the vocal mechanism, the buccal mechanism, and the dynamic mechanism. (6) The vocal mechanism, representing life, produces the inflection; buccal mechan-

[19] *Ibid.* p. 12.

ism, representing mind, produces the word; and the dynamic mechanism, representing soul, produces the gesture. (7) Gesture is the most important expression since it represents the soul or love. Gestures may be classified according to the zones of the body: the torso or vital zone, the head or intellectual zone, and the face or moral zone. (8) Movement itself may be either normal, concentric, or eccentric. (9) The vital zone is indicated by normal movement; the mental zone is indicated by eccentric movement; while the concentric movement represents the moral zone. (10) All expression may be analyzed according to its relationship to the two beings of man and results from a coordination of many different factors which are triune in pattern.

The system is neat and mechanical. It is not scientific but purely speculative. However, it became a fad which was quite generally recognized not only in the field of vocal expression but in the field of physical education. Its claim to curative powers, at least for such afflictions as lack of poise and awkwardness, may possibly be granted, because total bodily action was required for expression. This demand continues to be made of the speaker. In addition, Delsarte's emphasis upon an interrelation of man's soul, mind, and body has been accepted as a working principle for modern teachers of speech.

CHAPTER III

THE TRADITION OF WALKER, AUSTIN, AND RUSH REMAINS UNBROKEN

Although Delsarte and his followers succeeded in diverting many teachers from the study of the vocal mechanism to the study of physical culture and gesture as the most important means of expression, there were still a number who carried on the old traditions of the Mechanical school as embodied in the systems of Walker, Austin, and Rush. The desire to devise notations and to formulate rules for use in showing variation in pitch, quality, time, and force of this vocal expression still obtained.

The scientific emphasis which produced *The Philosophy of the Human Voice* continued to produce treatises based upon physiology. Eventually, this trend was to bring about a further dichotomy in the field of speech. Voice Science was soon to become a separate course apart from the Art of Interpretation, although still contributing to it. In the early period, Rhetoric, because of the emphasis upon *pronuntiatio*, was forced to accept a division which gave status to a study of Elocution. Now further specialization divided Elocution, and courses were offered in the college curriculum not only in *Voice Science*, but also in *Gesture* and *Pantomime*. Methods of teaching required vocal techniques and physical flexibility as prerequisites for the student who attempted to interpret literature. These techniques were often based on mechanical rules.

ALEXANDER MELVILLE BELL. Alexander Melville Bell was one of the great leaders in the perpetuation of the Walker-Rush tradition. He was best known for his system of *Visible Speech,* a physiological alphabet in which each symbol showed the position of the organs of speech necessary to make a particular sound. He delivered lectures on this subject before Lowell Institute in 1868. In 1871 his son Alexander Graham Bell came to Boston and used the system in teaching the deaf in Miss Fuller's School, the first day-school for the deaf.

The family was very much interested in elocution. Alexander Bell, the father, was a professor of elocution in London, while his brother, David Charles Bell, held a similar position in Dublin. Alexander Melville Bell was first a lecturer on elocution in Edinburgh University and after his father's death took his position in London. While in Edinburgh, he published *Principles of Elocution* (1849). He came to the United States in 1872. The book then went through its fourth, fifth, sixth, and seventh editions here, the last one appearing in 1899.[1]

Although Alexander Melville Bell taught only private lessons in this country, he exerted a great influence and seems to have been considered the dean of the profession. When, in 1899 at the age of eighty, he addressed the meeting of the National Association of Elocutionists at Chautauqua Lake, New York, President Trueblood, Rev. Francis T. Russell, and S. H. Clark all testified in flowery language concerning his great contribution to the development of elocution.

Although an attempt was always being made to reduce the task of teaching elocution to a system or a series of rules which would be scientific and reliable, the rather intangible influence of the personality of the teacher upon his students was greatly appreciated and was often mentioned during this period. Pedagogues were beginning to realize that the personal element entered into the teaching situation and also that the learning process was a most complex one. Curry shows this attitude very clearly in his tribute to Bell after the latter's death on August 7, 1905:

> Of all my teachers, numbering fifty or sixty in different parts of the world, he has perhaps had the greatest influence over me.
>
> * * *
>
> The work of a teacher of a subject so subjective as Vocal Training or Delivery can hardly be indicated in print. The sudden suggestion, the constant varying of the point of view, the giving of a clause incorrectly or with the exaggeration of a fault in order to awaken the student to a realization of his own mistakes, the endeavor to awaken the student's consciousness of himself, or of the real meaning of his mannerisms, of his failures to present the truth correctly, . . . how can a teacher's method of dealing with such psychological problems be even hinted at in cold type? The look, the inflexion, the delicate hint, the peculiar touch upon a word, the illustration, the criticism—in short, the living spirit of the truly great teacher who is called upon, as in Vocal Expression, to read the heart of his student and to make clear to the pupil himself his own failures to reveal his best self, can never be recorded.
>
> It is for this reason that Delivery—the right use of the voice, articulation, correct methods of breathing, faults of inflexion, and all the subtleties of Vocal Expression—must be taught by a living teacher. . . .
>
> This is not because Vocal Expression can ever be taught by imitation. Professor Bell, of all teachers I have ever known, was free from instruction by imitation.[2]

Bell's book, *The Principles of Elocution,* is divided into four parts: pronunciation, modulation and expressive delivery; emphasis; intona-

[1] *Dictionary of American Biography.* vol. 2. p. 149, 152, 153.
[2] Curry, Samuel Silas. *Alexander Melville Bell, Some Memories from Fragments from a Pupil's Notebook.* p. 10, 53.

tion and clausing; and looks and gestures. Throughout, a physiological approach to elocution is evident. His definition for elocution epitomizes his theory of teaching:

> Elocution may be defined as the *Effective Expression of Thought and Sentiment* by Speech, Intonation, and Gesture. Speech is wholly conventional in its expressiveness, and mechanical in its processes. Intonation and gesture constitute a Natural Language, which may be used either independently of, or as assistant to, speech. Speech, in all the diversities of tongues and dialects, consists of but a small number of articulated elementary sounds. These are produced by the agency of the lungs, the larynx, and the mouth.

* * *

> Elocution, as it involves the exercise of language, must embrace the Physiology of Speech—the mechanics of vocalization and articulation. . . . The student of Elocution, then, should be made acquainted with the instrument of Speech *as an instrument,* that all its parts may be under his control, as the stops, the keys, the pedals, and the bellows, are subject to the organist.

* * *

> There is scarcely a sentence which will not admit of just expression by half a dozen, or ten times as many, modes of vocal inflexion. What is wanted is not a Rule for this or that species of sentence, but a power over the voice generally, to redeem it from monotony; a knowledge of the various modes of conveying sense; and an appreciation of the special sense to be conveyed. To aim at anything more than this would be to destroy the speaker's individuality, and to substitute formality and mannerisms for versatility of natural manner.[3]

Although Bell was primarily interested in the physiological aspects of elocution, he was also interested in the psychological aspects of reading and interpretation. He considered the exercises of the mind in discovering the meaning of the author essential. However, he felt that the student often appreciated the sense of the material without having the technique to express his idea or emotion.

> What a student chiefly requires to know, is *how* to vary his voice; if his own judgment and appreciation of the sense, in connection with defined principles, do not inform him *when* to do so, the most minute direction by Rules will be of little service. The *mechanics* of expression are what he must master, if he would use and manifest his mind in reading; but he must be unfettered in their application, in order that he may develop and improve his manner without acquiring the formality of mannerisms.[4]

His position is not as paradoxical as it appears, because his insistence upon training allows for individual taste and does not bind him by rigid rules. The notations which are given are to be used in practice and elementary exercises to facilitate learning, rather than to dictate the entire procedure. In an address to the National Asso-

[3] Bell, Alexander Melville. *The Principles of Elocution.* p. 6-8.
[4] *Ibid.* p. 5.

ciation of Elocutionists in 1895, Bell made clear his position concerning the use of exercises.

The value of elementary exercise can hardly be overrated. Elocutionary pupils are apt to be impatient to get to reading and declamation, without being troubled with the elements. Here the skill and tact of the teacher are displayed, in giving interest to rudimentary drill, and in partially gratifying the young ambition by regulating indulgence in the practice of delivery. . . . There is no way by which the voice and the ear can be so effectively cultivated, as by the practice of scales and exercises. Every lesson should include a portion of such work. I may be allowed to say that I speak from a long experience in this matter. I commenced each of my class-lessons by a revival of the scales of articulate elements and tones. This occupied only a few minutes; but it made the pupils so familiar with all the relations of the sounds that practical application became spontaneous. And I am sure that weariness of that portion of the lesson was unknown.[5]

The practice of exercises was recommended to the student to improve the mechanics of expression so that he could "make the sound an echo to the sense." [6]

Throughout the book, *The Principles of Elocution,* Bell seems to be attempting a compromise between the *natural* and *mechanical* methods. He offers a more elaborate notation for variation in voice and gesture than those of Walker, Austin, and Rush. He offers a vowel wedge with numbers to indicate different sounds.

```
pool 17                                              1  eel
  pull 16                                          2  ill
    old  15                                      3  ale
      ore  14                                  4  air
        all   13                           5  ell
          doll 12                     6  an
            urn  11            7  a
              err   10     8  ask
                    9
                    ah
```

This system was used before by Sheridan in smaller groups of sounds which had the same orthographic symbols although not in wedge form.[7] Pitch is indicated as high, above middle, middle, below middle, and low. The following symbols indicate higher ⌐ and lower L . Force may be indicated by stronger < weaker > and break. . . . Time may be quicker V slower ⋀ and a pause is indicated by ⌒ . The language for the expression of the emotions resembles that of Austin. Abbreviations are used in the same way, for example, *Ch* for chuckle

    [5] Bell, Alexander Melville. *Address to the National Association of Elocutionists.* pamphlet. p. 9.
    [6] *Ibid.* p. 10.
    [7] Sheridan, Thomas. *The Art of Reading.* vol. 1. p. 7.

and *Sar* for sarcasm.[8]   Yet with all these mechanics, Bell repeatedly insists that he abhors imitation as a method and any manner that is artificial and unnatural.   He accepts the fact that there are individual differences.   Elocutionary rules are only to develop mechanical facility and definiteness of execution, and not uniformity of performance. Walker's rules are cited as demanding too great standardization.[9]   He does, however, defend notations as a useful tool in teaching.[10]

Good articulation and the ability to "speak out" are very important, according to Bell:

> Indistinctness of articulation, and smothering of the voice, are the two prevailing faults of public speaking, and they defeat its very object. Gentlemen who "read papers" come on the platform without the preparation for the reading. They ought to be so familiar with their subject that they do not need to keep the eye constantly on the writing; yet this is the habitual attitude of a large majority of readers.   Common courtesy dictates that a speaker should look at the person addressed.
>
> Here is the elocutionist's field.   Take in the whole scope of a sentence by the eye, but pronounce its parts one by one; with separation by pause, or pitch, or tone, or rate.[11]

In the preparation for public reading or speaking, several types of training are prescribed.   Breathing exercises are considered therapeutic just as they were by many previous writers.   The common fault of dropping the voice at the end of the sentence is traceable to faulty breathing, and exercises are given to correct this fault.   For example, the student tries to increase the number of times he is able to say *e, ah, aw,* etc. on one breath.   The following remedy is also given to strengthen breathing:

> To strengthen weak respiration, the practice of energetic reading in a strong, loud whisper, or "gruff" voice, will prove beneficial. Above all, exercise in the open air will be found of advantage.
>
> * * *
>
> Respiratory exercises should not be practiced immediately after a full meal.   The distension of the stomach prevents the free play of the diaphragm. The public speaker should therefore be sparing before any important oratorical effort, and defer making up the deficiency until he has made his bow to the audience.[12]

Emphasis is treated as one of the most important divisions.   Inflection is considered a servant of emphasis and if the important stress is regulated according to the sense to be conveyed, the inflection

[8] Bell, Alexander Melville. *The Principles of Elocution.* p. 112.
[9] *Ibid.* p. 8.
[10] Bell, Alexander Melville. *On the Use of Notations in Elocutionary Teaching.* p. 9.
[11] *Ibid.* p. 12.
[12] Bell, Alexander Melville. *The Principles of Elocution.* p. 22.

will not be far wrong. The context determines the stress, not the inherent grammatical rank. The term *accent* is used when the stress falls on syllables; *emphasis* refers to stress on words; and *modulation* is used when the unit considered is the sentence.[13]

Pausing is called *clausing* and is said to be one of the most important qualities in reading. It does not always coincide with the punctuation but is used to give the full sense of the material. Bell says:

> There can be no good reading without frequent and, sometimes, long pauses. They convey an effect of spontaneity, which rivets the attention of the hearer; while unbroken fluency, especially in the reading of complex sentences, will never sustain attention, because it is manifestly accompanied with no thought on the part of the reader. Appropriate clausular pausing will lead the reader to *THINK*, and it will make him *seem* to do so even when he does not.[14]

It is suggested that the student read the material carefully and mark the clauses with a straight up and down mark. The principles of verbal grouping are given with appropriate exercises for each stage. The rules for pausing are based upon grammatical construction. Ten pages of "clausing" exercises are given to make the voice more tractable. Bell says of this practice:

> The practice of clausular reading, with proper accentuation and with varied well-defined inflexions accompanying every utterance, will be found speedily and perfectly effectual in imparting FLEXIBILITY to the voice, and in removing habits of MONOTONY, or other inexpressive mannerisms in Reading.[15]

Modulation is defined as including the consideration of pitch and key and the expressive variations of force, time, and quality. The following distinctions require a change in pitch: questions from answers, assertions from proofs or illustrations, general statements from inferences, quotations, a new division of a subject, changes of sentiment, explanatory and parenthetic matter.[16]

The full expression of sentiment makes necessary twenty-seven different qualities: whisper, orotund, hoarseness, falsetto, monotone, plaintive, tremor, chuckle, staccato, smooth, prolongation, rhythm, restraint, straining, panting, inspiration, expiration, percussion, hem, imitation, sympathy, apathy, warmth, sarcasm.[17] The nasal quality is considered the most marked feature of American dialect. It results, Bell explains, from the relaxation of the soft palate so that

[13] *Ibid.* p. 9, 14.
[14] *Ibid.* p. 81, 82.
[15] *Ibid.* p. 84.
[16] *Ibid.* p. 107.
[17] *Ibid.* p. 112.

"the inner ends of the *nares* remain uncorked." [18]   In his discussion of quality he follows much of the Rush terminology and method of practice, although he often credits the exercises to M. Garcia of Paris.   The following is an example:

> The voice may be formed by a soft and gradual vibration, or by an abrupt and instantaneous explosiveness of sound.   The latter mechanism of voice is often employed in energetic, emphatic speech; and the orator should be able, at will, to adopt it with any degree of force from *piano* to *forte*.   The pronunciation of the vowel sounds with something of the effort of a cough, but without its breathiness, will develop the power of producing this intensive vocal effect. Thus:—inhale a full breath and eject the vowel sounds directly from the throat; avoiding in the most forcible effort, any bending or other action of the head or body. [19]

At the age of eighty, Bell was still writing books on elocution. Altogether he wrote forty-eight.   In his last one, *On the Use of Notations in Elocutionary Teaching,* he emphasized the need for ear-training in the teaching of interpretation.   Curry says in his tribute to Dr. Bell that the only man whom he had known who equalled Dr. Alexander Melville Bell in accuracy of ear was his son, Dr. Alexander Graham Bell. [20]

Bell went so far as to say that ear-training should be considered first.   His method of teaching is explained in the following excerpt from his book:

> The first point in elocutionary teaching should always be to train the ear, for it is of no use to speak of qualities of sound unless the pupils apprehend uniformly the qualities to which you refer.   This exactness of apprehension is rarely possessed naturally; it has to be developed by practice. . . .
>
> The tests of ear would proceed in this way: I would read a few lines and suddenly stop, and ask—Was my voice going up, or going down, or was it level when I stopped? . . .
>
> The next point to be settled by the ear was the relative pitch of the voice on successive words.   Reading again, I would say: Was the last accented syllable higher or lower than what preceded it? . . . .
>
> The answers to these two questions involved very important discriminations; namely, the distinction between pitch and inflexion, and between the two modes of every possible inflexion, namely, one mode in which the pitch *rises* to the accent, and the other in which the pitch *falls* to the accent. [21]

Alexander Melville Bell contributed a strong link in the evolution of methods of teaching based upon physiology.   He made a very important contribution when he introduced the hearing mechanism as an integral part of the speech process, and insisted upon ear-

[18] *Ibid.* p. 39.
[19] *Ibid.* p. 23, 24.
[20] Curry. *op. cit.* p. 9.
[21] Bell, Alexander Melville. *On the Use of Notations in Elocutionary Teaching.* p. 6.

training as a requisite part of the teaching of oral interpretation. He realized the importance of the mental understanding and emotional appreciation of the literature interpreted, and believed in individual work free from any imitation of the teacher. He insisted upon rules and notations mainly because he believed them useful in the preparatory work necessary before interpretation.

OTHER FOLLOWERS OF THE MECHANICAL SCHOOL. M. S. Mitchell's *Manual of Elocution* published first in 1867 and later in 1871 followed Rush, Murdoch, and Russell and added nothing new. Frank H. Fenno in 1878 compiled a book of recitations and readings which was called *The Science and Art of Elocution.* It contained about a hundred pages of the Rush system. S. S. Hamill denounced Delsarte and his gymnastics and adhered closely to Rush in *Easy Lessons in Vocal Culture* published in 1898. The outstanding book on gesture in the Austin tradition was Albert M. Bacon's *A Manual of Gesture* published first in 1872. It went into its eighth edition in 1893.

The most difficult task of all was attempted by Trueblood and Fulton, that of reconciling Delsarte and Rush. The attempt to classify the Rush elements according to the three natures of man was called the composite system.[22] (See page 161.)

Fulton and Trueblood were faithful followers of the Mechanical school as defined by Rush. They emphasized rules and believed in a thorough training in the use of the vocal mechanism as the best means of developing good speakers. The introduction of Delsarte's theory shows an attempt to make the system based on the study of the "elements" up-to-date but the result was a complicated scheme which must not have been very practical.

Several teachers used Mandeville's system of sentential delivery which based elocution upon the grammatical structure of the material read. Inflection and emphasis, in particular, were made dependent upon an understanding of the different forms of sentence structure. Brainard G. Smith wrote such a book, *Reading and Speaking,* 1891, for the students of Cornell. The demand for natural, unaffected speech shows itself in all these textbooks no matter how mechanical their basic theory may be. Smith states his aim as one of helping young men "to a natural, comfortable, manly, forceful manner of speech." He suggests that the student should read aloud to someone who would be responsible for telling him every time he departed from a natural conversational manner.[23]

[22] Fulton. Robert I. and Trueblood, Thomas C. *Practical Elements of Elocution.* p. 87.
[23] Smith, Brainard G. *Reading and Speaking.* p. v.

COMPOSITE SYSTEM

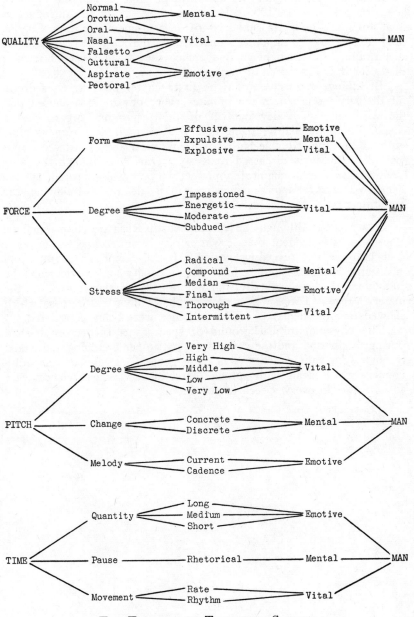

THE FULTON AND TRUEBLOOD SYSTEM

Erastus Palmer and Walter Sammis attempted to combine the mechanical and the natural approach in *The Principles of Oral English* published in 1906.   However, they say in the introduction that they are giving a standard of measurement for oral English and that since grammatical analysis is the only sure means of determining the thought in a sentence they have accepted it as a basis for their discussion of method.[24]

Breathing is considered in the first chapter and exercises given. If the student practices ten minutes every day he is promised that he will witness "a development of the respiratory organs and a facility in manipulating them that will be no less surprising than satisfactory and valuable both from a physical and an artistic stand-point." Quality is discussed in Rush's terms.[25]   Although the book shows that the mechanical approach is perhaps tempered by the increased attack upon artificiality, it is definitely following the tradition of the Mechanical school.

SUMMARY. Although the Walker-Austin-Rush tradition remained unbroken, it is evident that it was not as distinct or as strong as it had been in the preceding period. It still emphasized rules and notations but did not exclude the necessity of considering the individual reaction mentally and emotionally to the content of the material read. There was a new emphasis upon naturalness which showed that the demands of the audience were being considered.

The physiological background of speech was further established during this period and the emphasis upon proper breathing, cultivated through systematic practice, was quite general. Eventually, separate courses which dealt with speech correction and voice science were to be found in every speech department.

[24] Palmer, Erastus and Sammis, L. Walter. *The Principles of Oral English.* p. vi.
[25] *Ibid.* p. 5.

PSYCHOLOGICAL SANCTION FOR THE NATURAL SCHOOL

The impact of the new psychology which was destined to permeate every fibre of the twentieth century pedagogy, was beginning to be felt in most fields before the end of the nineteenth century. Titchener's belief in introspection as a technique for discovering the mind, Hall's theories of recapitulation as shown in the development of mental capacities, and James' laws of association and habit and his explanation of the "stream of consciousness" were rather widely discussed in academic circles. Some of these ideas were partially digested and applied to methods of teaching.

It is not surprising that the old idea of the teacher "drawing out" the natural capacities should come back with new vigor, claiming support from the psychologist. Rush and his mechanical system had relied upon physiology and physics to give credence and authority to a science of the voice. Under the influence of an interest in psychology, elocution seemed destined to become the "art of expression," the means of communicating the inner thoughts and feelings. The concept of *dualism,* or of the mind and body as two separate entities, was modified by the theory of *interactionism* or, as the Wundtians believed, a closely related *parallelism.* James and the pragmatists believed in a close relationship and defined the mind in terms of what it did, the theory of *functionalism.* Imprints of all of these different ideas are to be found in the methods which were used by those who did not emphasize the physiology of the voice, but rather the thought-processes behind speech. Occasionally the older philosophies of a transcendentalistic flavor were mingled with the newer philosophy of pragmatism, but they never really mixed. The result is confusing to the present-day reader; no doubt the techniques in teaching were not as contradictory as the expositions of the theories.

SAMUEL SILAS CURRY. Samuel Silas Curry was the outstanding example of the "think the thought" school. His interests were diverse and included the philosophy of transcendentalism, Delsarte's system, and psychology. As was quoted earlier, he believed that Bell exerted a great influence over him. These influences must have waged war at times and are responsible, no doubt, for much of the ambiguity in his books. However, his teaching methods must have been fairly clear and effective for he achieved considerable popularity as a teacher and textbook writer. According to Miller, of all the speech books on sale in 1928, *Foundations of Expression,* published in 1908, ranked second in sales.[1] The fact that the Curry books are mentioned in the surveys of speech training in teachers colleges [2] and of Texas colleges,[3] which will be mentioned in the next section, indicates a popularity even today.

Curry seemed to believe in a one-sided interactionism—the soul influencing the body. "We can see that all expression presupposes two things," he says, "first, a correct action of the faculties of the soul, and secondly, a normal action of the organic means which transmit the action of the soul." [4] In addition to a properly working mind he felt that there must be a plastic body and responsive voice. This coordination, Curry stated, could only be brought about by training.

Curry believed in a mysterious force within the soul, the "psychic nature." Sometimes he speaks of the *dramatic instinct* and its revelation through the body. One of his books was entitled *Imagination and Dramatic Instinct.* Although he discusses Delsarte in *The Province of Expression,* and credits his system with some truth, he discredits the idea of fitting everything into a trinity. He states that Delsarte's theories hamper the teacher in developing adequate methods, and labels his school as speculative.[5] Curry evidently used the two words *mind* and *soul* almost as synonyms: "When we come to study expression still more closely we find that man's entire organism is linguistic; that every part of the body is concerned in the manifestation of the conditions and actions of the mind; that the whole body breathes and thrills with the activity of the soul." [6]

Communicating one's thoughts and feelings implied for Curry only deepening of natural processes. Following James in his discussion of the stream of consciousness, Curry states the primary elements of thinking to be, first, concentration on one point; and second, a leap of the mind to another point. Thinking involved training in transitions and pausing. The pause must be a part of the mental action else it would be only a hesitation which is a grievous fault and reveals a chaotic state of thinking. He is sure that speakers rarely realized the value of pausing to stay the attention until the mind had

[1] Miller, M. Oclo. *The Psychology of Dr. S. S. Curry.* p. 1.
[2] "Speech Survey in Teacher-Training Institutions." *Quarterly Journal of Speech.* 16:56 (1930).
[3] Bryan, Earl C. "Speech Training in Texas Colleges." *Quarterly Journal of Speech.* 18:261-9 (1932).
[4] Curry, Samuel Silas. *The Province of Expression.* p. 251.
[5] *Ibid.* ch. 20.
[6] *Ibid.* p. 50.

received a definite impression. Directions for length of pausing are given in terms of thought values:

> The length of pause is due to the intensity of thinking or to the degree of clearness, vividness, and depth of the impression. In taking up a new subject, in weighing an idea before giving it, in the reception of all impressions, the length of pause will vary according to the degree of mental action, the extent of the change the mind is supposed to make, or the importance of the idea.[7]

According to his discussion, pauses determine phrasing—which gathers words together in a group and gives them the unity of a single word. This phrasing makes the same grouping of words as that found in conversation, but the process used is different. In reading, there is instant perception of the words, then concentration and conception; in conversation the idea comes first, and the mind chooses the words.[8]

Stress or accent is named *Touch*. It is also the result of the natural working of the mind:

> Each idea, each concentration of the mind receives a central touch as definite as the stroke of a hammer. As the stroke implies a lifting of the hammer so speech implies a pause for mental concentration, emotional realization, breathing, and the establishment of right conditions. But to the listener a pause is a mere blank unless intensified by a vigorous expression of the following phrase.[9]

Intensity exists in proportion to the depth and centrality of the command of force within.

The pitch varies, Curry states, according to the discrimination of the mind. The degree of variation between one idea and another will be expressed in a varying degree of pitch. There is some difference in the variations used in reading and talking which Curry explains thus:

> If we compare reading with talking, another difference noted is the constant variation of pitch in the talker while the reader calls successive words and phrases upon the same key. This is due to the fact that in talking we think an idea before we speak the words expressing it. In reading, however, we often get the idea after speaking the words.[10]

Although the emphasis throughout his books is upon the reaction of the mind upon the body, yet in vocal training, which is carefully distinguished from vocal expression as the "establishment of normal conditions of the body and voice," there are statements which imply a reaction of the body upon the mind. Like many earlier teachers, Curry placed emphasis upon proper breathing. He advocated the use of exclamations in practice to improve the voice because they were

[7] Curry. *Foundations of Expression.* p. 24.
[8] *Ibid.* p. 27.
[9] *Ibid.* p. 31.
[10] *Ibid.* p. 43.

closely associated with action and spontaneously established natural conditions of speaking and breathing. In the directions for the exercise he says:

Practise all kinds of exclamations and exclamatory phrases and passages with vivid individual ideas, not only pausing and concentrating the mind intensely, but feeling the co-ordination of the breath, and the opening of the tone passage, and the expansion of the body with the mental and emotional actions. Be sure that action of the mind, as far as possible, directly causes the sympathetic response of the body and the voice.[11]

But he says further that taking the breath properly and opening the tone passage are associated with the establishment of conditions that are fundamental to all right use of the voice. Faults of the voice are caused by the perversion or lack of the primary responses of breathing and of the tone passages to individual impressions.[12] And in *Mind and Voice,* Curry indicates that the emotions are best expressed or controlled by the breathing apparatus "is the diaphragm which is the central agent for the control of feeling."[13] This last statement also presupposes some reaction of the body upon the mind.

His attention to gesture and bodily action was very much influenced by the Delsartian gymnastic techniques in fashion. Miller, who was a student in the School of Expression, makes these statements concerning the physical exercises:

This activity of the body, the putting of "mind into muscles" as he termed it, was more characteristic of his teaching than it was of his theory. Rhythmical Balance, a course in dancing, in using the body rhythmically, in making it express with music, was always taught in the school. The student was made conscious of his body, its possibilities and sometimes its limitations. There seemed to be a general assumption, which was probably correct, that everyone's body was constricted and because of that fact exercises in relaxation were given from the start. The first exercises were what was sometimes called decomposing exercises, and consisted in relaxation of various parts of the body. Then after specific exercises, the organization of the body around a center, was begun.[14]

However, Curry did not put action first. He recognized the importance of the whole man expressing his thoughts and emotions and used the monologue as a good means of developing adequate expression because of its use of pantomime with voice. In *Browning and the Dramatic Monologue* he says, "Of all languages, action is the least noticeable,

[11] *Ibid.* p. 66.
[12] *Ibid.* p. 71.
[13] Curry, Samuel Silas. *Mind and Voice.* p. 88.
[14] Miller. *op. cit.* p. 41.

the most in the background, but, on the other hand, of all languages, it is the most continuous." [15]   Action was an integral part of speaking. Miller notes that in Curry's teaching great stress was placed upon physical transitions on the platform. She says that a great amount of time was spent in exercises for making the change in posture smooth and not distracting to the   attention. In the beginning of his plat- form work the student was urged to change position deliberately and to note the change made in his pitch and in his thought. This again implies some realization of the effect of bodily action upon mental processes. [16]

Tone-color was considered very important for literary interpreta- tion and "perhaps the most difficult element of vocal expression." It is defined in *Foundations of Expression* as the "modulation of the overtones of the human voice by imagination and feeling." [17]   To discover the presence of *tone-color*, Curry suggests that the student read over two very different passages—one didactic, and the other imaginative and sympathetic. He should note that the inflection, changes in pitch, pauses and touches are very similar and that the difference lies mainly in the quality of the voice. Many other methods are used to make the student conscious of the importance of quality and to help him to make his voice more responsive to the emotion expressed in the literature. [18]

In fact, Curry gave many excerpts from literature for the express purpose of encouraging the student to experiment and to discover his vocal reactions to different thoughts and emotions. In addition, he gave specific directions for the practice of exercises in reading which should be used for gaining flexibility in each one of the characteristics of speech.

From the first, Curry had objected to the mechanical schools. He disposes of the Rush school in the following manner:

The Rush system has come to be known as elocution and has made the name synonymous with the substitution of artificial tricks for nature. Such a system makes the whole art of expression a mere matter of mechanical stresses, waves, semitones and tremors, and a reading by this system is little more than an exhibition of mechanical actions miscalled "signs of emotion."

The greatest evil, however, of the whole system, is that it introduces mere rules, founded upon a mechanical mode of procedure. The whole action of the mind is focused upon the modes of execution by the voice, and not upon the successive ideas. There is thus a violation of the great law of nature which was formulated by Comenius, "from within, out." [19]

[15] Curry, Samuel Silas. *Browning and the Dramatic Monologue.* p. 176, 195.
[16] Miller. *op. cit.* p. 45.
[17] Curry, Samuel Silas. *Foundations of Expression.* p. 159.
[18] *Ibid.* ch. 12. "Tone-Color."
[19] Curry, Samuel Silas. *The Province of Expression.* p. 317.

The function of the teacher was magnified by Curry. He must be able to inspire the student and make him alive to cultural needs. He must be interested in the student as a person with definite problems and not as a mechanism to be trained. The teacher must be very well educated; the reasons Curry gives are as follows:

. . . a teacher of expression must be an educated man because he must be able to penetrate into the deepest needs of students. He must know something, therefore, of all departments of knowledge, especially in their relation to education, that is to say, he must understand the effect upon the personality of all subjects.

* * *

This breadth of culture, however, must be of a practical kind. It must be artistic and literary, as well as scientific. There must be insight and true love for all literature and art. It has been shown that delivery is essentially a department of art. Without such a love of art and literature he can never love this work, he can never inspire students, he can never awaken the creative faculties of their minds. . . . He must be enveloped by an artistic atmosphere; he needs not mere critical knowledge, but thoroughly trained artistic power for execution.[20]

Curry believed that his principles held for any kind of dramatic interpretation, even for the actor, because he must use his own imagination and feeling to be a real creative artist. He discusses the various forms of acting and speaking which were popular during this period. Charlotte Cushman is given as an example of an actress who read plays very effectively without the benefit of much action. She sat at a table and read from a book. He says: "Her intensity, her versatility and suggestiveness, the mobility of her face and the flexibility of her voice, enabled her to suggest the deepest subtleties of the highest literature with perfect ease and repose." Other readers of plays walked about and used pantomimic representation of acting. Professor Robert T. Raymond is given as a good example of this method of reading.[21]

The impersonator used properties and acted each character with fidelity to the stage. The exaggeration of "pantomimic bearings and vocal modulations" is explained as necessary to accent the opposition of characters to each other which had to be shown in moments and not in continuity as on the stage. The monologue resembled the impersonation except that only one character was impersonated and the others suggested indirectly. Both of these forms were memorized as were the recitations which Curry says were always called declamations in the colleges.[22]

[20] *Ibid.* p. 418-19.
[21] *Ibid.* p. 326.
[22] *Ibid.* p. 326-7.

The Curry School of Expression is still functioning. According to the last catalog, over ten thousand students have studied in the school and some well known teachers of speech are among them: Smiley Blanton, Sara Stinchfield Hawk, Lee Emerson Bassett, Azubah Latham, Gertrude Johnson. The purpose of this school remains much the same as that articulated by the founder.

> The Curry Method of training, which so successfully coordinated mind, body, and voice, is employed with the thoroughness and accuracy intended by its Founders. Now, as throughout its sixty years of training, Curry measures its educational value by its ability to take people where it finds them, and lead them into a realization of their individual powers.[23]

Curry's theories may seem confused at times, but they were clearly based upon the major premise that in order to express an idea the mind must actively hold the idea and dictate the means of expression. His methods indicated an appreciation for a training that would give flexibility in the use of the body and especially the voice, but the main interest was always in "thinking the thought."

Unity, to Curry, was not only the highest quality of art and the climax of artistic endeavor but it was also the test of the methods used.

> Where the method aims to regulate the modulations of the voice by rules, then inconsistencies and lack of organic coherence begin to take the place of that sense of life which lies at the heart of every true product of art. But where vocal expression is studied as a manifestation of the processes of thinking; where the teacher is able to see and to show the student, not only the chief fault in the action of the body and voice, but its ultimate cause in the action of the mind; and where he is able to awaken genuine thinking and assimilation, to inspire imaginative action and dramatic instinct,—then one of the first results to follow is the truer energy of the student's faculties and powers, and the higher and more natural unity of the complex elements of his expression.[24]

CHARLES WESLEY EMERSON. Charles Wesley Emerson, of the Emerson College of Oratory, worked out all of his methods on the principle of evolution. He held a kind of recapitulatory theory which stated that any art must be taught according to the natural development of the human mind. There are four stages of development according to Emerson: the Colossal, the Attractive or Melodramatic, the Realistic, and the Suggestive. The application of this theory to the development of a good delivery is explained below:

> For correct guidance in our search for the best methods, we must understand the order of the development of the human mind. A child before he arrives at an age where he can be taught definitely is simply a little palpitating mass of animation. Soon he begins to show an attraction toward surrounding

[23] Curry College. *Catalogue*, 1939-40. p. 10-11.
[24] Curry, Samuel Silas. *Imagination and the Dramatic Instinct*. p. 360.

objects. Next he begins to show a greater attraction for some things than for others. His hands clutch at and retain certain objects. He now enters the period of development where he makes selections, and thus is born the power of choice. Objects which, at first, appeared to him as a mass now begin to stand out clearly one from another, to become more and more differentiated, while the child begins to separate and to compare. Thus the brain of the child passes through the successive stages from simple animation to attraction, to selection or choice, to separation or analysis. This principle of evolution, operating along the same lines, is found in the race as in the individual. In all man's work he has but recorded his own life or evolution. All history, all religions, all governments, all forms of art bring their testimony to this truth, and in each the scholar may find these successive stages of development.[25]

According to this theory of learning, the teacher becomes a sort of husbandman for the growing process and must not "paralyze the unfolding mind by ill-advised dictation." The first stage is to teach the student to respond to his own thought with animation. "The Pied Piper" and "Lochinvar" are given as good selections for practice in this state. In the second stage the student must develop a smoothness of voice. The "Twenty-Third Psalm" is suggested for practice. Next, he concentrates upon the volume of the voice and suggests practice in reading "Spartacus to the Gladiators" and Byron's "The Ocean." In the last stage he considers the audience and he is prompted to study the elements, the musical slides and all the details of articulation and inflection which make the thoughts and sentiments intelligible and important to the hearer. In this stage, Hamlet's "Advice to the Players" is an appropriate selection for practice. The method consists mainly in selecting suitable materials for the different stages of development.[26]

In *Psycho Vox,* most unusual and scarcely scientific methods are explained for improving the quality or for giving the voice proper resonance:

Beauty of the voice is largely due to the fact that the vocal aperture is in the form of a curve. Unpleasant qualities in the voice are caused by the vocal column being made to move in angles instead of curves. The curve should become a fixed mental object during all vocal practice, whether in speaking or singing. Holding this object in mind must become a habit so firmly established that the mind will ultimately act above consciousness in forming it. The vocal organs react upon ideals held in mind. Thus, if a flat object is held in mind while using the voice, the tone tends to flatness, if a round one it tends to roundness. . . .

The tone must be idealized with reference to place and form. The student should imagine the tone outside that resonant chamber of the nares most distant from the vocal cords. This will bring the consciousness outside that part of the nose which is between the eyes. The anterior portion of the nares is, so far as place and consequent resonance are concerned, the dominant center of the voice. My reason for calling this the dominant center of the voice is that

[25] Emerson, Charles Wesley. *Evolution of Expression.* vol. 1. p. 8.
[26] *Ibid.* ch. 1, 2, 3, 4.

when the tone is perfectly directed toward this chamber, all the resonant passages open freely through the entire nares, mouth and pharynx to the vocal cords and also the tongue has a tendency to relax its rigidity. It is important, however, that the mind should not think of this locality as being in the nares, but outside, and think of it, too, as an ever expanding and luminous globe which moves forward and downward.[27]

Emerson believed in the therapeutic value of voice training and in gymnastics as a part of the course of training. The course entitled *Psychology and Philosophy* which was given in Emerson College in 1896 was based upon the system of Delsarte. Gesture drill was used rather than the usual form of gymnastics. According to the catalog, the college taught oratory as an art, "resting upon absolute laws of nature, explained and illustrated by exact rules of science." Its physical culture, it says, rarely failed to restore to health the weak and devitalized. The term *physical culture* is explained as "the development of the entire physical person, through cultivating it to express the purposes and emotions of the soul." [28]

His system is unique in that it is more interested in adapting to evolutionary principles than to psychological ones. His methods are unscientific and his theories very speculative, but his following was large. According to Fiske, his greatest contribution was made as a teacher who exemplified the finest personal qualities. His pedagogy was, according to her, one of character and employed literary interpretations which emphasized the artistic and idealistic values to the exclusion of other approaches. This was the era of highly revered teachers.[29]

WILLIAM B. CHAMBERLAIN and SOLOMON H. CLARK.   William B. Chamberlain of the Chicago Theological Seminary and Solomon H. Clark of the University of Chicago published *Principles of Vocal Expression* in 1897. Chamberlain was particularly interested in rhetoric as vocal expression while Clark was interested in the mental techniques of literary interpretation. The book follows rather closely the Curry principles and mention is made of his influence by Chamberlain. Their position is clearly one of two-sided interactionism and a two-fold training is set forth as necessary in the study of oral expression. It must contain, ". . . the measurement of thought as a process of communication, or the analysis of the expressional elements of thought; and the mastery of the physical means of expression. Both of these— the mental and the physical training—together constitute the technique

[27] Emerson, Charles Wesley. *Psycho Vox.* p. 73-4.
[28] Emerson College. *Catalogue,* 1896-97. p. 23.
[29] Fiske. Bertha V. "A Pioneer in Speech Training." *Emerson Quarterly.* 15, no. 1:7-8 (1934).

of expression." [30]   The interaction of mind and body is explained thus: "Mind and body so react upon each other, that we may not say, This part is only physical; that, simply mental." [31]

Expressional paraphrasing is the name applied to the method which Chamberlain offers for discovering the correct interpretation. This method is justified because interpretation implies translation: "All attempts at interpretation rest upon the essential principle of translating or carrying over into one's own realm of experience, observation, and communication, things that are found in some less familiar realm." [32]

Paraphrasing which is used as a preparation for expression may be objective, giving fuller content; or subjective, manifesting the intent. It may be expansive and the thought amplified, or it may be condensative and the thought abridged; or it may be prosaic and assist in sharpening intellectual processes which are dulled by conventional reading or obscured by the diction in poetry.   The purpose of the method is simply to "bring consciousness to those thought processes which must be present in vivid, fresh, suggestive, vocal interpretation."

There is quite a bit of discussion in *Principles of Vocal Expression* of the instinct of expression.   The term is used loosely as it was by Curry.   However, Chamberlain makes clear that instincts are regulated by reason.   The purpose of education in expression, he maintains, is to subordinate automatic action to genuine purpose and intention.   He quotes James as saying that there is no antagonism between reason and instinct, and that man does not work *automatically* as the animal does. [33]

Pure tone is called the vocal exponent of normal feeling.   It is explained as the simplest musical vibration which results from the normal action of the vocal organs.   When it is expanded, it becomes the orotund tone which is deeper and fuller and uses lower chest vibrations.   The muscular and nervous conditions of the body must agree on the quality of the tone and induce it.   The other vocal qualities described by Rush are mentioned and described in terms of the mental conditions producing them.   For example, the pectoral quality is characterized by deep vibrations held within the chest and gives an oppressed or shuddering quality typical of the emotion portrayed. Chamberlain believed in training the instrument so that it worked

[30] Chamberlain, William B. and Clark, Solomon H. *Principles of Vocal Expression.* p. 6.
[31] *Ibid.* loc. cit.
[32] *Ibid.* p. 9.
[33] *Ibid.* p. 22.

with ease and precision. He agreed with Curry in prescribing exercises for breathing, open throat, and articulation.[34]

Clark adds little that is new but presents his ideas and methods clearly. He states plainly that he believes the conversational manner to be the basis of all good reading and gives exercises which are made up of literature in colloquial diction as a starting place for the student. He recognizes the necessity for some association or identification of ideas.[35] His discussion of formulation, or the grouping of ideas, and of discrimination, or the locating of central and subordinate ideas, is very similar to that found in the textbooks written by Curry. He does not acknowledge Curry, but Raymond instead, and quotes freely from his *Orator's Manual.*[36]

Clark agrees with Chamberlain and Curry that the student must rely upon natural instincts and impulses which are demonstrated through the range, power, flexibility, and quality of the voice, and that they must be developed and controlled. He discusses energy of abruptness under studies in volition according to the principles of Rush, but insists that it is normal action. His description of it makes it seem less mechanical than the *abruptness* which was described as a mode in *The Philosophy of the Human Voice.*

It is the result of normal action of the vocal chords, which, coming together previous to syllabic impulses, suddenly part, causing a slight degree of explosion. Hence the term abruptness. Absence of this form of energy gives the delivery a kind of drawling effect. It is further to be noted that even in those utterances characterized by other forms of energy, this form yet manifests itself on most of the syllables. . . . He (student) will have noticed that the other forms are significant just in so far as they differ from this "abrupt" one, which is normal; and, further, that because the energy of abruptness *is* the normal, the expression of other forms of energy on a comparatively few (emphatic) syllables will give a very significant coloring to a whole paragraph.[37]

The student is advised to practice the exercises in colloquial form and the paradox of training that which is normal is explained in terms of individual differences :

It has been urged, that if the claim is true that the complete assimilation of the thought and feeling will, through practice, lead to adequate expression, why bother the student with such drills as these? The answer is plain. One's temperament may be of such a nature that he cannot express a single sentence without, say, the greatest insistency. The insistency I say, is temperamental, and it shows in everything the speaker does. By a careful study of "Volition," he is introduced to his own consciousness, soon recognizes his weakness, and his delivery is improved through his mental action. If this is true for the

[34] *Ibid.* p. 206.
[35] *Ibid.* p. 272.
[36] Raymond, George L. *The Orator's Manual.*
[37] Chamberlain and Clark. *op. cit.* p. 296.

creative speaker, the orator, how much more is it true of him who reads or recites the words of another.[38]

Clark considers *recitation* an art, a re-creative form, which may be classified with musical renditions. Artistic reading implies high intellectual and imaginative qualities in addition to technical ability. " . . . if he have not the genius to *select the significant details, and the ability to arrange them,* no matter what his technical ability, he falls short of being an artist." [39]

The discussion of literary forms and their demand upon the reader is most complete and interesting from the teacher's point of view. Clark goes far beyond the grammatical analysis with which many of the earlier books were filled. He does not discuss the emotions in an isolated literary or pantomimic form, but is concerned with literature as an experience. He speaks of atmosphere, climax, and tone-color, and states his theory of interpretation as related to the content thus:

> Literature contains two elements, the intellectual and the emotional. The intellectual part is that which deals with facts, for in the most ethereal poetry there must be a substantial basis. The intellectual side of literature deals with particulars, details. The contemplation of facts stimulates, under certain conditions, the poet's imagination: and that in turn stimulates his emotions. Now, the stirring of the poet's imagination is manifested in the language, style, and form in which his thought is clothed. Hence, it is our purpose to analyze literature in order that we may show that particular sounds or elements are uniformly used to express particular emotions. . . . Poetry is written to be read aloud. The poet listens to his verse as it rises in his brain, and his poetic insight and artistic training teach him that certain sounds are better avenues of expression for given emotions than others. One might say that tone-color is the avenue along which the emotion passes in its progress from within outward, or from the poet to his hearer. The mere fact is expressed by the words; the emotion is expressed by the various qualities of the voice, and these qualities of the voice may be more surely and easily manifested on certain elements than on others.[40]

This emphasis upon the literature itself is even more evident in his book, *Interpretation of the Printed Page,* published in 1915. In it, Clark takes the position that the appreciation of literature is the most important part of the process and even goes so far as to say that interpretation which is silent is of greater importance than that which is oral.[41] This seems to be an indication of a shift in emphasis from the technique of delivery to the subject matter itself.

This position indicates that *Elocution* has become *Interpretation;* the technique of delivery although important and capable of training

[38] *Ibid.* p. 297-8.
[39] *Ibid.* p. 321.
[40] *Ibid.* p. 386
[41] Clark, Solomon H. *Interpretation of the Printed Page.* p. 14.

is less important than the mental process which gives to the reader an impression of the literature which he reads. The book follows this theory concerning interpretation closely and devotes itself to methods for getting the thought and emotion. Exercises in grouping are considered the most important; the sequence of thought and the subordination and coordination of ideas are clearly explained and well illustrated in excerpts from literature. There is some explanation of the variety in the response of the voice to complete and incomplete thoughts as they appear in sequence. The analysis of *group motive* leads into a discussion of speech tunes. "As the motive changes your melody changes," he explains. These changes are made either by jumps or slides, and are distinguished from musical variations in that they are instinctive while song melodies are invented.[42]

Clark appreciated punctuation as one guide to the sense of the author and analyzed the uses of the different forms. Many exercises to give the student practice in such analysis are found in *Interpretation of the Printed Page*. He also includes practice in reading for the denotation of words and phrases. In his treatment of connotation, his real theory concerning the interpretation of literature is epitomized. It is a further elaboration of the ideas expressed in the earlier book in which the logical and emotional content of literature were differentiated.

It may be asked, then, why the reader needs to have his attention called to Connotation, since its appeal to the imagination is instantaneous, and doesn't have to be worked out like a problem in geometry. True, it doesn't: but I wanted to impress upon you that authors use words deliberately to touch the imagination; and, furthermore, I would convince you that while you can dig out the facts in books of information, the appeal that literature makes comes only to those who gaze and gaze. To catch the glory of one great line of poetry is forever to be poetic. It is experience we seek in literature, not knowledge; it is the joy, the ecstasy, the delight of sharing with an artist his vision of what most mortals would not see without him. You can't be examined on what is best in literature, on the soul of things; you can only like or dislike; appreciate or ignore.[43]

The Interpretation of the Printed Page shows the greatest divergence from the Mechanical school. Clark is completely converted to the "think the thought" school. In the last chapter he gives specific rules to teachers, which indicates that he believes in strenuous practice in reading aloud: "Drill, constant drill on interesting material, is indispensable for the formation of the habits necessary to proper interpretation and vocal expression." However, there is

[42] *Ibid.* p. 149.
[43] *Ibid.* p. 251.

no discussion of the different modes of the voice or any analysis of the vocal mechanism and how it works in expression of thoughts. Appreciation and understanding will lead to natural expression, he feels, and this will be the student's own interpretation. *"It is not of so much moment that the student's interpretation agree with mine or with the teacher's, as that he have an interpretation which he can defend."* [44]

HIRAM CORSON. Hiram Corson, professor of English in Cornell University, realized the importance of vocal expression in the appreciation of literature. His emphasis was different from that of Clark, in that he stressed the necessity of feeling above the intellectual understanding. He believed that at times feeling preceded rather than followed thought in the process of appreciation. *Spiritual education* is the term that he uses throughout his book for the ultimate purpose of reading. "By the spiritual I mean man's essential, absolute being; and I include in the term the emotional, the susceptible or impressible, the sympathetic, the instinctive, the intuitive,—in short—the whole domain of the non-intellectual, the non-discursive." [45]

Whately's position of favoring only that which is natural, he decried because he thought that natural reading was often imperfect and the conversational voice was inadequate for higher types of poetry or impassioned prose. Since the language must be idealized the voice should be also.[46] However, he did not believe in allowing the technique to intrude so he gives very little space to it in his book. *The Voice and Spiritual Education* did not purport to be an elocutionary manual but rather an analysis of the relationship of vocal interpretation to the enjoyment of literature. He says, "Reading must supply all the deficiencies of written or printed language. It must give life to the letter. . . . A poem is not truly a poem until it is voiced by an accomplished reader who has adequately assimilated it—in whom it has, to some extent, been born again, according to his individual spiritual constitution and experiences." [47]

If forced to choose between a reader who is technically trained but who has no inner preparation and one who has sympathetically assimilated that which he has read but has had no elocutionary training, Corson would choose the latter.

The exhibitory aspect of much of the reading of those trained in elocutionary schools, Corson condemned. Reading should not be act-

[44] *Ibid.* p. 309.
[45] Corson, Hiram. *The Voice and Spiritual Education.* p. 6.
[46] *Ibid.* p. 13-14.
[47] *Ibid.* p. 29-30.

ing; if people want to see acting, they go to the theater. He explains his position as follows:

When they listen to reading, they want serious interpretative vocalization; only that and nothing more is necessary, unless it be a spontaneous and graceful movement of the hands, occasionally, such as one makes in animated conversation.

Again, the most elegant way of vocally interpreting a poem, is to read it from a book, rather than to recite it. Recitation has much to do with this acting business. In fact, elocutionists recite in order to have their arms free to act— to illustrate the thought they are expressing. Thought should not be helped out by gesture. Gesture results, or should result, from emotion, and should, therefore be indefinite.

* * *

The trouble with many public readers is, that they don't truly know, have not inwardly experienced, what they attempt to interpret vocally; and, as a consequence, they resort to what disgusts people of real culture.[48]

In order to approach the real inner meaning of literature, Corson states that a student must have perspective which will enable him to synthesize and to group the thoughts properly. There is no better test of a student's knowledge of the organic structure of language and the extent to which thought is spiritualized than reading.[49] Not only did Corson think that reading was the test for the student, but also for the teacher, and said that the highest form of the literary lecture was interpretative reading.[50] He evidently was a fine reader himself and used that technique in teaching literature. Bassett mentions him as one of the finest readers he has ever heard.[51]

Corson believed in practice to improve the articulation and the flexibility of the voice but that these exercises should never be divorced from the fundamental aim of reading. He makes his position clear in this excerpt from his book:

Vocal exercise must not only be physiologically intelligent, but there must always be some conception back of it which it is the aim of the exercise to realize in the voice. One may have a conception, more or less distinct, of how some very significant sentence in Shakespeare, for example, should be uttered, and yet his voice is not sufficiently obedient to his will and his feelings. He therefore has something to work after, and in time may vocally realize, to his full satisfaction, his conception; and in doing so, he has acquired some new and valuable control of his voice which he can make use of, whenever required, in the rendering of other expressions.[52]

The whole book voices a protest against education that is too mechanized—which is interested in form but not in the spirit. He

[48] Ibid. p. 126-30.
[49] Ibid. p. 28, 29.
[50] Ibid. p. 37.
[51] Bassett, Lee Emerson. "Adapting Courses in Interpretation to the Academic Mind." Quarterly Journal of Speech. 18:186 (1932).
[52] Corson. op. cit. p. 62-3.

quotes Wordsworth, Coleridge and Browning and with them looks toward a better day when spiritual education will rank with intellectual training and discipline. Corson believed that education concerned itself almost exclusively with scientific ideas, and that a future education which will be more complete must consider the lack of spiritual values a great defect.

Corson was undoubtedly an inspirational teacher. He does not mention imitation, but the reader is confident that even though he read poetry to his students, he would never expect them to copy his interpretation. He idealized literature and the expression of it. His whole theory of education is permeated with a mystic's faith in "things unseen." His technique was neither mechanical nor imitative, but rather one which inspired the student to possess a full appreciation of good literature and a desire to read it aloud because of the resultant deepening of the experience.

ARTHUR E. PHILLIPS. Arthur E. Phillips, principal of the Phillips School of Oratory in Chicago, used what he called *natural* or *tone* drills to train students for the art of interpretation. His methods are similar to those used by Chamberlain and are based upon the value of paraphrasing for a clearer understanding of what is read. In his book, *Natural Drills in Expression* (1909) fifty-eight pages are devoted to Tone Drills which give in colloquial and classical form examples of different kinds of emotional expression. These are to be practiced with special attention paid to the tone used. After these drills are mastered, the student may read a new poem or bit of prose and as he reads jot down the states or tones required by the poem. He then tries to use the inflection and melody that he learned to use in the corresponding tone drill. In addition, he makes the associational ties with his own experiences which will make the literature come alive.

Some of his recommendations for the use of these drills show the results that were expected:

The Tone Drills help to *rid the pupil of artificiality and secure naturalness.* They do so by coming vividly into the pupil's experience and by showing him that the classical in literature has its similarities and equivalents in his own sensations, and vice versa. He sees that the colloquial "what a magnificent sunset!" and the classical "what a piece of work is man!" have an underlying relationship of feeling.

The Tone Drills *develop spontaneity. . . .*

The Tone Drills *reveal the expressional faults of the pupil. . . .*

The Tone Drills help to secure *the true expression of feeling* in both speech and literature. . . .

The Tone Drills help to *train the imagination. . . .*

The Tone Drills *rid the pupil of self consciousness. . . .*

The Tone Drills *develop a love for the best literature* and develop it in a *natural way.* . . .

The Tone Drills achieve the *coördination of the entire expressional organism.*[53]

The teacher is to be greatly benefited by this technique for teaching. For example, the drills economize time. Phillips suggests using chorus drills as well as individual drills in class as a short-cut. The method is up-to-date and based on the new psychology. He mentions the fact that the use of the laws of association is according to the principles set forth by Herbert Spencer and Henry James.[54] He seems overly enthusiastic over one rather specialized method, but undoubtedly felt that he had found something new which would be an effective and time-saving technique for teaching students to interpret literature. His basic idea is similar to that of Sheridan, the early leader of the Natural school, who based his technique of reading on conversational speech.

EDWARD N. KIRBY and EDWIN D. SHURTER. Edward N. Kirby's *Public Speaking and Reading* (1896) is an example of a textbook which proposes an eclectic method. Not only does *Kirby* discuss a style for reading poetry, but a style which is usable in rhetorical speaking. They are akin, he says, in that they demand a certain creative ability and are both based upon conversational speech. In fact, delivery is treated as the general subject and the examples and exercises are drawn from both fields.

The main problem before the student is to secure right mental action. When this is accomplished the body responds. This is not a unique idea, but the insistence that the mind and body work in double inter-actionism is perhaps more clearly explained than in most of the books which were contemporary:

For the solution of this Main Problem, both the *subjective* and the *objective* treatment are employed. The subjective treatment deals directly with the content of the mind; that is, with the thought and feeling.

The thought and feeling are analyzed and dwelt upon. Related ideas are brought forward; and thus, by dealing with the factors of the mind directly, we seek to promote right mental action with reference to the subject-matter and its expression.

* * *

In the objective treatment, however, we call attention to the agents (the chest, the mouth, the hands, etc.), and to the elements (emphasis, pitch, etc.), expressive of the thought and feeling.

The objective treatment is based upon the fact that bodily states affect mental states; hence, by assuming the physical attitude, the corresponding mental state is initiated and promoted. We not only entreat the angry man not to be angry, but also coax him to sit down and not speak so loudly. . . . This

[53] Phillips, Arthur Edward. *Natural Drills in Expression with Selections.* p. 3-7.
[54] *Ibid.* p. 5.

treatment, reaching the mind by calling attention to the physical states, is the shorthand method of every-day life. Just as the child is told to "quit whining" and "to straighten out" his face, so also in elocutionary training, we say "Speak louder," "Pause more frequently," "Speak on a lower pitch." [55]

The characteristics of delivery that are most to be desired are, according to Kirby: clearness, force, and elegance. The following *scheme* is proposed as a guide for the student:

THE SCHEME [56]

A. SOURCES OF CLEARNESS, FORCE, AND ELEGANCE.

    I. *Physical Vitality and Earnestness.*

    II. *Control and Reserved Force.*

    III. *The Audience* (Attention of—Communication), and *Goodwill* (Sympathy).

    IV. *Mental Content,*—Thought and Feeling (Attention).

    V. *Variety in Unity,*—Differentiation.

B. ELEMENTS OF CLEARNESS, FORCE, AND ELEGANCE.

    I. *Of Clearness.*
      1. Enunciation (Syllables, Vowels, Consonants).
      2. Emphasis.
      3. Phrasing or Grouping.
      4. Transition.

    II. *Of Force.*
      1. Strong, Pure, Flexible Tones.
      2. Appropriate Voice.
      3. Inflection (Slides).
      4. Melody of Speech.
      5. Rhythm.
      6. Loudness.
      7. Stress.
      8. Rate.
      9. Climax.
      10. Imitative Modulation.
      11. Gesture.

    III. *Of Elegance.*
      1. Harmony of Parts.
      2. Pronunciation.

In the discussion of control and reserved force, the following indications of their presence are listed:

In the physical bearing. It is strong, and every movement has a purpose and is without excess. It is closely identified with physical control; the co-ordinations are accurate and timely. . . .

In the use of the voice. The breath is all converted into tone. The chest is active, the lungs are well filled. Breathing is never labored nor obtrusive. There is an absence of noisiness.

[55] Kirby, Edward N. *Public Speaking and Reading.* p. 18-19.
[56] *Ibid.* p. 31.

In suppressed emotion. In reserved force, there is the impression given of strong and vital thought, and feeling. The speaker seems to express less emotion than he feels.

In a masterful hold upon the audience. The speaker seems to hold the audience by direct effort of will. This hold upon the audience seems to reflect its power upon the speaker, and he in turn is restrained or held by the audience. . . .

In specialized effort. This gives the impression of ease and grace.[57]

A whole chapter is given over to the discussion of the relation of the speaker to the audience. The communicative attitude, which precludes *speaking before* an audience but rather for it, and the deferential attitude, which implies a direct and simple manner, are considered requisites. The speaker must objectify the thoughts he is speaking and hold the attention of the audience, not only because of the demands of the audience, but because of the stimulating effect of an attentive audience upon him.[58]

In his discussion of the elements of clearness, force, and elegance, Kirby takes his information and his suggestions for practice from many writers. He uses much of the Rush terminology. He uses the three-fold division for the voice, modifying the Delsarte terms somewhat and calling them: *intellective, vital,* and *affectional.* The laws of gesture he attributes to the Delsarte system and gives a series of relaxing exercises and also Swedish gymnastics recommended by Sargent. The list of vowels and consonants is the list made by Alexander Melville Bell.[59] Probably Kirby's contribution lies in the broadening of the scope of *elocution* or rather *delivery* so that it is applicable to all forms of public speech. He seems to have exerted an influence of considerable scope. Winans mentions him in the preface to his *Public Speaking* as being the chief source for his treatment of delivery.[60]

Shurter follows Kirby in the belief that delivery is an important part of rhetoric. He advocates as one of the best ways to train inexperienced speakers in the art of conversational delivery the memorization of "choice selections from the best literature." The exercise furnishes the speaker with illustrations and aids his memory as well as his practice in delivery.[61]

Robert McLean Cumnock. Another teacher who used an eclectic method was Robert McLean Cumnock who founded the School of Speech at Northwestern University in 1878 and remained

---

[57] *Ibid.* p. 64.
[58] Cf. ch. 7.
[59] *Ibid.* p. 78, 100, 119.
[60] Winans, James A. *Public Speaking.* p. xiv.
[61] Shurter, Edwin DuBois. *Public Speaking.* p. 9.

its head until 1913. According to Ralph Dennis, present dean of the school, he did not believe in many rules. He says of Cumnock:

> Many times I have seen him draw a line on the blackboard, said line three feet long, said line representing the entire field of oral reading, of interpretation. He would then say, "Many people make rules which cover this line from the left to the right, through its entire distance. I tell you that you can have rules which will carry you out about three inches and the rest of the distance is up to you and your individuality and your ability."

* * *

> We are still an eclectic school. We follow no set pattern. We endeavor to develop the abilities of the student in the way and manner best suited to the student's gifts. Certain basic processes of development are fundamentally the same for all students. But we have no hard-and-fast rules by which to measure the work finally done by these students. We judge things by results. If the work pleases discriminating people, then it is good work.[62]

Unfortunately, Cumnock did not write a textbook, but his *Choice Readings* was a very popular anthology. It was published first in 1882, again in 1905, and in 1938 a "new and definitive" edition was published.[63]

[62] Dennis, Ralph. Personal letter, April 10, 1940.
[63] Cumnock, Robert McLean. *Choice Readings for Public and Private Entertainment Arranged for the Exercises of the School, College and Public Reader wi'h Elocutionary Advice.*

SUMMARY

At the beginning of the period when the American plutocracy and all of its excesses were in evidence, there was a great demand for adult education and entertainment through lyceums and Chautauquas. Since there was a puritanical objection in many groups against the theatre, and the moving pictures had not yet appeared, platform readings of plays and other literary programs were much in demand. It was during this time that the fad of Delsartism flourished and that many professional schools of elocution were founded. The elocution like the architecture was often in bad taste. Occasionally, it was mere exhibitionism.

Because of the bad reputation which it had made for itself in many quarters and because of the reaction against the old classical curriculum, rhetoric and the related forms of public speaking were no longer required and sometimes were dropped completely from the curriculum in the institutions of higher learning. If rhetoric remained, it usually emphasized written rather than oral communication of ideas. Professional schools of elocution filled the gap, training professional readers and teachers. Often the only training in elocution in the colleges and universities was carried on by itinerant teachers. Many of these teachers established departments of speech when the subject was reinstated in the curriculum toward the end of the period. In 1914, the National Association of Academic Teachers of Public Speaking was formed. This organization indicated perhaps better than anything else the reinstatement of speech education in the program of higher education. In the middle of the period, speech work had been combined with English in many schools. A separation was effected as speech became more important and diversified. With the addition of more courses to meet the varied needs of an increasingly heterogeneous student population, interpretation of literature became more specialized. To teach appreciation of literature became the primary aim of many of the teachers of this subject, and the entertainment value, although present, was minimized.

The most significant tendency during this period from 1870-1915 was to base methods of teaching upon new psychological theories. The teaching of interpretation was noticeably affected by this new trend. "An art must rest upon a science" had been preached by teachers from the beginning, but psychology had never before assumed the rank of a science. The so-called Natural school received the most help from the new psychological emphasis. To start with the individual and his natural reactions to literature had always been their basic principle. Psychology made clearer the nature of mental processes. The method of "thinking the thought" before attempting to read anything became the most popular method and the one that carried over into the next period.

The sciences which had supported the Rush school succeeded in evolving a *voice science* which was eventually to develop into a separate field from that of interpretation. In fact, one of the most surprising developments was to be the addition of many new courses to the department of speech, once the department was firmly established. The period was interesting and eventful in the study of the evolution of methods used in teaching the interpretation of literature. It demonstrated probably better than any other period the remarkable vitality of the subject itself. If it had not contained essential values which are important to students in colleges and universities, it could not have survived from 1870 to 1915.

PART IV

THE SPEECH PROGRAM IS ENLARGED:
1915–1940

CHAPTER I

SPEECH EDUCATION BECOMES MORE EXTENSIVE

This period has been called the Period of Disillusionment or the Realistic Period. Wars and depressions and a gradual realization of the complexity of twentieth century life succeeded in destroying most of the Utopian dreams of the previous century. Since it was evident that everyone could not be rich and happy by merely working and planning to that end, it became necessary to pare down to fundamentals, to take inventory of the human and economic resources, to recognize the problems that plagued the nation as a whole. The long adolescence was over and the time for sober and thoughtful living had come.

There was much unrest throughout this period but also much creative activity. The United States had been shocked into maturity by World War I and would not again be astonished when World War II threatened in 1939. The Roaring Twenties gave place quickly to the Depression Years. There had been a thorough unsettling, psychologically as well as economically; new political ideologies were popularized and democratic ideals were questioned. H. L. Mencken prodded men into thinking, if only to oppose his views. Irving Babbitt in *The Critic and American Life* explains the Mencken influence during the twenties:

It is of the utmost importance however, if one is to understand Mr. Mencken, to discriminate between two types of temperamentalist—the soft and sentimental type, who cherishes various "ideals" and the hard, or Nietzschean type, who piques himself on being realistic. As a matter of fact, if one sees in the escape from traditional controls merely an opportunity to live temperamentally, it would seem advantageous to pass promptly from the idealistic to the Nietzschean phase, sparing onself as many as possible of the intermediary disillusions. It is at all events undeniable that the rise of Menckenism had been marked by a certain collapse of romantic idealism in the political field and elsewhere. The numerous disillusions that have supervened upon the War have provided a favoring atmosphere.[1]

Although there was understandable pessimism in the writing of the period (for example, T. S. Eliot assumed his important place in poetry with *The Waste Land,* 1922), there was also a new kind of affirmation growing from an almost satiric attitude toward life. Changes could be made to improve man's lot if he were forced to see realistically the source of the trouble.

World War I brought a great emancipation from old restrictions and any traditional puritanism which had lingered. In the literary world, great freedom was given to writers and no subject seemed to be taboo. However, the catharsis did not cure all the problems. Although many realistic and pessimistic writers clarified the social ills, there were few who proposed solutions. It would seem, though, that the dissidence which was so characteristic of the letters of the period was indicative of intellectual energy rather than of decay. The size and diversity of the literary output showed a culture which might be a bit crude at times but was surely vigorous and unmistakably native-born. There were then encouraging developments both in letters and in education. The old formulas had not worked too successfully and it was time for a change; many optimistic and imaginative people worked hard to effect that change.

Granville Hicks maintained that the American tradition must be a revolutionary one. He cited Willa Cather and Robert Frost as examples of writers who, because they did not recognize the problems of industrialism, found the creation of vital literature difficult. He chose Dos Passos as the best example of the new tradition, said to deal with "representative American men and women in representative situations."[2] There were also those critics who looked for the old traditional values. Norman Foerster represented this humanistic tradition, and contrary to Hicks, he found literary values in the works of Frost and Cather. Thus the two opposing points of view of literary critics were quite clearly defined, and literature affected accordingly.

HUMANISTS VERSUS PROGRESSIVES. In the colleges and universities, there were similar disagreements concerning education. Foerster and Babbitt, in accordance with their humanistic philosophy, favored a liberal arts education through a cultural curriculum for the selected few. Administrators such as President Hutchins of The University of Chicago agreed with this concept. On the other hand, the progressives saw education as a means of raising the cultural level of all the people rather

---

[1] *Literary Opinion in America,* ed. by Morton Dauwen Zabel. vol. 1, p. 135.
[2] Hicks, Granville. *The Great Tradition.* p. 303. See also "Liberalism in the Fifties." *American Scholar.* 25:283–296 (1956).

than merely training the leaders. The curriculum, they thought, should be extended to include any subject that would be useful in solving the practical and social problems of a democracy; this plan admitted many vocational subjects along with the so-called cultural ones. John Dewey was the recognized leader of the progressive group.

Although the elective system was still functioning, there had been a small regression since President Eliot of Harvard had succeeded in abolishing all prescribed subjects. Most educators agreed that some prescription was necessary, and the amount of prescription depended upon the concept of education. If the educator belonged to the humanist oriented group, the prescription might well be the hundred great books of the Hutchins Plan as used in St. John's College. If the purpose of education was to fit the individual to fill his place in society, the requirement might be survey courses in Modern Civilization, Modern Science, Modern Languages, and the Humanities, such as those required of freshmen at Columbia University.[3]

The predictions, which Mr. Winans made in 1914, concerning the development of speech work offered to college students were accurate.[4] Speech was reinstated in the curriculum and did attain a reputable status during this period. In 1928, the charter members of the Association of the Academic Teachers of Public Speaking, now called the National Association of Teachers of Speech, reviewed their progress in accomplishing the original aims of the organization. They agreed that the results were more gratifying than they had dreamed possible in 1914. James Lardner was quoted in the *Quarterly Journal of Speech,* as saying:

As I recall the arguments in favor of organizing the National Association of Teachers of Speech, the outstanding issue was this: we needed an independent organization through which we could unify the university and college teachers of speech, and through which we could improve the scholastic standing of speech education in our colleges and universities. We felt the need for recognition, and for higher standards of excellence in our teaching, but we had no adequate organization that we could use to help us gain these ends. The National Speech Arts Association was practically dead, and furthermore, its purpose had been mainly to develop a platform type of Elocution and not Speech as a part of an educational program of a university.[5]

Speech during this period became a part of the educational program. A survey of speech curricula was made in 1932; data were gathered from a study of the catalogues of 356 colleges and universities listed in the *Educational Directory* of the Federal Bureau of Education for 1929. A grand total of 2,083 courses was found to be offered in *Speech* under

[3] Cf. Butts, R. Freeman. *The College Charts its Course.* Ch. 19, 20, 21, 25.
[4] Winans, James A. "Report of the Eastern Public Speaking Conference." *Public Speaking Review.* 4:12 (1914).
[5] O'Neill, James M. "After Thirteen Years." *Quarterly Journal of Speech.* 14:246 (1928).

694 different course titles. In the division of *Interpretation*, there were 414 courses offered under 179 different titles. The titles which appeared most frequently were: *Interpretative Reading, Dramatic Interpretation, Story Telling, Literary Interpretation, Interpretation of Literature, Interpretation, Advanced Interpretation,* and *Oral Reading. Declamation* and *Elocution* were seldom mentioned.[6]

A similar survey was made of the Teacher Training Institutions in 1930. This survey revealed that the academic training of instructors had been extended since an earlier survey made in 1922. More institutions were requiring speech and following the system of prerequisites for advanced courses. There was also more uniformity of nomenclature and standardization of approach, showing an unmistakable improvement.[7]

Coulton found that in the period 1920–30 seven additional courses were mentioned in the catalogues which he examined. The basic course in speech appeared under such titles as *Fundamentals of Speech* and *Elements of Oral English.* Distinct courses were being offered in *Argumentation, Group Discussion,* and *Debate.* Under the heading *Science,* courses were offered in the physiology and psychology of speech. *Speech Correction* was a new area in many speech departments, and clinics were established in connection with this work. Instead of one course, usually called *Dramatic Production,* now there were courses entitled *Stage Lighting, Scenic Designing, Costuming.* A course in *Radio* was perhaps the newest course that was added during this period.[8] The basic course became more and more important. Since it was a prerequisite for advanced courses, to it was given the responsibility for training the student in the simplest vocal techniques. For example, voice and action received seven chapters of *Basic Principles of Speech* by Sarett and Foster, Woolbert gave them nine out of the eighteen chapters in his book, *The Fundamentals of Speech,* and Avery, Dorsey, and Sickels were concerned chiefly with training in voice and diction in *First Principles of Speech Training.*

Many courses in the interpretation of literature appeared during this period. In 1926, Wilson made a study of college catalogues to discover the extent of work offered in this phase of speech education. She found that 120 colleges and universities and 23 normal schools offered courses in the oral interpretation of literature. In fact, she found that 203 separate courses whose titles included either *interpretation* or *reading* were listed. Furthermore, she found that interpretative reading was

[6] Weaver, J. Clark. "A Survey of Speech Curricula." *Quarterly Journal of Speech.* 18:607–8 (1932).
[7] Speech Survey in Teacher-Training Institutions." *Quarterly Journal of Speech.* 16:42–61 (1930).
[8] Coulton, Thomas E. *Trends in Speech Education in American Colleges 1835–1935.* p. 52.

often included in courses labeled Literature, Public Speaking, Voice, Oratory, Dramatics, and very often in beginning Speech courses.[9] This overlapping was due, of course, to the unusual expansion of the speech departments during this period.

There were special courses in the interpretation of literature that were rather generally offered. In the teacher-training institutions surveyed in 1930, *Story Telling* was offered by 110 of the 181 institutions.[10] *Choral Reading,* although an old form of interpretation inherited from the Greeks, was revived first in England through the efforts of Marjorie Gullan of the University of London, and later through her students in the United States. According to the *Bibliography of Speech Education,* some twenty-five books concerned with choral reading were published after 1935.[11] Many teachers used this form of interpretation for different purposes. It added a new interest and was an enjoyable group activity for students of all ages, even those in the elementary schools. Keppie, in her book *The Teaching of Choric Speech,* emphasized the particular value to the timid student.[12] De Banke, in her book, *The Act of Choral Speaking,* listed many uses for this kind of training, such as an aid to the study of phonetics and as a cure for speech defects, especially stuttering, and also as a help in the teaching of a foreign language.[13]

In this period it was evident that the colleges and universities had resumed their responsibility for speech training. Their program had been extended far beyond any previous plan. Interpretation of literature, as it fitted into this program, shifted its purpose somewhat. Kramer stated, in 1936, that the true aim of oral interpretation was the appreciation of literature.[14] Most teachers probably agreed with her.

PROFESSIONAL SCHOOLS OF SPEECH. The lyceum and Chautauqua were no longer the chief source of education and entertainment in the rural communities; the radio, the "talking" pictures, and community dramatics had gradually superseded them. Platform-reading, which had been most popular, was no longer in vogue, and that meant, of course, a change in the training offered by the professional schools of speech.

They had to adapt themselves to the decreased demand for public readers, to offer training for the entertainment now popular, or to change the whole purpose of their organization. Emerson College of Oratory became a liberal arts college in 1936. Leland Powers School of Oratory became the Leland Powers School of the Theatre, and Columbia College

---

[9] Wilson, Helene. "Some Statistics Concerning Interpretation Courses." *Quarterly Journal of Speech.* 12:343–52 (1926).

[10] *Quarterly Journal of Speech.* 16:42–61 (1930).

[11] Thonssen, Lester and Fatherson, Elizabeth. *Bibliography of Speech Education.* p. 269–73.

[12] Keppie, Elizabeth E. *The Teaching of Choric Speech.* p. 13.

[13] DeBanke, Cecile. *The Art of Choral Speaking.* p. 23.

[14] Kramer, Magdalene and McCarthy, Margaret M. "The Development of Personality." *Emerson Quarterly.* 16:16+ (March, 1936).

of Expression now advertised training for actors and radio performers. The Curry School of Expression became Curry College and has been granting degrees since 1939.[15] Many similar schools went out of existence.

The entertainment values of oral interpretation were never discounted but were found in new forms. Since the problems of unemployment and enforced leisure were nagging most communities during this period, any effort to entertain and inform through oral reading was welcomed. Many students were trained to be radio performers; others, interested in the drama, became actors or directors. Skill in interpretive reading was recognized as an important part of their training.

PSYCHOLOGY CONTINUED TO EXERT AN INFLUENCE. The influence of current theories of psychology upon methods of teaching continued. It did not alter the methods so much as it explained them to the teacher, who presumably knew better how to teach because he understood the processes of learning more clearly.

The old idea of a dualism of mind and body was outmoded, and modern teachers accepted a monistic theory as a basis of all speech training. Woolbert subscribed to this theory in the preface to *The Fundamentals of Speech* when he explained the purpose of the book:

> . . . it aims to offer speech training for the whole man: body, voice, and mental mechanism. It is frankly psychological in foundation, and of psychologies is outspokenly behavioristic—that is to say, it insists that speech is a matter of the whole man, the cooperative activity of the entire organism; that it is a revelation of personality, but that the true definition of personality gives a picture compounded of thinking apparatus, emotional machinery, muscular activity, and body-wide participating parts—voice, brain, muscles, trunk, and limbs. Its essential thesis is that no speaking is good speaking which is not of the whole machine and which does not establish the desired relationship between the one speaking and the one listening.[16]

Functional psychology, which was called the "new" psychology in the last period, exerted great influence in changing the theories of education. Educators saw their work now primarily as the facilitating of student adaptation to his environment and were not concerned with the development of different mental faculties through disciplinary subjects. The mind was described by Dewey as "the power to understand things in terms of the use made of them."[17] This made it necessary for a teacher to consider the background of the student as well as the educational

---

15 See 1940 catalogues for the above-mentioned schools.
16 Woolbert, Charles H. *The Fundamentals of Speech.* p. xi.
17 Dewey, John. *Democracy and Education.* p. 39.

materials offered to him. Bode summarized this theory of learning as follows:

> . . . the distinctive features of this theory of learning all flow from what Dewey calls the continuity of experience. According to this principle of continuity, school experiences are educative only in so far as they serve to modify or "reconstruct" the background of experience which the pupil brings with him to school. . . . A school operating on the basis of this theory will protect the continuity of the school with the life outside of the school and it will provide various kinds of experiences, both with things and social relations, so as to serve the overarching purpose of reconstruction. On the negative side it will avoid the fallacies of faculty psychology and rote learning and mechanistic conceptions of habit formation; on the positive side it will stress insight and the practice of thinking which is required if these insights are to serve the purpose of giving our experience a new quality and a deeper meaning.[18]

This modern theory of education when applied to the teaching of oral interpretation of literature changed the purpose of the course to one which was more individualized and not primarily concerned with the entertainment of an audience. It made it impossible for a teacher to use imitative methods or to give assignments which did not allow for individual differences. It made it necessary to put the emphasis upon thinking and upon making the reading of literature a vivid and contributory experience for the student. The concept of oral expression became larger and more complex and speech was seen as a function of thought.

A closer relationship between thought and speech made current such definitions of thought as "sub-vocal speech" and of speech as "overt thought." There was no longer authority for believing that the mind sat supreme, dictating to the larynx what it should do. The process was considered more complex than ever before, and mechanical exercises were thought not adequate to train effective readers. Methods now must take an account of a larger pattern.

Psychologists attempted to carry the objective attitude to its last limits and succeeded. Watson's *Behaviorism* (1925) set forth a theory that all human behavior could be reduced to the same terms as those used in natural science. It allowed no recognition of motivation of behavior to purpose, foresight, or desire. Behaviorism, according to Hartman, oversimplified the process of learning to the mere acquisition of reflex habits. The Gestaltist however, refused to believe that mental processes were simple bridges over the gap between stimulus and response, but rather defined them as a part of an all-inclusive dynamic field. "Altering the 'field' alters the mind; modifying the environment (in essentials) modifies the child."[19]

[18] Bode, Boyd H. *How We Learn.* p. 251–2.
[19] Hartman, George W. *Gestalt Psychology.* p. 270.

Jastrow explained the difference between Behaviorism and the Gestalt psychology in the following manner:

Behaviorism proposed the S-R (stimulus-response) formula as the simplest pattern of all behavior and assumed that this formal statement was adequate. It ignored the vital factor of the organism, which decisively, and in each type of organism distinctively, determines which of all the physical and generally environmental forces shall act as a stimulus (S), and what the manner (including the absence) of response shall be. The true formula is S-O-R, stimulus-organism-response. The "Gestaltist" recognized that the integration pattern—which is the Gestalt—is present from the outset. Accepting the same emphasis, others speak of an organismic psychology; still others emphasize that since all behavior is active, the "act" psychology, the completing motor phase, is the proper point of approach and the consummation of behavior is the unit of response.[20]

Hartman said that teachers of speech in particular were drawn to Gestalt psychology as a workable pedagogical theory. In fact, he saw this psychology exemplified in philology and oral and written language:

Philologists have long known that syntax is the heart of human language and that individual words can be comprehended only in connection with the whole. The famous classical scholar, August Boeckh is said to have formulated something like a *Gestalttheorie* a century ago, and Grimm's law may be but a statement of the transformations which typical configurations undergo.

Effective oral and written composition both illustrate this point.[21]

It is easy to see why a teacher of interpretation who followed the Gestalt theory of psychology would develop methods which emphasized the emotional and the logical content of the material read rather than mechanical details of voice production. Parrish discussed the matter in an article titled "Implications of Gestalt Psychology". He said:

. . . to the Gestaltist, trial and error is not a method of learning at all. Unless such random movements succeed in forming a configuration they do not even amount to a "differentiation". . . . More intelligent methods are, first, "assimilation," in which two already known acts or perceptions enter into a new situation and become at once members of a new pattern of behavior; second, "gradation," where a direction of change (in brightness, quantity, loudness, and the like) once learned is transferred to a new situation; third, "re-definition," in which a perception is re-defined by a process of re-centering or re-focusing, as when one is able to see in a flat drawing of a cube either a corner or a hexagon, or when the same gesture or facial expression may have different meanings in different contexts.[22]

The fact that psychic combinations never repeat themselves with complete exactness is mentioned by Hartman as a principle which finds its best expression in the field of aesthetics.

Just as some colors are more colorful than others, so some patterns are more "figured" than others. A heap of sand or a lump of earth has less *form* than a

[20] Jastrow, Joseph. "Psychology," in *Encyclopedia of Social Sciences*. vol. 12. p. 595.
[21] Hartman. *op. cit.* p. 264.
[22] Parrish, Wayland Maxfield. "Implications of Gestalt Psychology." *Quarterly Journal of Speech*. 14:18–19 (1928).

tulip or a swallow. This is what Ehrenfels terms "height" or "degree" of Gestalt—a feature which increases with the product of the constituents, their unity and multiplicity of parts. In fact, it is suggested that what we call beauty is none other than "degree" of Gestalt.[23]

Cornelius Cunningham was one of the first teachers to see the importance of aesthetic theory as explained in his discussion of "Interpretative Reading as a Fine Art."

> . . . When interpretative reading is analyzed carefully as to the particular method of the application and development of the underlying principles in a given form of art, it is found to demand precisely the same qualities or characteristics of technic as do the major fine arts. . . . Nor can artistic interpretative reading be secured by the application of secret mathematical formulae of gesture and use of the voice, despite the ingenuity of such well-known men as Delsarte. . . . Interpretative reading is again like the major fine arts in that it baffles all efforts to reduce it to an exact science.[24]

Thus, the whole problem of teaching interpretation became much more complicated than it had been for the early teachers who understood method as a following of nature or saw it as the implementation of numerous mechanical rules and notations.

It will be remembered that the early teachers tried to standardize the action which indicated different emotional states. The modern teacher knew more about the physiology of emotions and realized that there were many subliminal and supraliminal stimuli which an audience could receive and that these were more subtle than the action which the early writers describe. The fact that changes in blood content, muscle tension and tonicity accompanied emotional disturbances suggested that a teacher must observe all the visible details of emotional reaction to get a complete picture. Simon made the following observation:

> As we read, many things happen within us, our entire selves respond in some way. The selection is grasped in terms of action. There are observable bodily movements of one kind and another as well as less observable, but none the less real, strains, tensions, and contractions. Muscles, nerves, glands, all do their part in our reaction to literature. . . . It is this "doing something" that *is* the appreciation.[25]

Woolbert also said that "the speech teacher functioning as psychologist comes to accept as his simplest and surest 'givens' the clear evidence he gets of muscular action and tension. . . ."[26]

The modern teacher because of his increased information became more observant. He was more mindful of the difficulty which a student might

[23] Hartman. *op. cit.* p. 12.
[24] Cunningham, Cornelius. "Interpretative Reading As a Fine Art." *Journal of Expression.* 2:78–9 (1928).
[25] Simon, Clarence T. "Appreciation in Reading." *Quarterly Journal of Speech.* 16:185 (1930).
[26] Woolbert, Charles H. "Psychology." *Quarterly Journal of Speech.* 16:16 (1930).

have in appreciating literature in terms of his own experience and also of the difficulty of stimulating an emotional response in an audience. Modern methods, therefore, are presumably more effective because of greater knowledge in the fields of physiology and psychology. Since the individual and his adaptation to his environment are the chief concern of educators, the teacher found it necessary to follow a functional psychology which engendered a disdain for learning by rote, by imitation, and by mechanical rules.

New methods of research prompted many studies which added to this knowledge of physiology and psychology as it affected the speaking situation. Barnes conducted an experiment, at the University of Wisconsin, to determine the relation between the vital capacity and ability in oral reading. The *vital capacity* was defined as "the maximum of air an individual is able to expel from the lungs by voluntary effort, after taking the deepest possible inspiration." According to this study, the correlation between vital capacity and ability in oral reading was insignificant.[27] Knower and Dusenbury made experimental studies, at the University of Minnesota, of the symbolism of action and voice. Their conclusions attested to the reliability of the interpretation of both facial expression and tonal symbols. In the second study they found: (1) one may communicate meaning suggestive of emotional states by the use of a tone code with a high degree of accuracy; (2) women appear to be more sensitive to the reception of tone codes than are men; (3) the communication of emotional meanings by the tone code is influenced by the pattern of stimulus; (4) there are marked differences in the ability of individuals to use codes which suggest different moods; (5) although the visible code appears to be more specific than the tone code, the differences in the communicative values of these codes depend upon the performers, meaning to be suggested, and the persons who react to the codes.[28]

It is evident, therefore, that speech teachers in this period were cognizant of new developments in related fields and eager to integrate this knowledge with that which had been passed down to them. The departments of speech in the colleges and universities were enlarged into specialized fields to meet the demands of modern education. Oral Interpretation, as a course offering, was to a degree revamped. Its organization and restatement in the curriculum evidenced a sensitivity to the value of the subject in cultural training.

[27] Barnes, John. "Vital Capacity in Oral Reading." *Quarterly Journal of Speech Education.* 12:176–82 (1926).

[28] Dusenbury, Delwin, and Knower, Franklin. "Experimental Studies of the Symbolism of Action and Voice: A Study of the Specificity of Meaning in Facial Expression." *Quarterly Journal of Speech.* I. 24:424–35 (1938). II. "A Study of Meaning in Abstract Tonal Symbols" 25:67–75 (1939).

CHAPTER II

METHODS USED IN TEACHING ORAL INTERPRETATION

There is a noticeable agreement in the methods outlined in the textbooks of this period. They are all based on some kind of natural approach and emphasize the necessity of getting the basic thought of the literature to be interpreted. They agree that the interpreter acts as an entity and that his whole body functions in communicating the ideas held in the symbols of the printed page. The audience is considered an important part of the speech situation. Effective speech, therefore, implies communication of ideas. However, the value of oral reading for the student himself, even when an audience is not present, is considered significant.

No unique or unusual system or theory, such as those of Delsarte or Rush, evolved. In fact, one might say that the contribution of these teachers consisted more of using wisely established methods and adding to the traditional materials, than in devising anything which might be called new. The textbooks were written for use and not to defend or explain a new theory. They are all replete with suggestions for the analysis of the intellectual and the emotional content of literature. There is a noticeable tendency to spend less time on training in voice and gesture and more on ways of finding the full implications of the material to be read.

TEXTBOOKS. The output of textbooks on oral interpretation was not great during this period. Lee Emerson Bassett's *A Handbook of Oral Reading* appeared in 1917. It followed the natural approach very closely. "Correct the thought, arouse interest, awaken the mind to clear, vigorous action, and the speech will take care of itself pretty well." This was his key idea, and his methods all depended upon the stimulation of mental processes. In 1922, Rollo Anson Tallcott wrote *The Art of Acting and Public Reading*, in which he tried to show that the two had much in common and should not be divorced. Algernon de V. Tassin was interested in the relation of oral interpretation to the study of literature. His book, *Oral Study of Literature*, 1923, is chiefly an anthology of selections for delivery. *The Art of Interpretative Speech* by Charles H. Woolbert and Severina E. Nelson, published first in 1927 and later revised by Nelson in 1935, reflected the same theories articulated earlier in Woolbert's *The Fundamentals of Speech*. *The Spoken Word in Life and Art* by Estelle H. Davis and Edward W. Mammen, 1935, stressed training in voice and diction, as did Margaret P. McLean's *Oral Interpretation of Forms of Literature,* 1936. Wayland Maxfield Parrish published *Reading Aloud* which was to become a kind of classic in its field in 1932. It followed the Natural school more closely than any of the others and quoted freely from Corson, Whately, and Curry. Maud May Babcock rewrote Clark's *Interpretation of the Printed Page* in 1940, but altered only slightly the general thesis of the book. Argue Tresidder's *Reading for Others,* 1940, included, in addition to discussions of the mechanics of speech and oral interpretation, chapters on acting, radio, and choral speaking. Several notable collections of material were made to supplement the textbooks used. Outstanding among these were Gertrude Johnson's *Modern Literature for Oral Interpretation,* 1926, and William J. Farma's *Prose, Poetry, and Drama for Oral Interpretation,* I and II 1930, 1935.

THE "NATURAL METHOD" REDEFINED. Twentieth century teachers did not have the wholehearted reverence for nature that the eighteenth century followers of Rousseau had. They believed that man's nature depended greatly upon the environment in which he developed. Speech was *learned* and although the basis was good conversational speech, Parrish said, "We must follow not what is natural for us but what is normal, what is *standard* in expression."[1] Woolbert was even more restricting in his explanation. To him interpretation was an art and therefore the interpreter did not speak naturally but appeared to speak naturally. He said:

Drop the notion that art comes by nature and is "natural," when finally it comes. Art is mastery. It is control, management, command. . . . So then if interpretation is an art, it is a matter of planning and foresight by a person who knows what he is doing and of execution by a person skilled in speaking and reading.[2]

Tallcott, who favored training in acting for the student who would read orally, agreed with Woolbert. He proceeded on the thesis that acting was an art and demanded certain techniques which were not natural but learned.[3] Tassin and Bassett were particularly concerned with adequate comprehension. What the mind comprehended it could communicate, they believed. All of these teachers agreed that there are certain speech skills which cannot be overlooked because they are necessary to communicate ideas and emotions to the audience.

Although Parrish stated in his chapter on method, "In learning to read, then, we shall give our attention not to manipulating the voice, but to the analysis of thought, the grouping and inter-relations of logical

---

[1] Parrish, Wayland Maxfield. *Reading Aloud.* p. 35.
[2] Woolbert, Charles H. and Nelson, Severina E. *The Art of Interpretative Speech.* p. 31–4.
[3] Tallcott, Rollo Anson. "Teaching Public Reading." *Quarterly Journal of Speech Education.* 9:53–66 (1923).

elements, and later to the analysis of the more subtle elements of mood, emotion, and imagination," he gave a chapter to voice improvement and one to pronunciation. However, he did not give as much consideration to the techniques of reading as did many others because he had a great fear of becoming too mechanical.

It is scarcely to be questioned that variety in all these elements is desirable, but it *is* to be questioned whether it can best be secured by giving attention to them separately, or whether any *system* of rules or principles of variation will not lead to affectation and artificiality.

Attempts have sometimes been made to standardize the expression of a given sentence, on the theory that there must be one, and only one, correct way to speak it. A kind of musical score is sometimes used, on which is indicated, as for singing, the pitch and duration of each syllable, with legatos and crescendos as in musical notation. All such attempts must end in absurdity. English is not a language which can be so trapped and stereotyped.[4]

The natural method is re-defined, therefore, to mean that method which has its basis in functional psychology, which will make the literature real and stimulating to the individual who reads. Those methods which are used to give flexibility to voice and body are only servants · to the process of interpretation. They can never be emphasized at the expense of the process of understanding and appreciating which involves the whole man and stimulates him to communicate the ideas and emotions which he has found.

VARIATIONS AND ELABORATIONS OF OLD METHODS. As was said before, very little that can be called original was introduced by the writers of this period, but they did make an attempt to write usable and complete textbooks. The variations and elaborations may be rather conveniently grouped under the following headings: the mechanics of speech, the logical content, the emotional content, and interpretation for an audience.

(a) *Mechanics of Speech.* Although Woolbert stressed practice in order to use quality, pitch, stress, and time correctly, he did not emphasize the mechanics of speech as much as did McLean, and Davis and Mammen. They were very much interested in the improvement of speech habits—in training the voice from the point of view of its physical properties. During this period the International Phonetic Alphabet became more commonly used; it was a useful tool in improving diction and pronunciation. Klinghardt's system of recording intonation was used by Davis and Mammen, and by McLean. An example follows:

A straight line indicates the general pitch level, whether high or low. Dots above or below this line indicate the relation to that pitch level of the syllables of a word or sentence. A heavy dot is a stressed syllable; a light one, an unstressed

4 Parrish. *op. cit.* p. 100.

syllable. The comma-like tail indicates the more important inflections. The sentence "I like this now book very much" would be recorded:[5]

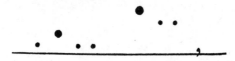

This notation is similar to those devised in the earliest period, 1762–1827. Its use by students was not generally encouraged, however, and it appeared in textbooks rather in an illustrative fashion in the discussion of intonation. It was now possible to make recordings of the spoken word, and the necessity of finding an exact notation for speech variations was gone.

Parrish suggested the use of the chanted monotone as one method for establishing a resonant voice. After the selection is intoned, it is read, first retaining the same tempo and rhythm, then as "rational reading." In the final reading, there should remain much of the initial intonation, or monopitch. It was suggested that this exercise was good for poetry, since it was originally written to be sung and still retains many of the same qualities as music. However, he adds at the end of the explanation of the exercise, that the student should remember that it is possible to get the same results without mechanical means, by a free, imaginative responsiveness to the mood and feeling of the selection.[6]

Tresidder, in his definition of "oral interpretation," defines the words separately and says that *oral* means "everything relating to the speaking apparatus: the physiology of voice plus diction, which includes the proper shaping of sounds, the proper choice of sounds, and the whole pattern of speaking."[7] He included five chapters on voice and gesture. Davis and Mammen discuss the physics and physiology of speech and give more than half of their textbook to mechanical aspects. Most teachers of oral interpretation, however, although they believe that a student must have skill in using the voice and body, are not preoccupied with the mechanics of speech. The study of the speech mechanism has become the core of other courses in the speech department—courses which are often prerequisites for the course in oral interpretation of literature.

(b) *Logical Content.* The logical content of the literature read is important to all teachers. Reading must be meaningful, not merely beautiful. Tassin, Bassett, and Babcock are particularly emphatic in their

[5] Davis, Estelle H. and Mammen, Edward W. *The Spoken Word in Life and Art.* p. 80.
[6] Parrish. *op. cit.* p. 167.
[7] Tresidder, Argus. *Reading to Others.* p. 3.

demands that a reader understand clearly the material he is reading for himself or for an audience. According to all of the textbook writers, the starting place for the reader is a consideration of the intellectual content of the material—the meanings of the words or symbols on the page. It is not only necessary, the student was told, to know the denotation but also the connotation of these written symbols. This ability depends in part upon the previous experience of the reader, especially his experience in reading. After the reader understands, the next problem is, of course, to convey the meaning clearly to an audience. As the student selects his material, it is thought necessary for the instructor to consider his ability rather than to follow any plan that is concerned with the history or form of literature. Parrish begins with prose because he thinks it is easier for the student to grasp.[8]

Both Parrish and Tresidder suggest the writing of a précis of the material to be read. A précis is defined, by Tresidder, as a condensation of the original, not a paraphrase or critical estimate. "The précis," he says, "must be unequivocally clear, omitting no significant point of the original, but discarding all ornamentation. It should as far as possible depart from the wording of the original without changing the person, the attitude, or the emphasis." He also suggested that it might be beneficial to make an oral précis before attempting to write one.[9]

Grouping of words is considered important, not only for meaning but for rhythm. Babcock, in her edition of Clark's *Interpretation of the Printed Page,* treated unit grouping, paragraph sequence, and group value in the first three chapters. Tresidder suggested the old technique of marking the pauses with vertical bars, a single one for short pauses and a double one for long ones.[10] McLean used the same method and also suggested that the student copy the selection, if it is prose, on typewriting paper assigning one main breath group to a line.[11]

The writers agreed that in addition to grouping, important words must be emphasized. Tresidder called this process "centering." He suggested underlining key words.[12] This was an old but useful technique. The concept of reading ideas instead of words was generally accepted by this time; along with it, came the necessity of making a distinction between weak and strong or important and unimportant words. Rhythm was described as depending upon emphasis and timing to a great extent, but it could not be confined to the discussion of the logical meaning since it had strong emotional values. Nevertheless, the principle of elision

---

[8] Parrish. *op. cit.* p. 48.
[9] Tresidder. *op. cit.* p. 46–51.
[10] *Ibid.* p. 32. Sheridan also suggested this notation in *Art of Reading* (1775).
[11] McLean. *op. cit.* p. 69, 116.
[12] Tresidder. *op. cit.* p. 32–9.

in order to make the important idea stand out is related to rhythm, and the jerky, unpleasant kind of rhythm results from emphasizing each word equally. Woolbert and Nelson explained the relationship as follows:

> Inability to secure a broken rhythm often occurs if the student has been urged to give every syllable equal value in the interest of distinct enunciation. But no sensible or sensitive person talks all words and syllables evenly spaced like a typewriter or metronome. . . . Monometer as this is called is the chief cause of "indirectness" and is altogether abominable. It is not communication.[13]

Some textbooks gave space to the discussion of meter and scansion. McLean, in addition to placing emphasis upon metrical forms, mentioned the caesura as a principal pause. Walker, in *Elements of Elocution,* published in 1781, insisted upon this pause in or near the middle of the line for distinctness and harmony,[14] but McLean considered the caesura as usually a sense pause, not often indicated by punctuation marks.[15] Other texts of this period are more concerned with rhythm than with meter. Woolbert and Nelson saw no value in scansion for the reader but considered rhythm an important element: "Meter has no surprises; rhythm never gives away its secrets. . . . It titillates attention and interest by the everlasting uncertainty of what is going to happen next." The pattern that the reader gives to his reading through a skillful use of pauses, emphasis, and intonation will vary according to his ingenuity and understanding of the material.[16]

Paraphrasing was prescribed to help the student understand what he read and to overcome unnaturalness in his manner of reading. It was not used in any standardized form as in Phillips' tone drills. Parrish, for example, suggested "thinking into" the context various transitional words which would ease the reading and make it more expressive. He even suggested that, if necessary, the student might speak under his breath such words as *so, then, hence, that is, therefore,* etc., if they aided him in the preparation of a selection.[17]

The habit of close observations of details, such as exact meanings of words, punctuation, and grammatical construction was considered important. The most important of all was grasping the meaning of larger units—of seeing the poem as a whole with all its overtones of meaning. This emphasis upon comprehension of the meaning of the whole led to clearly outlined procedures for memorization which insisted upon the "whole method." Immel listed ten steps in memorization which

---

[13] Woolbert and Nelson. *op. cit.* 2nd ed. p. 214.
[14] Walker. *op. cit.* p. 250.
[15] McLean. *op. cit.* p. 182.
[16] Woolbert and Nelson. *loc. cit.* It is interesting to note that in the 1934 edition of Woolbert and Nelson's *Art of Interpretative Speech,* Dr. Rush's terms "expulsive," "explosive," and "effusive" are still being used.
[17] Parrish. *op. cit.* p. 48.

are typical of the methods used. They have their roots in the psychology of learning. In shortened form, they are:

1. If the material to be memorized is part of a larger whole *read the entire selection.* . . .
2. *Begin memorizing early and spread the work over as long a time as possible.*
3. . . . *memorize your material as a whole,* never sentence by sentence.
4. *There is an advantage in reading or repeating out loud* as you learn.
5. Always read or repeat the selection *thoughtfully.*
6. Try to *feel* the content of the selection as you read or repeat it.
7. Read or repeat the selection as *to an audience.*
8. Have the selection in a convenient place and read it at *different times during the day.*
9. As the selection becomes a little more familiar, *repeat as much as possible without looking at the page.*
10. For value in practice, *a selection should be absolutely word perfect.*[18]

(c) *Emotional Content.* It is more difficult for the student to communicate the emotional content than the logical content when he reads. Without it, however, the reading is dull and lifeless. The problem becomes greater for the modern reader because he cannot depend much upon physical action. Perhaps in an attempt to make a distinction between reading and acting, or in a reaction against the extravagant gestures of the Delsartians, the amount of action considered in good taste had been decreased. Parrish said: "The reader should yield himself to the feeling of the poet, but had best avoid gesticulation. He must find a happy mean between abandon and indifference, keeping the thought-content always dominant but maintaining a high excitement."[19] This maintaining of a high excitement through being emotionally responsive to the feeling of the author becomes a much more understandable process than before. Nevertheless, it still eludes definition.

The James-Lange theory of emotion forms the basis for the methods of inducing emotional reactions. James, in his *Briefer Course of Psychology,* set forth the theory convincingly when he said:

Everyone knows how panic is increased by flight, and how the giving way to the symptoms of grief or anger increases those passions themselves. . . . Whistling to keep up courage is no mere figure of speech. On the other hand, sit all day in a moping posture, sigh, and reply to everything with a dismal voice, and your melancholy lingers. . . . Smooth the brow, brighten the eye, contract the dorsal rather than the ventral aspect of the frame, and speak in a major key, pass the genial compliment, and your heart must be frigid indeed if it do not gradually thaw![20]

[18] Immel, Ray K. "A Note on Memorization for Delivery" in *A Course of Study in Speech Training and Public Speaking for Secondary Schools,* ed. by A. M. Drummond. p. 257–9.
[19] Parrish. *op. cit.* p. 217.
[20] James, William. *Briefer Course of Psychology.* p. 382–3.

In line with this theory, Parrish stated that stimulated interest in reading may become real and that the reader must "keep his body alive."

General bodily tension, alertness, or readiness will facilitate appropriate emotional responses, and sympathetically affect the intricate complex of small muscles which control the voice. It is well to bear in mind that these muscles, like any other part of the body, reflect general bodily slackness or tonicity.

* * *

We need not bother our heads about traditional systems of gesture, about stereo-typed positions of hands and head, except to avoid them. It is these that have helped to make public elocution a reproach. But we do need to concern ourselves with general bodily responsiveness, especially with the cultivation of a "lively play of facial expression."

* * *

We must try to recover some of the normal spontaneity of childhood.[21]

The reader must have the ability for sympathy or empathy with the author. Discovering the emotions implied in the poem to be read requires much more ability than expressing these emotions once they are discovered. The personality and experience of the reader must be reckoned along with his imaginative and creative abilities.

Teachers of this period generally agreed that oral interpretation at its best involved a creative process and could become an art. Dennis asked that they not quibble over terms or even over methods. "Let's get a better, bigger understanding of what this life is all about," he said, "let's find a meaning in it, let's learn how to re-translate, into living words and actions that will be understood by all, the thoughts, the life values, the life interpretations which writing men have put into books."[22] This necessity for experience and an understanding of life involved a sharpening of the perception, a development of the imagination, an indulgence in contemplation. The reader was told that he must re-create the poet's image in his own mind out of images which he already possessed. "Imagination is hindered," Parrish said, "by unfamiliar terms, when we allow them to pass without analysis; by triteness, when we neglect to revivify a too familiar passage; and by our lack of concentration and deliberation. . . . Vivid and correct expression depends upon correct and vivid impression."[23]

Woolbert and Nelson gave some definite suggestions for the study of the emotional quality of writing. One chapter is devoted to the emotional setting. The discussion includes the study of the author's character and

---

[21] Parrish. *op. cit.* p. 95, 96, 97.
[22] Dennis, Ralph. "One Imperative Plus." *Quarterly Journal of Speech Education.* 8:222–3 (1922).
[23] Parrish. *op. cit.* p. 239.

philosophy of life, his mood at the time of writing, and the environment in which he wrote. The facts involved in this background study may be very useful in understanding and feeling with the author.[24] It is also accepted that one of the best ways to enlarge one's emotional responsiveness and to develop creative ability is by practice in reading. Kerfoot is insistent upon that fact in his book, *How to Read.* "Learning to read," he says, "in the real sense, means enlarging our equipment and learning creatively to use it." He reiterates at different times during the book that a reader reads in terms of his own equipment and not in terms of the author's equipment.

> For reading consists of our making—with the aid of the pattern and the hints supplied by the author, but out of *our* mental stock, which we have produced by living—something that never existed before; something that only exists at all in so far as we make it; something that can never be duplicated by any other reader; something that we ourselves can never wholly reproduce.[25]

Visual communication was still considered important but required a more subtle analysis of technique. Since the reader no longer depended upon the use of a special gesture to interpret each emotion, he must rely upon developing an emotional responsiveness which would enliven the whole interpretation spontaneously. The detailed study of action had become the art of pantomime. Blake made a study at Columbia University, in 1933, of the interpretation of bodily expression, which showed the great communicative powers of action without benefit of voice.[26] Two significant textbooks were written for use in classes where this type of interpretation was emphasized: Alberti's *A Handbook of Acting Based upon the New Pantomime* (1934) and Pardoe's *Pantomimes for Stage and Study* (1931). The study of action had been separated from oral interpretation, and it was now much more closely related to acting.

(d) *Interpretation for an Audience.* Reading for an audience became an art in itself and was distinguished rather clearly from other related arts. Woolbert and Nelson made the differentiation on the basis of the amount of activity used:

> Acting uses the whole man: voice, arms, body, face—everything. In addition, it may employ costuming, lighting, movement, and one's relation to other people on the stage. It is the fullest form of expression dealing with the reading of "lines." Impersonation is a little less full in its demands; it is acting with the omission of costuming, lighting, stage pictures. Interpretation is impersonation with the omission of walking about, change of posture, and fullness of gesture and facial expression.[27]

[24] Woolbert and Nelson. *op. cit.* Ch. 6.
[25] Kerfoot, John B. *How to Read.* p. 20.
[26] Blake, William H. *A Preliminary Study of the Interpretation of Bodily Expression.*
[27] Woolbert and Nelson. *op. cit.* p. 38.

The attempt on the part of the teacher to make distinctions between acting, impersonation, and oral interpretation continued throughout the period and into the next one.

Parrish was firm in his belief that the artist must idealize and universalize the emotion and that his own personality must not intrude. He felt that much harm had been done by the modern doctrine of self-expression. "It is never safe for the young actor or reader," he said, "to fall back upon a mere 'That's the way I feel about the passage,' or 'That's the way I think it ought to be read.' A great art is universal instead of personal." The aesthetic theory that demanded that the interpreter act only as a medium for communication, and with a certain amount of "aesthetic distance" from the audience, was generally accepted by the teachers of this period. As a result, the exhibitional performances of the previous period were frowned upon.

A very good summary of the principles which were considered important in establishing oral interpretation as an art is given by Parrish in his textbook:

> Mastery of the art of interpretation should be governed by well understood general principles, which should enable one to interpret competently any kind of literature. In dramatic poetry one must interpret not only idea and emotion but also character and situation. The interpreter should not pretend to *be* the poet or character whom he represents. The arts are forms of imitation. They do not, however, literally copy natural objects; they represent what is typical, universal, or ideal in them.

* * *

> The interpreter may create as genuinely as the poet whose work he represents. He should try to give us, not real life, but a representation of life, the appearance or image of life. . . . In such representation his own personality has no place. He discovers significant tones and gestures by long patient study of his own and others' reactions and emotions, getting what he can from inspiration. If he follows this objective method, the method of the scientist, his own character should not be injured even by the representation of evil persons. The difference between reading, impersonation, and acting are largely conventional. Good taste should tell one how much he may relay on theatrical accessories on a given occasion.[28]

The class in oral interpretation, because of the functions assigned to it, usually gave little time to acting or impersonation. That reduced its importance as a place of training for public performers. Nevertheless, oral reading was always allied to acting and impersonation, and a student interested in the latter forms discovered that a preliminary study of oral interpretation was very useful.

[28] Parrish. *op. cit.* p. 331.

SUMMARY. Speech returned to the curriculum of higher education during this period. Separate departments were formed in many colleges and universities, and an attempt was made to satisfy a diversity of student needs. This diversification of needs made an extension of the offerings in speech necessary. As a result, special courses in Dramatic Production, in Voice Science and Corrective Speech, in Public Speaking, in Debate and Discussion, in Oral Interpretation, in Verse Speaking, and in Radio were offered.

Oral Interpretation as it became an academic study was limited to a sincere and unpretentious communication of the intellectual and emotional content of literature. The conventional idea of this type of interpretation restricted the amount of action which might be used and put a premium upon a careful study of the printed page and the mental activity that that demanded. There was a belief that the process was a creative one in which the experience, the imagination, and the emotional sensitivity of the reader were the chief determinants. The reader, however, could not capitalize upon his own personal charms but must suppress his own personality in favor of the power and effectiveness of the literature. The development of new methods for and attitudes toward oral interpretation was due primarily to a wider knowledge of psychology. More attention was now given to the individual student, to his special interests and background. The development of an appreciation and understanding of the literature became the main purpose of the course in Oral Interpretation of Literature.

PART V

ORAL INTERPRETATION IMPROVES ITS ACADEMIC STATUS: 1940–1965

CHAPTER I

ARTS AND HUMANITIES IN
A SCIENTIFIC AGE

The United States emerged from the Second World War a major power but found it difficult to assume a position of leadership. Because of her wealth, her motives were suspect, and because of her technological superiority, she was feared. Here was an affluent society which offered man more comforts but at the same time more anxieties. He felt threatened by the new scientific discoveries which might possibly, in time, prove his destruction. Eiseley, an anthropologist and historian of science, observed that "never in human history has the mind soared higher and seen less to cheer its complacency."[1]

The exploration of space stimulated an emphasis upon science and technology. There were new frontiers beyond the weary world, and the Federal government was willing to finance their exploration: Men were sent in spacecraft to orbit the earth and to gather scientific data; the moon was no longer Luna, the moon-goddess, but a target for astronauts. But in spite of scientific progress, a new pessimism, born of fear of the unknown and a sense of imbalance caused by changing scientific theories and ethical principles, settled upon the leaders in all strata of society. With the rapid changes came an unsureness. Eiseley explained this phenomenon as follows:

We have heard much of science as the endless frontier, but we whose immediate ancestors were seekers of gold among great mountains and gloomy forests are easily susceptible to a simplistic conception of the word *frontier* as something conquerable in its totality. . . .
Not so the wilderness beyond the stars or concealed in the infinitesimal world beneath the atom. Wise reflection will lead us to recognize that we have come upon a different and less conquerable region. Forays across its border already

[1] Eiseley, Loren. "Science and the Unexpected Universe." *The American Scholar.* 35:425–426 (1966).

suggest that man's dream of mastering all aspects of Nature takes no account of his limitations in time, space, or even his own senses, augmented though they may be by his technological devices. Even the thought that he can bring to bear upon that frontier is limited in quantity by the number of trained minds that can sustain such an adventure. Ever more expensive grow the tools with which research can be sustained, ever more diverse the social problems which that research, in its technological phase, promotes.[1]

Although man found that he could adjust to new environments and carry out difficult experimentation, the truth remained that he could not adjust to other men with better grace and understanding than before. He seemed to become more mechanical and less human in his attitudes, knowledgeable but not wise, sophisticated but uncultured. The President's Commission on National Goals stated, in 1960, that ultimately the success of the United States as a civilized society would be judged in terms of the creative activities of its citizens: in art, architecture, literature, music, and the sciences. Because of a concern that science might become too powerful at the expense of the humanities, a commission on the Humanities was founded in 1963, sponsored by the American Council of Learned Societies, The Council of Graduate Schools in the United States, and the United Chapters of Phi Beta Kappa. Their report delivered on April 30, 1964, stated that expansion and improvement of activities in the arts and humanities was in the national interest and consequently deserved financial support by the Federal government.[2]

The success of the National Science Foundation, established in 1950, was well-known and stimulated interest in the arts and humanities as another worthy field for encouragement. In 1965, The Arts and Humanities Act became law and twenty-one million dollars were appropriated for each of the fiscal years, 1966 through 1968, "to develop and promote a broadly conceived national policy of support for the humanities and the arts."[3] The task assigned to the educators in this field might well be more difficult than that of the scientists exploring new frontiers. The results would be less tangible because the subject was man himself and the intent was to strengthen his moral fiber. For all who were interested either as creators or interpreters, a new incentive had been provided to make a contribution to American culture.

LITERATURE IN A CRITICAL AGE. Writers were faced with the formidable tasks of reflecting a complicated and secular society and of criticizing the standardization and automation which modern life nourished.

---

[2] Report of the Commission on the Humanities (The American Council of Learned Societies, 1964). p. v.
[3] Grove, Richard. "National Foundation on the Arts and the Humanities Act." *U. S. Department of Health, Education and Welfare Indicators.* Nov. 1965. p. 46.

Nevertheless, there was an increase in the number and the variety of books written. Competition in the publishing business was intensified. An attempt to reach a larger reading public produced a multiplicity of books, both hardback and paperback, encouraged book clubs and best-seller lists, and made it difficult for the creative writer to do his work without looking often toward the marketplace.

The readers showed a greater diversity of taste than ever before but. also a conformity within groups. The young readers, those under twenty-five, exerted a new influence: because of their increased number (it was predicted that they would soon outnumber the elder group), they could make a book, or the movie based on the book, a financial success. Erich Fromm, in his analysis of the human condition, found that the present culture demanded men "who cooperate smoothly in large groups; who want to consume more and more, and whose tastes are standardized and can be easily influenced and anticipated."[4] The paperback made more books available to more people, but the ability to select and enjoy the best literature became a concern of many people. The possibility of assisting students in developing taste for literature that would be individualistic and not conformative, and the necessity of standards for selection concerned the educator.

Fromm observed that modern man often found himself alienated from the world in which he lived because his life forces flowed into things and institutions to which he found himself forced to bow. The creative artist resisted in different ways, sometimes by withdrawing from society, but often by rebelling against it. The inevitable search for identity produced nonconformist groups among writers, readers, and playgoers. It is difficult to find identity in a world that man believes inimical to his well-being. Many "anti" attitudes developed, and such terms as "anti-establishment," "anti-hero," "anti-novel," and "anti-drama," became common. The older pessimism seemed to give place to an active negativism—a rebellion against traditional standards both for social conduct and artistic endeavor.

As early as 1921, Van Wyck Brooks observed that the optimistic adolescence of the last century had been replaced by a more mature and realistic attitude. "America is the only country," he said, "where, until recent years, the prosperous middle class has gone unchallenged, where the Philistines have never been aroused to a sense of their limitations."[5] By the beginning of the second half of the twentieth century, the pendu-

---

[4] Fromm, Erich. "The Present Human Condition." *The American Scholar.* 25:31 (1955).
[5] Brooks, Van Wyck. "The Critical Movement in America" in *Literary Opinion in America.* vol. 1. p. 81.

lum had swung far toward a critical realization of our shortcomings. It was difficult to find writers who affirmed life or critics who encouraged such affirmation.

In spite of a plethora of literature critical of mass culture in the present-day civilization, there were literary critics who found encouragement in the changing scene. Trilling saw a new kind of intellectual developing with a potentiality which could not be disregarded. "The members of the newly expanded intellectual class," he said "partly by reason of the old cultural sanctions, which may operate only as a kind of snobbery . . . partly because they know that the mental life of practical reality does have a relation to the mental life of theory and free imagination, are at least potentially supporters and consumers of high culture."[6]

Because of the increasing number of so-called intellectuals, the demand for diversity of literature became compelling. There was an enlarged demand for nonfiction, especially for biography and history which are written with a fictionist's touch, and for books from the fields of sociology and psychology. Notable among the latter are David Riesman's *The Lonely Crowd,* James Baldwin's *Nobody Knows My Name,* and Vance Packard's *The Hidden Persuaders.* There was a lament that the novel fell short of its traditional aim—to give the reader an insight into the common problems and experiences of man. Langbaum suggested that criticism might bring a new unity and find values that could be organized into a new tradition. He deplored the fact that novelists of his generation, unlike the writers of the Twenties, had been unable to show "our style, our sense of ourselves."[7] The Southern writer, although considered in the vanguard during this period, struggled with pressures growing out of civil rights legislation and agitation. Eudora Welty resented the demand that the fiction writer become a propagandist and insisted that the great novelist, for example, William Faulkner, spoke for all men.[8]

In 1966, Truman Capote reported a multiple murder in the mode of the novel and called it a new form; Hersey's *Hiroshima,* a similar report had appeared in 1946.[9] Public interest in this kind of factual book seemed to be increasing, and magazines that formerly gave preference to the short story became primarily nonfiction, the *Atlantic* and *Harper's* among them.

Perhaps the paperback book was the most noteworthy contribution to the development of a larger reading public. Literature was available to everyone; teachers and students benefited, and publishers profited.

[6] Trilling, Lionel. *A Gathering of Fugitives.* p. 68.
[7] Langbaum, Robert. "This Literary Generation." *The American Scholar.* 25:87–94 (1955).
[8] Welty, Eudora. "Must the Novelist Crusade?" *Atlantic.* 216:104–108 (1965).
[9] Capote, Truman. *In Cold Blood;* and Hersey, John. *Hiroshima.*

Criticism, however, was the imprint of the period which was sometimes called "The Age of Criticism."[10] The diversity of literature complicated the task of the critic and gave him undue importance.

American criticism developed slowly but became a necessary adjunct to the study of literature. At its best, it added a new dimension for the reader or oral interpreter. The emphasis was clearly upon analysis of the writing with attention to the technical skill of the writer. Sometimes there seemed to be a breach between form and content. Often students became so engrossed in "symbol-finding" that they lost sight of the entire plan and purpose of the writer.

Kenneth Burke exerted immeasurable influence throughout the period. *The Philosophy of Literary Form: Studies in Symbolic Action*, 1941, set forth a theory of criticism which had a dramatic perspective. Burke believed that the most relevant analysis of the structure of writing was in terms of its function revealed in symbolic action. This was a pragmatic approach which assumed, for example, that a poem was designed "to do something" for the poet and for his readers; the similarity of the action depended upon the degree to which the situation of the poet overlapped with the situation of the reader. The critic in his task of analysis, he said, must discover the "dramatic alignment"—the conflict— and identify the roles of the speakers through the "associational clusters" —the kinds of acts, images, personalities, and situations which the writer uses to represent his ideas of heroism, despair, etc. He explained that it was possible to analyze the poem without reference to the poet, but it would be more fruitful to begin with the poem as a symbolic act of the poet. "If we try to discover," he says, "what the poem is doing for the poet, we may discover a set of generalizations as to what poems do for everybody. With these in mind, we have cues for analyzing the sort of *eventfulness* that the poem contains. And in analyzing this eventfulness we shall make basic discoveries about the structures of the work itself."[11] There were other theories of criticism, of course, but all seemed to put a premium upon the intellectual approach rather than an intuitive one and to focus upon the art object rather than on the artist.

Although criticism focused upon the technical aspects of writing and tried to be objective, perhaps scientific, in its aesthetic judgment, the personal reactions of the critic were never entirely missing and often added interest for the reader. This was especially true of the dramatic criticisms, for example, the criticisms of George Jean Nathan and more recently those of the English critic, Kenneth Tynan.[12] F. R. Leavis re-

---

[10] Jarrell, Randall. *Poetry and The Age*. p. 63–86.
[11] Burke, Kenneth. 2nd ed. p. 62.
[12] Nathan, George Jean. *The Theatre of the Fifties*. Tynan, Kenneth. *Curtains: Selections from the Drama Criticism and Related Writings.*

vealed his personal reactions in much of his criticism of English literature, and Alfred Kazin's reviews of contemporary American literature often resembled the personal essay.[13]

The process of careful analysis of literature along with an attempt to identify with the writer at work was a useful concept for the oral interpreter of literature. Emotional sensitivity to art requires the development of a critical taste which is the result of careful study and analytical thought. In addition there must be a certain vitality—an aliveness. It is not enough to analyze, the reader must be able to recreate some of the original energy of the artist.

THE GROWTH OF SPEECH EDUCATION. Education was affected by all the forces mentioned above. Immediately after the war, the colleges and universities were flooded by ex-soldiers who added a new maturity to the student population. The faculties of these institutions were stimulated and also taxed by these men who were eager to prepare themselves for good jobs. It was a period of self-appraisal and self-analysis for educators. The growth in the number of students was phenomenal and inevitable. It seemed that the inflation which the economists deplored had a counterpart in education. How could the educator safeguard the idea of education as a process of self-development for the "good life" against a materialistic philosophy that demanded that every graduate be prepared to make a good living?

Speech departments were challenged to train more people for more diverse positions. To the training of teachers, lawyers, preachers, and actors was added training for specialized positions in speech therapy, in radio and TV. Although not a new area, Speech Science became one of the most popular fields in speech. A pattern of proliferation of courses and increased specialization was followed in the other areas. Departments grew in size, but at the same time the lines of division became clearer.

The problems of growth and specialization and the relationship of Speech to other disciplines became a concern of the Speech Association of America. An *ad hoc* committee was formed to make recommendations and, as a result of the committee's report, the constitution was revised. One change provided for the formation of small interest groups within the organization, each with some administrative functions. The new constitution was adopted at the national convention in 1954.[14] The Oral Interpretation Interest Group was the first of many which were formed

---

[13] Leavis, F. R. *Two Cultures? The Significance of C. P. Snow.* Kazin, Alfred. *Contemporaries.*

[14] Jeffrey, Robert C. "The History of the Speech Association of America, 1914–1964." *Quarterly Journal of Speech.* 50:442 (1964). The name *Speech Association of America* was adopted at the 1945 convention.

to discuss common problems, plan convention programs, and serve as a clearing-house for new ideas.[15]

Although specialization had caused the withdrawal of two groups from the parent organization,[16] the membership in the Speech Association of America grew steadily: in 1940 it was 3,265 and in 1963, 6,775. In 1964, this organization celebrated its Golden Anniversary and honored the seventeen men who formed it with the purpose "of promoting research in Speech and improvement of the teaching of the discipline."[17]

Between 1940 and 1965, many separate speech departments were formed, and those well-established celebrated anniversaries. The University of Michigan carries the distinction of having the first speech department offering credit-bearing courses; a fiftieth anniversary celebration was held in 1942. Thomas Clarkson Trueblood, the founder, participated in the celebration.[18] In 1965, universities and colleges were accustomed to separate speech departments. If a division occurred, it was usually not a speech department leaving the English department but a split within the speech department itself. There were some examples of speech clinics finding homes in medical schools or of theatres becoming part of fine arts departments. In its growth, the speech department mothered many different kinds of study: art at one end and technical science at the other. It was obvious that the speech department poached on many fields "with the eye of doing what other groups were not in the position to do: apply the knowledge of human communication."[19]

[15] This group was authorized by the Executive Committee in 1952. Helen G. Hicks was the first chairman and planned the oral interpretation programs for the 1953 national convention.
[16] The American Speech and Hearing Association was formed in 1933, and the American Educational Theatre Association in 1936.
[17] Jeffrey. *op. cit.* p. 444.
[18] Program of Speech Honors Assembly held April 24, 1942, in the Lydia Mendelssohn Theatre on the campus of the University of Michigan.
[19] Jeffrey. *op. cit.* p. 442.

CHAPTER II

ORAL INTERPRETATION STRENGTHENS ITS POSITION IN THE LIBERAL ARTS

Oral interpretation was always an integral part of the speech curriculum. At the first meeting in 1915 of the National Association of Academic Teachers of Public Speaking, Maude May Babcock spoke on the subject, "Interpretative Presentation versus Impersonative Presentation." Although this subject continued to be discussed and may never be ignored, the significance of the discussion lay in the early effort to limit and define oral interpretation. From the beginning, the emphasis was placed upon the intellectual activity involved and not upon entertainment values, and only after long experience were teachers convinced that the two were compatible. Making the words come to life and allowing the author to speak clearly was the general aim of the academic courses in interpretation.

In 1940, Gertrude Johnson, a teacher of long experience, stated her belief that teachers of oral interpretation should have a longer and more adequate training than had previously been required. "Persons who wish to teach interpretation," she said, "should have as complete knowledge of English literature as those who are to teach in the latter field, . . ."[1]

In the forties, although oral interpretation had a fairly firm position in the undergraduate program, few graduate students were able to do their work in this field. Usually, if they were interested in oral interpretation, they majored in English or in the theatre. Within the subsequent years, the master's degree became a requisite for the teacher in many academic positions, and the Ph.D. degree was rapidly becoming necessary for the teacher in colleges and universities. With the demand for well-trained teachers as the impetus, established teachers presented the case for graduate work in oral interpretation. In 1949, Wallace Bacon made such a plea, pointing out the relationship to other fields of inquiry: English, foreign languages, philosophy, esthetics, psychology, and history. He suggested graduate studies be: critical analyses of literary texts in preparation for reading, studies in prosody, bibliographical studies, and historical research. "The exact balance of fine scholarship and fine oral skill," he said, ". . . is the goal toward which the work in

---

[1] Johnson, Gertrude E., ed. *Studies in the Art of Interpretation.* p. 5.

interpretation ought to move."[2] In 1965, Klyn urged more scholarly work, suggesting experimental research for this area of speech.[3]

Eighty-five Ph.D. degrees were granted in the field of oral interpretation by 1966, of which five were awarded before 1940. According to Simon, in 1949, eight-hundred eighty-five Master's degrees and forty-seven Ph.D.s had been awarded in Speech.[4] In 1966, *Speech Monographs* reported that the total had risen to twenty-two thousand, seven hundred and eleven M.A. degrees and three thousand and sixty-seven Ph.D. degrees. Oral Interpretation was credited with a modest two percent of the total. The research journal, *Speech Monographs,* published first in 1934, was important in encouraging research and in keeping the membership informed of the various fields of investigation that are important to teachers and students.

As the number of graduate students increased, so did the offerings in the curriculum. Many courses designed for the study of one author or of one form were added to the basic course of oral interpretation: for example, "Interpretation of Shakespeare" and "Oral Interpretation of Modern Poetry." Courses for teacher preparation in the history of the subject, in studies in literary criticism as it relates to oral interpretation, and in readers theatre were added to many curricula. In some institutions, courses in oral interpretation were required of students being trained as English teachers, and many English offerings were required of students majoring in Speech; especially was this true of graduate students in oral interpretation. It is believed that as a result of these requirements, there was more cooperation and respect shown between the departments of English and Speech than ever before.

One of the most encouraging developments was the inclusion of oral interpretation as an elective satisfying the humanities requirement in many liberal arts programs. The remarkable growth in this subject at the University of California, Berkeley, was due to this status. Wilson credited good teaching for part of the expansion but explained that it was also due to "the adoption of an approach to Oral Interpretation which serves the liberal arts college and furthers the aims of general education."[5] Don Geiger, a member of the same department, in an article entitled "Oral Interpretation in the Liberal Arts Context," discussed the

[2] Bacon, Wallace. "Graduate Studies in Interpretation." *Quarterly Journal of Speech.* 35:316–319 (1949).

[3] Klyn, Mark S. "Potentials for Research in Oral Interpretation." *Western Speech.* 29:108–114 (Spring 1965).

[4] Simon, Clarence T., "Graduate Studies in Speech." *Quarterly Journal of Speech.* 36:462–470 (Dec. 1950). Since 1946, in addition to the annual report of advanced degrees awarded, abstracts of dissertations and a listing of works in progress have been added in *Speech Monographs.* See Appendix for report of research in the History of Oral Interpretation.

[5] Wilson, Garff B. "The Growth of Oral Interpretation at the University of California." *Speech Teacher.* 1:187–192 (1952).

emphasis upon literature and its analysis and justified the appointment of creative writers as teachers.[6] Although vocal techniques were always important, they were subordinated to concern for the literature.

Although it is reported in *Speech Monographs,* August, 1966, that forty-eight institutions grant Ph.D. degrees in speech, only eighteen grant the degree in oral interpretation. The School of Speech, Northwestern University, claims the largest number. This is not surprising because it offers the largest program of courses. In the 1965 catalogue, twelve courses are listed, including "Interpretation of Biography and History," "Studies in Individual Styles," and "Chamber Theatre."[7] The research contributed has been chiefly in the history of the teaching of oral interpretation and in the critical analysis of literature. A good example of the latter is Trissolini's "An Analysis of the Structure of Hart Crane's *The Bridge.*"[8] A few departments have encouraged scientific inquiries in the psychological and sociological implications of the oral reading of literature.[9] There are other related fields, for example, linguistics and aesthetics, which suggest new directions for research.

The phenomenon of creativity, the character of artistic talent, and the qualities of an aesthetic appreciation of art are not clearly understood, and many studies of audience participation in the public reading of literature are still to be made. It is probably safe to assume, however, that the majority of teachers regard their field as one of artistic rather than scientific endeavor, but undoubtedly would be happy to make use of any research findings which were applicable.

TEXTBOOKS. A number of textbooks were written during this period, especially during the last fifteen years. As in other periods, textbooks give a kind of overview of the work done in the classroom and a glimpse of the different approaches used by the teachers. Marcoux concluded from a study of textbooks, articles, and theses written from 1950 to 1963 that there was more agreement than disagreement concerning principles and that theories of interpretation had become standardized. There was, however, a noticeable difference in the emphasis given to

---

[6] Geiger, Don. *Quarterly Journal of Speech.* 40:137–144 (1954).

[7] Chamber theatre was developed by Robert Breen, Northwestern University to present prose narratives in a dramatic manner with the narrator as an important performer.

[8] Trissolini, Anthony, "An Analysis of the Structure of Hart Crane's *The Bridge"* Unpublished Ph.D. dissertation, Northwestern University, 1959.

[9] See

Brooks, Keith and Wulftange, Sr. I. Marie, "Listener Response to Oral Interpretation." *Speech Monographs* 31:73–75 (1964).
Snidecor, John C. "An Objective Study of Phrasing in Impromptu Reading and Oral Reading." *Speech Monographs* 11:97–104 (1944).
Shepherd, John R. and Scheidel, Thomas M. "A Study of Personality Configuration of Effective Oral Readers." *Speech Monographs* 23:298–304 (1956).
Cobin, Martin T. and Clevenger, Theodore Jr. "Television Instruction, Course Content, and Teaching Experience Level: An Experimental Study in the Basic Course in Oral Interpretation." *Speech Monographs* 28:16–20 (1961).

different parts of the whole process.[10] The agreement lay in the general purpose defined as illuminating literature for the reader and for the listener. The differences were found in the manner of preparation to accomplish this objective. The distinctions were similar to those made between the Natural and Mechanical Schools in that, again, the purpose was the same but the methods were different. Consequently the approach of the textbook writer determined what the various emphases would be.

Continuity in the history of this subject has depended upon the carrying on, as of a family tradition, the most worthwhile and serviceable methods and concepts. Three old books were revised during this period, which is a testimony to the soundness of their theories and practice. S. H. Clark's *Interpretation of the Printed Page,* first published in 1915, was revised by Maud May Babcock in 1940. It discussed the importance of discovering the exact meaning and attitude of the author through attention to grouping of words, sequence and subordination of ideas, construction of paragraphs, and denotation and connotation of words. *The Art of Interpretative Speech* by Charles H. Woolbert and Severina Nelson was first published in 1927, later in 1934, and 1945. The fourth edition appeared in 1956 and the fifth is promised for 1967.[11] Wayland Maxfield Parrish's *Reading Aloud,* 1932, exerted great influence in the previous period and continues to do so in this period. A fourth edition was published in 1966. Often the revision of a textbook means primarily changing the literary selections.

An effort has been made to facilitate the discussion of the new textbooks by dividing them according to three different approaches and selecting representative books for each group. The first approach will be termed *traditional;* it is concerned primarily with training students to become effective readers. The *communicative* approach describes those textbooks which emphasize the experience of literature and its recreation for an audience. The third approach, the *literary,* emphasizes the literature and finds some of the theories of modern literary criticism applicable to oral interpretation. There is much overlapping between the three groups and the division is useful mainly to show the effect of other disciplines.

The four textbooks selected to show the traditional approach with its emphasis upon improving the techniques of oral reading are: Sara Lowrey and Gertrude E. Johnson, *Interpretative Reading: Techniques and Selections,* 1942, second edition 1953; Lionel C. Crocker and Louis M. Eich, *Oral Reading,* 1947; Otis J. Aggert and Elbert R. Bowen,

---

[10] Marcoux, Paul Albert. Abstract of dissertation. *Speech Monographs.* 32:288–289 (1965).
[11] Letter from Martin S. Stanford of Appleton-Century-Crofts dated December 21, 1965. He states that the book has sold well over a 100,000 copies. The new edition will contain more than one-third new selections from literature.

Communicative Reading, 1956, second edition 1963 ; Joseph F. Smith and James R. Linn, *Skill in Reading Aloud,* 1960. All stress the stimulation of the imagination through sensory imagery, as a key to the emotional meaning, and the understanding of words and their relationships to each other and to the whole as the way to logical meaning. Many suggestions and selections are given to assist the student in learning to control pitch, quality, time, and emphasis, and for developing freedom of movement. As the title of one book suggests, communication with an audience is the reason for interpretative reading. The definition given in *Communicative Reading* is representative of the credo of these teachers and perhaps of all teachers : "Interpretative reading is the communication of the reader's impression of the author's ideas and feelings to the eyes and ears of an audience so that the audience understands the ideas, experiences the feelings, and appreciates the author's literary skill."[12] The traditional approach has always emphasized training to perfect skill in delivery, but this does not exclude from the textbooks considered discussions of the different forms of literature and the new developments in various kinds of group readings and lecture recitals.

The second group shows the influence of behavioral psychology. They discuss the communicative importance of oral interpretation in giving a literary experience reality for an audience. Some books show the influence of modern theories of aesthetics and, to a lesser degree, linguistics. Martin Cobin, in *Theory and Technique of Interpretation,* 1959, is concerned with the manner in which "signaling units" of speech, vocal sounds and visual actions, handle the lexical, functional, and acoustic values of language. He suggests that when other methods of discovering the meaning fails an analysis of the language might be helpful. Two chapters of the book are devoted to methods of linquistic study. The main emphasis of the book is upon the student's responsiveness to literature and his skill in stimulating comparable responses in others.

Chloe Armstrong and Paul Brandes, in *Oral Interpretation of Literature,* 1963, assert that oral reading of literature can make a contribution to the larger province of communication. The emphasis is on the effect of oral interpretation upon human behavior. The titles of the first two chapters indicate the relationship to the communication theory : "How does oral reading affect human behavior ?" and "How does the oral reader prepare himself to modify human behavior ?" It is important that the experience of the writer be transferred to the listener. Not only

[12] Aggert and Bowen. 2nd ed. p. 6. See Appendix for information concerning publication of other textbooks.

are the questions Who? What? Where? and To Whom? asked, but the student is urged to study the life of the author, his other writings, and critical comments on his work. The preparation must be as thorough as possible, if the interpreter is to influence the behavior of others.

Another textbook with an emphasis upon communication is *Literature as Experience,* 1959, written by Wallace Bacon and Robert Breen. The experience of reading literature as an analogue of human life is discussed; to understand the nature of man's literature it is necessary to know something about the nature of man himself. The theory, therefore, is basically a psychological one and rests heavily on the concept that man can and does adapt himself to different experiences. "The whole social process is a continuous modification and restraint of primitive impulses and drives in which man's emotional life becomes inextricably associated with his sense of values. Literature is concerned with man's emotional evaluation of human experience."[13]

The section which is attributed to Bacon states that literature by its very nature modifies, clarifies, and extends experience. But as an art form it is unique and must not be considered identical with either writer or reader. The manner of communication is stressed as important.

In *Interpretation: Reader, Writer, Audience,* 1961, Wilma H. Grimes and Alethea S. Mattingly present a good blend of the communicative and the literary approach. The purpose of the book is stated as "an aid and guide to the full understanding of literature, to the aesthetic appreciation of the arts of literature and interpretation, and to the attainment of bodily and vocal skills for the communication of meanings of literature."[14] They subscribe, as do others in this group, to the belief that all art is an organization of experience and that the reader's experience and that of his audience may be highly important as an educative and recreative process.

The books selected as representative of the literary approach are: Charlotte Lee, *Oral Interpretation,* 1952, 3rd edition, 1965; Don Geiger, *The Sound, Sense, and Performance of Literature,* 1963; Wallace A. Bacon, *The Art of Interpretation,* 1966; and Robert Beloof, *The Performing Voice in Literature,* 1966. In these textbooks, the emphasis is upon the exploration of literature rather than upon its communication to an audience. The New Criticism has contributed much to the theories of these teachers, and the poet (he is usually the representative for all writers) is viewed as a maker and consolidator of experience. Thus the art object is unique and self-contained, and, in order to be understood, its design must be observed in all its essential parts. Because the writer,

[13] Bacon and Breen. p. 39, 120.
[14] Grimes and Mattingly. p. vii.

especially is this true of the modern poet, often depends upon shifts in tone, upon irony and suggestion, upon symbol and indirection, rather than upon logical development and direct statement, he often presents the reader with a kind of puzzle. For this reason, the explication of the text became the basis of modern literary criticism, and these teachers of oral interpretation find it useful. The questions the critic asked, about the voice speaking, to whom? and for what purpose? are those that the interpreter must ask if he is to solve the puzzle.

The new theories of criticism with their stress on attitudes, tonal qualities, and the dramatistic character of literature developed rather slowly. The need that begot them, according to Ray B. West, was the absence of background myth or established moral order in which writers of other ages worked and a consequent lack of communal awareness. Because of this lack, it was necessary to rely upon the private sensibility of the artist himself. The critic must "educate himself in every possible technique for discovery and examination of the 'private' and often 'unconscious' intention."[15]

Although oral interpretation may well be the last step in the explication of the text, both Geiger and Beloof warn against equating the two. The teachers in this group, although interested in the work of the critic, prefer to develop their own perspective. It is possible to become so involved in critical techniques that the literature and its appreciation take a back seat, and sometimes the critic becomes a kind of symbol hunter.[16] The example of Robert Frost, forced to deny that his poem "Dust of Snow" revealed a death wish but is rather a celebration of his joy in existence, warned teachers that it is quite possible to make a simple poem complex and to read into it meaning that is not there.[17]

The emphasis upon the attitude, the tone of voice, and the relationship of the speaker to the situation was easy for the oral interpreter to accept. An interest in the theory of symbolic language as presented by the philosopher and critic, Kenneth Burke, is found in some textbooks. Thompson and Fredericks, in *Oral Interpretation of Fiction: A Dramatistic Approach*, 1964, are deeply indebted to this source and use dramatic terms—scene, role, gesture—in their analysis of literature. Geiger devotes one chapter to the dramatic analysis of literature.[18]

Charlotte Lee, although not an avowed follower of any theory of criticism, focuses attention on the different forms of literature—prose, poetry, and drama—and the need for an analysis of organization, struc-

[15] West, Ray B ., ed. *Essays in Modern Literary Criticism.* p. 324–325.
[16] Geiger, Don. *The Sound, Sense, and Performance of Literature.* p. 10, 76.
[17] Beloof, Robert. "Explicative Analysis" in *The Oral Study of Literature,* ed. by Thomas O. Sloan. p. 75.
[18] Geiger, Don. *op. cit.* Chap. 6.

ture, and style. She follows Cornelius Carmen Cunningham,[19] a former teacher, in stressing an analysis which would appraise the intrinsic and extrinsic factors of literary art: the intrinsic factors of unity and harmony, variety and contrast, balance and proportion, and rhythm; the extrinsic factors of universality, individuality, and association. Lee devotes two chapters to the training of the voice and body. A close rapport is maintained with the student. In the third edition, the selected materials were changed noticeably, and supplementary lists of related books, many of them on literary criticism, were placed at the ends of chapters. The text itself remains much the same.

In *The Art of Interpretation,* Bacon followed the same emphasis upon literature, dividing the book into three sections: "Principles of Interpretation," "Analysis of Literature" and "Special Kinds and Modes of Interpretation." He followed his theory of interpretation as experience as stated in the earlier book with Breen. In this book, the term "presence" is used to indicate the experiencial relationship to the *persona* in the literature. Although he gives no space to training the voice and the body, he seems to assume that the interpreter must have the necessary techniques. A trend is indicated in this omission and perhaps shows that this kind of discussion is not so necessary as it once was, since classes in voice and diction may well be prerequisites for courses in oral interpretation. Both Lee and Bacon give attention to group readings—readers theatre and chamber theatre—and the peculiar demands which these forms make. They both considered "character placement" a necessary technique, especially when reading dialogue.

The textbook which presents the most eclectic approach is Robert Beloof's *The Performing Voice in Literature.* His concept of the reader tuning his voice and body to the text which he has carefully analyzed colours the text throughout. He followed the others in believing that literary criticism is a necessary adjunct to the teaching of oral interpretation and credits I. A. Richards with making teachers aware that students have little trouble with basic, biologically oriented tones of hate, love, greed, and pain, but miss the tones of irony, ambiguity which is deliberate, and other complex attitudes. Beloof believed that when the tone was discovered, it was necessary to become involved bodily in order to have a sympathetic understanding. Literary analysis must have a unity of mind and body. And since he believed with Burke that language is gesture, he states that the only logical conclusion of the literary

---

[19] Cunningham, C. C. *Literature as a Fine Art,* Early in the period Cunningham and Frank R. Rarig emphasized the relationship between aesthetics and oral interpretation. See Frank R. Rarig. "Some Elementary Contribution of Aesthetics to Interpretative Speech." *Quarterly Journal of Speech.* 24:527–39 (Dec. 1940).

analysis of a piece of literature is "an oral, a living expression of the text."[20]

This book contains a wide selection of literature with a balance between the old and the new. Reference to a selection is made many times in order to assure a deeper study of the selection. One novel idea proposed is that the terms "fiction" and "fictive" be used to refer to all literature which is not factual reporting but the result of creative imagination and that prose and poetry be treated together not as separate forms. The same desire to unify, to relate, to see the parts but make them function together smoothly is necessary for writer, critic, and reader. Beloof believes that help must be found in a number of places, that along with literary criticism the student should be aware of the philogical, biographical, and historical backgrounds that may shed light on literature.

The teachers who have been included in the literary approach see their discipline as an educative and aesthetic one. Geiger states that the teacher's job is often "to help the student participate imaginatively in what he does not like, or what is, in many particulars, foreign to his experience. This is to share in the task of the humanities."[21]

There was enough difference in approach and enough misunderstanding about procedure among the textbook writers and teachers of this period to have caused some to think themselves in opposition. The traditionalists feared that oral interpretation might become too "literary" and lose the ground it had gained, and comments that certain research problems had nothing to do with oral interpretation were sometimes heard in convention corridors. But the agreements far outweighted the differences. Sometimes it was a matter of using new names for old ideas, and generally it was a case of drawing upon another field for new approaches to an old subject. It must be considered salutory that in this period we have listened to many other voices and that we are living nearer, if not under the same roof, with those whose lives are devoted to the study of literature.

READING PROGRAMS. Although lecture recitals and reading programs were never discontinued, and public recitals were required in many departments of seniors and/or M.A. candidates, the professional reader had almost disappeared until the middle forties. Charles Laughton is usually credited with the revival. He said that he began giving programs in hospitals to salve a feeling of uselessness during the war but continued because of the unusually warm reception he received from both general

---

[20] Beloof, Robert. p. 12.
[21] Geiger, Don. *op. cit.* p. 76.

and college audiences.[22] His program was miscellaneous, including stories from the Bible as well as modern materials. Although he used the actor's skill in convincing the audience that he was selecting materials on the spur of the moment, when the program was carefully planned, and in using his full range of vocal skill, he did not lose his identity as Charles Laughton, the reader.

In the nineteenth century, two literary personages, Charles Dickens and Mark Twain, delighted audiences with readings, usually from their own books. These performances were revived. Emelyn Williams impersonated Dickens and used a replica of the red plush reading-stand he had used. Mark Twain was presented again by Hal Holbrook in *Mark Twain, Tonight,* which was well received in the early fifties and revived in New York in 1966. Both actors used careful make-up and attempted to use voice and gesture that recalled the original performer. When Williams gave a memorial program of Dylan Thomas' stories and poems, however, he made no attempt at impersonation—too many people remembered Thomas' readings. He appeared before a screen on which appeared Dylan Thomas' signature and held an armful of worn copybooks to suggest the poet's early years. He titled his program, *A Boy Growing Up.* He chose the manner of presentation appropriate for his subject.

Sir John Gielgud arranged a program of readings from Shakespeare which was very popular in England and America and was taped for educational TV. He used no costumes or staging except appropriate lighting. The drama critics appreciated his performance and recognized it as a different kind of entertainment. Clurman remarked that Gielgud was an "actor of high rank but his readings are *readings;* they are not acting."[23]

It is not surprising that reading programs became popular on college campuses. Professor Baxter gave afternoon readings of Shakespeare at the University of Southern California which were well received and later televised. Many poets gave programs of their own poetry, and recordings were generally available. The Y.M.H.A. in New York gave a series of readings, including poets and prose writers, that was supported by subscription. But for teachers of interpretation the most interesting development was the series of reading hours sponsored by departments of English and/or Speech. These programs usually included as readers both professors and students.[24] At the University of Colorado such a series

[22] Laughton, Charles. *Tell Me A Story.* p. 1–2.
[23] Clurman, Harold. *The Nation.* 188:39 (1959). See also, Linn, James R. L. "A Historical Study of Oral Interpretation in London 1951–1962." *Speech Monographs.* 21:288; and Keith Brooks. "Readers Theatre as Defined by New York Critics." *Southern Speech Journal.* 29:288–302 (1964).
[24] McCoard, William B. "An Interpretation of the Times." *Quarterly Journal of Speech.* 35:489–495 (1949).

has flourished for ten years; the programs are held on Tuesday afternoons in the Student Union and draw a sizeable audience from the town as well as from the university.

Readers Theatre, sometimes called The Interpreters Theatre, developed in the Fifties. Again Charles Laughton led the way with The Quartette—Charles Boyer, Agnes Moorhead, Cedric Hardwick, and Laughton—reading the third act of Shaw's *Man and Superman.* It was titled *Don Juan in Hell.* This program was given in both commercial theatres and college auditoriums across the country and later in Great Britain. The readers sat on stools before reading stands. The emphasis was upon the play. Later, Laughton directed *John Brown's Body,* a program based upon the epic poem by Stephen Vincent Benét. In this presentation he used three readers, who read from reading stands, and a reading chorus of twenty voices. Since that time, many group-readings both professional and amateur have entertained audiences who found they could accept the absence of full theatrical production and enjoy the literature itself. It was not a substitute for the conventional theatre but a different form of entertainment.[25]

Many students and some professors who were unable to participate in the university theatre found readers theatre a good substitute. Teachers of oral interpretation welcomed not only the opportunity for good training in reading before an audience but also the chance for experimentation in the arrangement of materials and the manner of presentation. There were discussions of techniques, many of them deriving from the definition of oral interpretation, but no strict rules were formed. Some teachers warned that the reader must not impersonate. Others forbade interplay between readers; characters are placed in the mind of the audience, not on the stage. Other directors believed that the manner of presentation must fit the material and allowed freedom of movement. Sometimes suggestions of costume and setting were used. Since the visual and the aural experiences are interrelated, it is possible for the mind to slip easily from one to the other. For this reason, some directors insisted that the scene for readers theatre might well shift from the stage to the audience from time to time, without the audience being aware, and to the advantage of the interpretation as a whole. Perhaps the most valuable advice for directors and readers was to suit the technique to the genre being interpreted.[26]

Readers theatre will probably continue to brighten the professional stage. It has already become an approved and recommended activity for

[25] Coger, Irene. "Interpreter's Theatre: Theatre of the Mind." *Quarterly Journal of Speech.* 49:157–164 (1963).
[26] Kleinau, Marion L. and Marvin D. "Scene Location in Readers Theatre: Static or Dynamic?" *Speech Teacher.* 14:193–199 (1965).

students and has given new interest to classes in oral interpretation of literature. The primary aim will always be to increase the understanding of and appreciation for literature, but the desire to train readers who can make oral interpretation a performing art in lecture recital or other solo performances and in group readings is compatible with this aim. It is hoped that teachers and students will continue to be experimental in their design of programs, that the emphasis upon the *word* will continue, and that there be a minimum of attention to external effects.

If the reader is obscured by too elaborate staging or if he is displayed at the expense of the author he is reading, the whole discipline will suffer. Our history is filled with examples of misguided training which resulted in exhibition rather than in interpretation. The focus must be on the literature and it must be worthy of time and effort on the part of the reader and the listener.

SUMMARY. Many changes were evident in higher education during the last twenty-five years; they reflected those taking place in all areas of American life. The advance of science and the improvement in technological processes led to more standardization but, on the other hand, stimulated growth and diversity of cultural opportunities. It was a period of anxiety and of criticism because humane values seemed threatened by scientific and mechanical progress.

Although lagging a bit, the arts and the humanities became more concerned with finding a secure place in the cultural pattern. Teachers of Speech looked for relationships with other fields and found many of them contributory to a better understanding of their students and their subject-matter. Oral interpretation benefited by graduate research that drew upon these fields for knowledge and stimulation. More courses were offered in oral interpretation, many of them in special fields of literature.

In this period, oral interpretation enjoyed a revival of interest in performances for public entertainment. As a performing art, solo-reading and group-reading entered both the professional and the amateur stage. Oral interpretation widened its base and increased its influence in the liberal arts curriculum.

CONCLUSION

The historical study of the methods used in teaching Oral Interpretation in the colleges and universities reveals four important facts: (1) Oral Interpretation has had a continuous history as a part of the training of American students; (2) The background of the times has influenced the curriculum and has changed the form and the methods used in teaching this particular subject; (3) There has been a gradual evolution of methods; (4) Oral Interpretation has a contribution to make in the area of the liberal arts.

The study of Oral Interpretation shows that it began as an emphasis upon that part of Rhetoric known as "pronuntiatio." The need for better delivery, especially among the clergy, and the desire to find adequate notations to record speech were the main influences which produced the Elocutionary School in England. This school soon developed two methods of teaching delivery: the Natural School under the leadership of Sheridan and the Mechanical school under the leadership of Walker. The first group looked to nature for examples of good technique and based its methods upon an imitation of *natural* speech forms, such as conversational variations in pitch, force, time, and quality. The Mechanical school devised many rules and notations and postulated the idea that if the rules were carefully followed the techniques of good oral communication could be learned and also recorded for future students. However, the two methods were never distinct one from the other. Both Sheridan and Walker wanted speech to seem natural. Gradually there was a merging of ideas, and the concept that the reader must understand and appreciate what he reads and that his technique must be motivated from within became generally accepted. The mechanical devices for the reader might be used successfully at times, but only as they contributed to the interpretation.

Higher education has tried to keep pace with the changing demands placed upon it. It has expanded from the idea that only a few leaders should be educated in the colleges and universities to mass education and now offers many different kinds of practical training instead of the disciplinary program of the old liberal arts studies. The whole process has been democratized and the curriculum enlarged to meet the diverse needs of a large and heterogeneous group of students. The two philosophies of education, one that education is the passing down of the wisdom of the past, the other that it is the development of the individual to his fullest potentialities, have guided the educators in shaping different kinds of curricula. The latter philosophy has been the more important in present-day education. Adult education has become a part of the program, and preparation for leisure an accepted responsibility. Oral Interpretation has responded to the different demands made upon it, and the methods of teaching it have responded to the latest scientific findings, especially in physiology and psychology. It has become more specialized as the curriculum has enlarged and has passed from specific emphasis upon entertainment values to an emphasis upon its function as a vitalizing and satisfying way of understanding and appreciating literature.

The five periods into which the study is divided show steps in the evolution of the methods used in teaching Oral Interpretation. In the first period, the English elocutionists directed the growth of a separate course in the teaching of delivery as an adjunct to Rhetoric. The Natural school defined its method rather hazily and depended either upon a lack ,of method or an imitation of nature. The Mechanical school taught by rules and notations. Many rules were based upon grammatical constructions; rules for gesture found their basis in the analysis of the outward manifestation of emotion. Practice of elementary exercises was required.

During the second period, the beginnings of scientific inquiry and the desire on the part of teachers to base their art upon scientific rules evolved. Since science in its beginnings was primarily interested in the isolation of facts and the classification of them, the science of the voice was chiefly an elaborate scheme of labeling. Dr. Rush's *Philosophy of the Human Voice* was the first attempt to study the voice scientifically. It was really not a textbook but a scientific treatise, which was most important because it influenced the majority of writers from 1827 to 1870.

The third period witnessed more variation than any other. Delsarte's system, which was neatly worked out in formula, was perhaps the most original, different and extravagant, of any plans for training the elocutionist. It was in vogue chiefly in the latter part of the nineteenth century. The Mechanical school was continued. Alexander Melville Bell was its outstanding teacher; he established a fairly successful compromise between the Natural and Mechanical schools. The philosophy of pragmatism and the new psychology were the most potent factors in designing pedagogical methods. Even the mechanical emphasis included some consideration of the importance of mental processes necessary for good interpretation. However, it was the Natural school which accepted most wholeheartedly the concept of monism. From Curry, with his principle of "thinking the thought," to Clark, who believed in the validity of shifting the emphasis from the reading techniques to the appreciation of the intellectual and emotional content, there were many other variations of the same school. It presaged modern methods of teaching Oral Interpretation of Literature.

Speech became a separate department in many colleges and universities during the fourth period. Oral Interpretation became an important subject independent of rhetoric or dramatic production; in fact, specialization began in almost all areas within the speech field. The methods used in teaching put an emphasis upon the careful, analytical study of the literature to be read. The textbooks shifted from preparing entertainers to stimulating interpreters of literature.

In the last period, Oral Interpretation improved its academic status. A noteworthy amount of research was done in this field. The purpose continued to be that of improving skill in reading so that the reader and the audience might have a greater appreciation for literature, but the study itself was deepened and made more complex through alliances with outside fields, such as aesthetics and literary criticism. There was a general belief that oral interpretation made a significant contribution toward strengthening the arts and humanities in the educational program of the United States.

It is well to remember that the oral presentation of poetry and prose preceded all written literature and that man naturally tells stories and responds to rhythmical expressions of emotion. What is called the Oral Interpretation of Literature is really an attempt to recreate the spontaneous and lively quality that the written word often seems to lose. If in this book the history of the teaching of oral interpretation seems to show the subject as a part of classical rhetoric or as a handmaiden to both written and oral expression, this is only a part of its larger history. And using a wider angle for a view of Man as he attempts to convey his experiences or those of his people to other men, it becomes clear that it is impossible to separate the manner from the matter, or as Yeats says, "to know the dancer from the dance."

APPENDIX

The following bibliography of the history of oral interpretation is offered as a supplement to the text. It is divided in three parts: dissertations and theses, articles from the three primary speech journals, and textbooks and reference books. The material is arranged chronologically so that the reader can easily survey the work that has been done during the period 1940–1965, with a few items from 1966 for good measure.

I. DISSERTATIONS AND THESES

Virginia Morris, *The Influence of Delsarte Philosophy of Expression as Revealed through the Lectures of Steele Mackaye*. M.A. thesis, Louisiana State University, 1941.

Lester Leonard Hale, *Re-evaluation of the Vocal Philosophy of Dr. James Rush as Based on a Study of His Sources*. Ph.D. dissertation, Louisiana State University, 1942.

Helen K. Philips, *The Influence of Samuel Silas Curry on Modern Interpretation Textbooks*. M.A. thesis, University of Alabama, 1942.

George Albert Neely, *The School of Delsarte*. M.A. thesis, Louisiana State University, 1942.

Anne Christine Drake, *The Elocutionary Theories of S. S. Curry and Their Application*. M.A. thesis, Louisiana State University, 1943.

Gail Jordan Tousey, *The Elocutionary Teachings of William Holmes McGuffey*. M.A. thesis, Louisiana State University, 1946.

Rayda W. Dillport, *The Pupils of Delsarte*. M.A. thesis, Louisiana State University, 1946.

James J. Barry, *Ralph Brownell Dennis, Lecturer, Interpreter, and Dean of the School of Speech*. M.A. thesis, Northwestern University, 1947.

Milton Joel Wiksell, *Social Aspects of Nineteenth Century American Elocution*. Ph.D. dissertation, Louisiana State University, 1948.

Frederick L. Kolch, *The Philosophies of Elocution in the Nineteenth Century*. M.A. thesis, Wayne State University, 1949.

Daniel E. R. Vandraegen, *The Natural School of Oral Reading in England 1748–1828*. Ph.D. dissertation, Northwestern University, 1949.

John B. Newman, *Joshua Steele: Prosody in Speech Education*. Ph.D. dissertation, New York University, 1950.

Edyth Renshaw, *Three Schools of Speech: The Emerson College of Oratory, The School of Expression, and The Leland Powers School of the Spoken Word*. Ph.D. dissertation, Columbia University, 1950.

Helen Pauline Roach, *History of Speech Education at Columbia College 1754–1940*. Ph.D. dissertation, Columbia University, 1950.

Dugan Laird, *American and English Theories in the Natural Tradition of Oral Reading 1880–1915*. Ph.D. dissertation, Northwestern University, 1952.

Kenneth Burns, *A Survey of the Contemporary Outlook Relative to the Basic Aspects of Oral Interpretation as it is Evidenced in Selected Writings in the Field*. Ph.D. dissertation, Northwestern University, 1952.

Frances E. Bowyer, *James Murdoch, the Elocutionist*. M.A. thesis, University of Colorado, 1952.

Leslie Irene Coger, *A Comparison for the Oral Interpreter of the Teaching Methods of Curry and Stanislavsky*. Ph.D. dissertation, Northwestern University, 1952.

Stanley A. Weintraub, *A Comparison of Textbooks in Oral Interpretation of Literature 1760–1952*. Ph.D. dissertation, Columbia University, 1953.

Alethea Smith Mattingly, *The Mechanical School of Oral Reading in England 1761–1821*. Ph.D. dissertation, Northwestern University, 1954.

Alban F. Varnado, *The Reverend Gilbert Austin's "Chironomia"*. Ph.D. dissertation, Louisiana State University, 1954.

Herbert R. Gillis, *The American College and University Literary Societies at Selected Institutions of the Mid-Atlantic Area 1875–1950*. Ph.D. dissertation, Western Reserve University, 1955.

Lloyd S. Jones, *Trends in Oral Interpretation as Seen through the Professional Journals from 1940–1955*. Ph.D. dissertation, University of Denver, 1955.

Dorothy S. Hadley, *Oral Interpretation at the Chautauqua Institution and the Chautauqua School of Expression 1874–1900*. Ph.D. dissertation, Northwestern University, 1956.

James W. Cleary, *John Bulwer's "Chirologia . . . Chironomia". A Facsimile Edition with Introduction and Notes*. Ph.D. dissertation, University of Wisconsin, 1956.

Ronald John Matlon, *The Life and Elocutionary Teaching of Jonathan Barber*. M.A. thesis, Purdue University, 1962.

Bill Rambin, *The Inventions and Innovations of Steele Mackaye*. M.A. thesis, Louisiana State University, 1962.

M. Leon Dodez, *An Examination of the Theories and Methodologies of John Walker (1732–1807) with Emphasis upon Gesturing*. Ph.D. dissertation, Ohio State University, 1963.

Nancy Hartung, *The Contributions of Hiram Corson to the Field of Oral Interpretation.* M.A. thesis, Wayne State University, 1963.

Kathleen E. Torsey, *The Application of the Tenets of Austin, Rush, and Curry by Writers of Representative Collegiate Speech Texts, 1925–1955.* Ph.D. dissertation, University of Florida, 1964.

Audrey S. Kirkland, *The Elocutionary Theory and Practice of James Edward Murdoch.* Ph.D. dissertation, Wayne State University, 1964.

J. Paul Albert Marcoux, *An Analysis of Current Trends Concerning Basic Aspects of Oral Interpretation as Evidenced in Selected Writings in the Field, 1950–1963, with Implications for Speech Education.* Ph.D. dissertation, Northwestern University, 1964.

John Hall Lamb, *John Walker: Elocutionist and Student of the English Language.* Ph.D. dissertation, University of Iowa, 1964.

Ronald Q. Frederickson, *Maud May Babcock and the Department of Elocution at the University of Utah.* M.A. thesis, University of Utah, 1965.

Edwin A. Hollatz, *The Development of Literary Societies in Selected Illinois Colleges in the 19th Century and their Role in Speech Training.* Ph.D. dissertation, Northwestern University, 1965.

II. ARTICLES FROM *The Quarterly Journal of Speech, Speech Monographs,* AND *The Speech Teacher*

Thomas Clarkson Trueblood, "Pioneering in Speech" *QJS* 27:503–511, Dec., 1941.

Mary Margaret Robb, "Looking Backward!" *QJS* 28:323–327, Oct., 1942.

Frank M. Rarig, "Ralph Dennis" *QJS* 29:234–240, April, 1943.

Giles W. Gray, "The 'Voice Qualities' in the History of Elocution" *QJS* 29:475–480, Dec., 1943.

Marion P. Robinson, "Diary of a Problem Child" *QJS* 32:357–367, Oct., 1946.

Warren Guthrie, "The Development of Rhetorical Theory in America: 1635–1850" *SM* 13:14–22, no. 1, 1946; 14:38–54, 1947; 15:61–71, no. 1, 1948; 16:98–113, no. 1, 1949.

Gail J. Tousey, "McGuffey's Elocutionary Teachings" *QJS* 34:80–87, Feb., 1948.

Warren Guthrie, "The Elocution Movement in England" *SM* 18:17–30, no. 1, 1951.

W. M. Parrish, "The Concept of 'Naturalness'" *OJS* 37:448–454, Dec., 1951.

John B. Newman, "The Phonetic Aspect of Joshua Steele's System of Prosody" *SM* 18:279–287, Nov., 1951.

W. M. Parrish, "The Burglarizing of Burghor, The Case of the Purloined Passions" *QJS* 38:431–434, Dec., 1952.

John B. Newman, "Steele's Role in American Speech Education" *SM* 20:65–73, March, 1953.

Daniel E. Vandraegen, "Thomas Sheridan and the Natural School" *SM* 20:58–64, March, 1953.

W. M. Parrish, "Elocution: A Definition and a Challenge" *QJS* 43:1–11, Feb., 1957.

Donald E. Hargis, "James Burgh and *The Art of Speaking*" *SM* 24:275–284, Nov., 1957.

Wilbur S. Howell, "Sources of the Elocutionary Movement in England: 1700–1748" *QJS* 45:1–18, Feb., 1959.

James W. Cleary, "John Bulwer: Renaissance Communication" *QJS* 45:391–398, Dec., 1959.

Nydia J. Reynolds, "It Wasn't Elocution: Five Professional Oral Interpreters, 1900–1925" *QJS* 47:244–252, Oct., 1961.

Robert C. Jeffrey, "History of the Speech Association of America 1914–1964" *QJS* 50:432–444, Dec., 1964.

Wallace A. Bacon, "The Elocutionary Career of Thomas Sheridan (1719–1788)" *SM* 31:1–53, March, 1964.

Alethea S. Mattingly, "Follow Nature: A Synthesis of Eighteenth Century Views" *SM* 31:80–84, March, 1964.

John Hall Lamb, "John Walker and Joshua Steele" *SM* 32:411–419, Nov., 1965.

GREAT TEACHERS

Severina Nelson, "Great Teacher of Speech: Charles Henry Woolbert" *ST* 4:113–117, March, 1953.

Marie Hochmuth, "Great Teacher of Speech: Wayland Maxfield Parrish" *ST* 4:159–160, Sept., 1953.

Joseph F. Smith, "Maud May Babcock 1867–1954" *ST* 11:105–107, March, 1962.

Stanley T. Donner, "Ralph Dennis: A Great Teacher" *ST* 11:214–220, Sept., 1962.

A. G. Kershner, Jr., "John Dolman, Jr." *ST* 11:290–292, Nov., 1962.

David W. Thompson, "Frank M. Rarig" *ST* 11:292–294, Nov., 1962.
Edna Gilbert, "Ralph Dennis" *ST* 11:294–297, Nov., 1962.
Charlotte Lee, "Cornelius Carmen Cunningham" *ST* 11:297–299, Nov., 1962.
Lawrence H. Mouat, "Lee Emerson Bassett" *ST* 11:299–302, Nov., 1962.
Severina E. Nelson, "Charles Henry Woolbert" *ST* 11:302–304, Nov., 1962.
Joseph F. Smith, "Maud May Babcock" *ST* 11:304–307, Nov., 1962.
Richard Murphy, "Wayland Maxfield Parrish" *ST* 11:307–310, Nov., 1962.
Magdalene Kramer, "Azubah J. Latham: Creative Teacher" *ST* 12:187–190, Sept., 1963.
Olive B. Davis, "Samuel Silas Curry—1847–1921" *ST* 12:304–307, Nov., 1963.

III. TEXTBOOKS AND REFERENCE BOOKS

Gertrude Johnson, ed., *Studies in the Art of Interpretation* (New York: Appleton-Century, 1940).
Argus Tressider, *Reading to Others* (New York: Scott, Foresman, 1940).
Sara Lowrey and Gertrude Johnson, *Interpretative Reading* (New York: Appleton-Century, 1942; 2nd. ed., 1953).
Jane E. Herendeen, *Speech Quality and Interpretation* (New York: Harpers, 1946).
Moiree Compere, *Living Literature for Oral Interpretation* (New York: Appleton, 1949).
Lester Thonssen, Mary Margaret Robb, and Dorothea Thonssen, *Bibliography of Speech Education* (Supplement 1939–1948) (New York: H. W. Wilson, 1950).
Lionel G. Crocker and Louis M. Eich, *Oral Reading* (New York: Prentice-Hall, 1947; 2nd. ed., 1955).
Cornelius Carmen Cunningham, *Making Words Come Alive* (Dubuque, Iowa: W. C. Brown Co., 1951).
Charlotte Lee, *Oral Interpretation* (Boston: Houghton, Mifflin, 1952; 2nd. ed., 1959; 3rd. ed., 1965).
Lionel Crocker, *Interpretative Speech* (New York: Prentice-Hall, 1952).
Gail Boardman, *Oral Communication of Literature* (Englewood Cliffs, N. J.: Prentice-Hall, 1952).

Karl R. Wallace, ed., *Speech Education in America* (New York: Appleton-Century-Crofts, 1954).

Ben Graf Henneke, *Reading Aloud Effectively* (New York: Rinehart, 1954).

Otis J. Aggertt and Elbert R. Bowen, *Communicative Reading* (New York: Macmillan Co., 1956).

John Dolman Jr., *The Art of Reading Aloud* (New York: Harpers, 1956).

Wilbur Samuel Howell, *Logic and Rhetoric in England 1500–1700* (Princeton, New Jersey: Princeton University Press, 1956).

Martin Cobin, *Theory and Technique of Interpretation* (New York: Prentice-Hall, 1959).

Wallace A. Bacon and Robert S. Breen, *Literature as Experience* (New York: McGraw-Hill Book Co., 1959).

Gladys E. Lynch and Harold C. Crain, *Projects in Oral Interpretation* (New York: Henry Holt and Company, 1959).

Joseph F. Smith and James R. Linn, *Skill in Reading Aloud* (New York: Harper Bros., 1960).

Wilma H. Grimes and Alethea S. Mattingly, *Interpretation: Writer, Reader, Audience* (San Francisco: Wadsworth Publishing Co., 1961).

Lawrence Mouat, *Reading Literature Aloud* (New York: Oxford University Press, 1962).

Don Geiger, *The Sound and Sense of Performance of Literature* (Chicago: Scott-Foresman, 1963).

Chloe Armstrong and Paul D. Brandes, *The Oral Interpretation of Literature* (New York: McGraw-Hill Book Co., 1963).

David Thompson and Virginia Fredericks, *Oral Interpretation of Fiction; a Dramatistic Approach* (Minneapolis: Burgess Publishing Co., 1964).

Wallace A. Bacon, *The Art of Interpretation* (New York: Holt, Rinehart, Winston, 1966).

Thomas O. Sloan, editor, *The Oral Study of Literature* (New York: Random House, 1966).

Paul N. Campbell, *Oral Interpretation* (New York: Macmillan Co., 1966).

Mary Margaret Robb and Lester Thonssen, ed., *Chironomia* by Gilbert Austin (Carbondale: Southern Illinois University Press, 1966).

Robert Beloof, *The Performing Voice in Literature* (Boston: Little Brown Co., 1966).

BIBLIOGRAPHY

I. MATERIALS ON SPEECH

A. Books, Monographs, and Pamphlets

Armstrong, Chloe and Brandes, Paul. *The Oral Interpretation of Literature.* New York, McGraw-Hill. 1963. 330p.

Aubert, Charles. *The Art of Pantomime.* New York, Henry Holt. 1927. 210p.

Austin, Gilbert. *Chironomia; or a Treatise on Rhetorical Delivery: Comprehending Many Precepts Both Ancient and Modern, for the Proper Regulation of the Voice, the Countenance and Gesture.* London, T. Cadell and W. Davies. 1806. 583p.

Bacon, Albert M. *A Manual of Gesture.* New York, Silver, Burdett. 1893. 260p.

Bacon, Wallace. *The Art of Interpretation.* New York, Holt, Rinehart, Winston. 1966. 396p.

Barber, Jonathan. *Exercises in Reading and Recitation.* York, Pa., Barber and Mason. 1825. 208p.

————. *A Grammar of Elocution.* New Haven, A. H. Maltby. 1830. 344p.

Bassett, Lee Emerson. *Handbook of Oral Reading.* Boston, Houghton Mifflin. 1917. 342p.

Bayly, Anselm. *A Practical Treatise on Singing and Playing with Just Expression and Real Elegance.* London, J. Ridley. 1771. 28p.

Bell, Alexander Melville. *Address to the National Association of Elocutionists.* Washington, D. C., Volta Bureau. 1895. pam. 25p.

————. *On the Use of Notations in Elocutionary Teaching.* Washington, D. C., Volta Bureau. 1899. 59p.

————. *The Principles of Elocution.* New York, Edgar S. Werner. 1887. Fifth ed. 240p.

Beloof, Robert. *The Performing Voice in Literature.* Boston, Little Brown and Co. 1966. 514p.

Bingham, Caleb. *The American Preceptor.* Boston, Thomas and Andrews. 1794. 228p.

————. *The Columbian Orator.* Boston, Manning and Loring. 1797. 300p.

Bishop, Emily M. *Americanized Delsarte Culture.* Meadville, Pa., Chautauqua-Century Press. 1892. 202p.

Blair, Hugh. *Lectures on Rhetoric and Belles Lettres.* London, Wm. Tegg. n.d. 602p.

Blake, William H. *A Preliminary Study of the Interpretation of Bodily Expression.* New York, Teachers College Contributions to Education. 1933. 54p.

Blanks, Anthony F. *An Introductory Study in the History of the Teaching of Public Speaking in the United States.* Unpublished Ph.D. dissertation. Stanford University. 1928.

Bronson, C. P. *Elocution; or Mental and Vocal Philosophy: Involving the Principles of Reading and Speaking; and Designed for the Development and Cultivation of Both Body and Mind, in Accordance with the Nature, Uses, and Destiny of Man.* Louisville, Ky., John P. Morton. 1845. Fifth ed. 384p.

Brown, Moses True. *The Synthetic Philosophy of Expression—As Applied to the Arts of Reading, Oratory, and Personation.* Boston, Houghton, Mifflin. 1886. 297p.

Bulwer, John. *Chirologia . . . Chironomia.* London, T. Harper. 1644. 2v. in 1.

Burgh, James. *The Art of Speaking Containing an Essay in Which Are Given Rules for Expressing Properly the Principal Passions and Humors, Which Occur in Reading, or Public Speaking, Taken from the Ancients and Moderns; Exhibiting a Variety of Matter for Practice; the Emphatical Words Printed in Italics; with Notes of Direction Referring to the Essay.* Baltimore, Warner and Hanna. 1804. 291p.

Caldwell, Merritt. *A Practical Manual of Elocution.* Philadelphia, Sorin and Ball. 1845. 342p.

Campbell, George. *The Philosophy of Rhetoric.* Boston, J. H. Wilkins. 1835. 396p.

Campbell, Hugh, Brewer, R. F., and Neville, Henry. *Voice, Speech and Gesture: Practical Handbook to the Elocutionary Art.* New York, G. P. Putnam. 1895. 840p.

Chamberlain, William B. and Clark, Solomon H. *Principles of Vocal Expression.* Chicago, Scott, Foresman. 1897. 473p.

Clark, Solomon H. *Interpretation of the Printed Page.* New York, Row, Peterson. 1915. 317p. Rev. ed. with M. M. Babcock, 1940.

Cobin, Martin. *Theory and Technique of Interpretation.* New York, Prentice-Hall. 1959. 256p.

Cockin, William. *The Art of Delivering Written Language; or, an Essay on Reading.* London, J. Dodsley. 1775. 152p.

Comstock, Andrew. *A System of Elocution.* Philadelphia, E. H. Butler. 1851. Third ed. 364p.

Corson, Hiram. *The Voice and Spiritual Education.* New York, Macmillan. 1897. 181p.

Coulton, Thomas E. *Trends in Speech Education in American Colleges 1835–1935.* Unpublished Ph.D. dissertation. New York University. 1935.

Crocker, Lionel G. and Eich, Louis M. *Oral Reading.* New York, Prentice-Hall. 1947. 507p.

Cumnock, Robert McLean. *Choice Readings for Public and Private Entertainment Arranged for the Exercises of the School, College and Public Reader, with Elocutionary Advice.* Chicago, A. C. McClurg. Ninth ed. 1905. 422p.

Curry, Samuel Silas. *Alexander Melville Bell, Some Memories from Fragments from a Pupil's Notebook.* Boston, Expression Co. 1906. 53p.

————. *Browning and the Dramatic Monologue.* Boston, Expression Co. 1908. 308p.

————. *Foundations of Expression.* Boston, Expression Co. 1907. 319p.

————. *Imagination and the Dramatic Instinct.* Boston, Expression Co. 1896. 369p.

————. *Lessons in Vocal Expression.* Boston, Expression Co. 1895. 310p.

————. *Mind and Voice.* Boston, Expression Co. 1910. 446p.

————. *The Province of Expression.* Boston, Expression Co. 1891. 452p.

Davis, Estelle H. and Mammen, Edward W. *The Spoken Word in Life and Art.* New York, Prentice-Hall. 1935. 512p.

Day, Henry N. *The Art of Elocution Exemplified in a Systematic Course of Exercises.* Cincinnati, Moore, Wilstach and Baldwin. Second ed. 1867. 384p.

De Banke, Cecile. *The Art of Choral Speaking.* Boston, Baker's Plays. 1937. 227p.

Delaumosne, L'Abbé. "The Delsarte System" *in The Delsarte System of Oratory.* New York, Edgar S. Werner. 1893. p. 1–163.

Diehl, Anna Randall. *A Practical Delsarte Primer.* Syracuse, C. W. Bardeen. 1890. 66p.

Drummond, Alexander M. (ed.) *A Course of Study in Speech Training and Public Speaking for Secondary Schools.* New York, Century. 1925. 291p.

Dwyer, John H. *An Essay on Elocution.* New York, G. and C. Carvill and E. Bliss. 1828. 298p.

Emerson, Charles Wesley. *Evolution of Expression*. Boston, Emerson College of Oratory Publishing Department. 1913. Twenty-Ninth ed. 4 vols.

———. *Psycho Vox*. Millis, Mass., Emerson College of Oratory. Publishing Department. 1897. 117p.

Enfield, William. *The Speaker; or Miscellaneous Pieces, Selected from the Best English Writers, Disposed under Proper Heads for the Improvement of Youth in Reading and Speaking to Which Is Prefixed an Essay on Elocution*. Boston, Joseph Larkin. 1808. 400p.

Farma, William Joseph. *Prose, Poetry and Drama for Oral Interpretation*. New York, Harper. 1930. 533p.

———. *Prose, Poetry and Drama for Oral Interpretation*. Second ser. New York, Harper. 1936. 529p.

Fenno, Frank H. *The Science and Art of Elocution*. New York, Hinds, Noble and Eldredge. 1878. 414p.

Fritz, Charles Andrew. *The Content of the Teaching of Speech in the American Colleges before 1850*. Unpublished Ph.D. dissertation. New York University. 1928.

Fulton, Robert I. and Trueblood, Thomas C. *Practical Elements of Elocution*. Boston, Ginn and Co. 1898. 235p.

Geiger, Don. *The Sound and Sense of Performance of Literature*. Chicago, Scott-Foresman. 1963. 115p. paper.

Grimes, Wilma H. and Mattingly, Alethea S. *Interpretation: Writer, Reader, Audience*. San Francisco, Wadsworth Publishing Co. 1961. 358p.

Hamill, S. S. *Easy Lessons in Vocal Culture and Vocal Expression*. New York, Eaton and Mains. 1898. 198p.

Johnson, Gertrude E. *Modern Literature for Oral Interpretation*. New York, Century. 1926. 413p.

———. ed. *Studies in the Art of Interpretation*. New York, D. Appleton-Century. 1940. 254p.

Keppie, Elizabeth E. *The Teaching of Choric Speech*. Boston, Expression Co. 1931. 147p.

Kerfoot, John B. *How to Read*. Boston, Houghton Mifflin. 1916. 297p.

King, Byron W. *Practice of Speech and Successful Selections*. Pittsburgh, Pa., W. T. Nicholson. 1882. Second ed. 216p.

Kirby, Edward N. *Public Speaking and Reading*. Boston, Lee and Shepard. 1896. 211p.

Kirkham, Samuel. *Essay on Elocution*. New York, Pratt, Woodford and Company. 1846. 357p.

Laughton, Charles. *How to Tell a Story*. New York, McGraw-Hill. 1957. 392p.

Lee, Charlotte. *Oral Interpretation*. Boston, Houghton, Mifflin. 1952. 3rd ed. 1965. 596p.

Leverton, Garrett H. *"The Philosophy of the Human Voice" by James Rush: an Analysis and Evaluation*. Unpublished Master's thesis. Northwestern University. 1925.

Lowrey, Sara and Johnson, Gertrude. *Interpretative Reading*. New York, Appleton-Century. 1942. 2nd ed. 1953. 607p.

McGuffey, William H. *McGuffey's Rhetorical Guide; or Fifth Reader of the Eclectic Series*. Cincinnati, Winthrop B. Smith. 1844. 480p.

McIlvaine, Joshua H. *Elocution: the Sources and Elements of Its Power*. New York, Scribner. 1870. 406p.

McLean, Margaret P. *Oral Interpretation of Forms of Literature*. New York, E. P. Dutton. 1936. 380p.

Maglathlin, Henry B. *The Practical Elocutionist*. New York, G. F. Coolidge and Bros. 1850. Fourth ed. 58p.

Mandeville, Henry. *The Elements of Reading and Oratory*. New York, D. Appleton. 1887. 354p.

Mason, John. *An Essay on Elocution or Pronunciation, Intended Chiefly for the Assistance of Those Who Instruct Others in the Art of Reading and of Those Who Are Often Called To Speak in Public*. London, R. Hett. 1751. 43p.

Miller, M. Oclo. *The Psychology of Dr. S. S. Curry as Revealed by His Attitude Toward the Mind-Body Problem*. Unpublished Master's thesis. University of Iowa. 1929.

Mitchell, M. S. *A Manual of Elocution Founded upon the Philosophy of the Human Voice*. Philadelphia, Eldredge and Brothers. 1871. 396p.

Monroe, Lewis B. *Manual of Physical and Vocal Training for the Use of Schools*. Philadelphia, Cowperthwait and Co. 1869. 102p.

Mouat, Lawrence. *Reading Aloud*. New York, Oxford University. 1962. 205p. paper.

Murdoch, James E. *Address Delivered at Steinert Hall to the Visiting Committee and Pupils of the Murdoch School of Voice Culture*. Lawrence, Mass., Lawrence Daily Eagle. 1889. pam. 29p.

———. *Analytic Elocution*. New York, American Book Co. 1884. 500p.

———. *A Plea for Spoken Language*. New York, Van Antwerp, Bragg and Co. 1883. 320p.

Murdoch, James E. and Russell, William. *Orthophony or Vocal Culture*. Boston, William D. Ticknor and Co. 1845. 336p. Re-edited in seventy-ninth edition by William Russell and Francis Russell. Houghton Mifflin and Co. 1896. Dedicated to James E. Murdoch, Esq.

Murray, John. *Elocution for Advanced Pupils.* New York, G. P. Putnam's Sons. 1888. 143p.

Murray, Lindley. *The English Reader; or Pieces in Prose and Poetry Selected from the Best Writers.* New York, Isaac Collins. 1800. 366p.

North, Erasmus Darwin. *Practical Speaking as Taught at Yale College.* New Haven, T. H. Pease. 1846. 440p.

Northrop, Henry Davenport. *The Delsarte Speaker.* Philadelphia, National Publishing Co. 1895. 512p.

Osgood, Lucius. *Progressive Fourth Reader.* Pittsburgh, A. H. English. 1856. 352p.

Palmer, Erastus and Sammis, L. Walter. *The Principles of Oral English.* New York, Macmillan. 1906. 222p.

Pardoe, T. Earl. *Pantomimes for Stage and Study.* New York, D. Appleton. 1931. 394p.

Parrish, Wayland Maxfield. *Reading Aloud.* New York, Thomas Nelson and Sons. 1932. 391p.

Perrin, Porter Gale. *The Teaching of Rhetoric in the American Colleges Before 1750.* Unpublished Ph.D. dissertation. University of Chicago. 1936.

Phillips, Arthur Edward. *Natural Drills in Expression with Selections.* Chicago, The Newton Co. 1917. 358p.

Porter, Ebenezer. *Analysis of Principles of Rhetorical Delivery as Applied in Reading and Speaking.* Andover, Gould and Newman. 1836. Fifth ed. 404p.

————. *Analysis of Vocal Inflections as Used in Reading and Speaking.* Andover, Flagg and Gould. 1824. pam. 21p.

————. *The Rhetorical Reader.* New York, Mark Newman. 1835. Two hundred twentieth ed. 304p.

Raymond, George L. *The Orator's Manual.* Boston, Silver Burdett. 1897. Ninth ed. 342p.

Rice, John. *An Introduction to the Art of Reading with Energy and Propriety.* London, J. and R. Tonson. 1765. 322p.

Rush, James. *The Philosophy of the Human Voice.* Philadelphia, Lippincott, Grambo and Co. 1855. Fourth ed. 559p.

Russell, William. *The American Elocutionist.* Boston, Jenks, Hickling and Swan. 1854. Fifth ed. 380p.

Sandford, William P. *English Theories of Public Address 1530–1828.* Columbus, H. L. Hedrick. 1931. pam. 211p.

Sarett, Lew and Foster, William Trufant. *Basic Principles of Speech.* Boston, Houghton Mifflin. 1936. 577p.

Sargent, Epes. *The Intermediate Standard Speaker.* Philadelphia, T. Cowperthwait. 1852. 558p.

Scott, William. *Lessons in Elocution or a Selection of Pieces in Prose and Verse for the Improvement of Youth in Reading and Speaking.* Leicester, Hori Brown. 1817. 407p.

Shaver, Claude Lester. *The Delsarte System of Expression as Seen Through the Notes of Steele Mackaye.* Unpublished Ph.D. dissertation. University of Wisconsin. 1938.

Sheridan, Thomas. *Course of Lectures on Elocution.* London, J. Dodsley. 1796. 320p.

————. *Discourse Delivered in the Theatre at Oxford. . . . Being Introductory to His Course of Lectures on Elocution and the English Language.* London, A. Millar. 1759. pam. 59p.

————. *Lectures on the Art of Reading.* London, J. Dodsley. 1775. 2 vols.

————. *A Rhetorical Grammar of the English Language.* Dublin, W. Price and H. Whitestone *et al.* 1781. 238p.

Shurter, Edwin DuBois. *Public Speaking, a Treatise on Delivery With Selections for Declaiming.* Boston, Allyn and Bacon. 1903. 254p.

Sloan, Thomas O. ed. *The Oral Study of Literature.* New York, Random House, 1966. 209p. paper.

Smith, Brainard Gardner. *Reading and Speaking.* Boston, D. C. Heath. 1891. 165p.

Smith, Joseph F. and Linn, James R. *Skill in Reading Aloud.* New York, Harper Bros. 1960. 463p.

Stebbins, Genevieve. *Delsarte System of Dramatic Expression.* New York, Edgar S. Werner. 1886. 252p.

Steele, Sir Joshua. *Prosodia Rationalis, An Essay Towards Establishing the Melody and Measure of Speech to be Expressed and Perpetuated by Peculiar Symbols.* London, J. Almon. 1775. 193p.

Tallcott, Rollo Anson. *The Art of Acting and Public Reading.* Indianapolis, Bobbs-Merrill Co. 1922. 224p.

Tassin, Algernon de V. *The Oral Study of Literature.* New York, Crofts. 1930. Fourth ed. 483p.

Thonssen, Lester and Fatherson, Elizabeth. *Bibliography of Speech Education.* New York, H. W. Wilson. 1939. 800p.

Town, Salem and Holbrook, Nelson. *The Progressive Fifth or Elocutionary Reader.* Boston, Sanborn, Carter, Bozin. 1856. 504p.

Tresidder, Argus. *Reading to Others*. Chicago, Scott, Foresman. 1940. 529p.

Vandenhoff, George. *The Art of Elocution As an Essential Part of Rhetoric with Instructions in Gesture and an Appendix of Oratorical, Poetical and Dramatic Extracts*. New York, Spalding and Shepard. 1847. 383p.

Walker, John. *Elements of Elocution*. Boston, D. Mallory and Co. 1810. 379p.

————. *The Melody of Speaking Delineated or Elocution Taught Like Music by Visible Signs*. London, J. J. Robinson and T. Cadell. 1787. 70p.

————. *The Rhetorical Grammar*. Boston, J. T. Buckingham. 1814. 356p.

Whately, Richard. *Elements of Rhetoric*. Boston and Cambridge, James Munroe. 1861. 538p.

Winans, James A. *Public Speaking*. New York, Century. 1910. 526p.

Woolbert, Charles H. *The Fundamentals of Speech*. New York, Harper. 1927. 523p.

Woolbert, Charles H. and Nelson, Severina E. *The Art of Interpretative Speech*. New York, Crofts. 1927. 541p. 5th ed. 1968. 586p.

B. Periodicals

Bacon, Wallace. "Graduate.Studies in Interpretation." *Quarterly Journal of Speech*. 35:316–319. 1949.

Barnes, John. "Vital Capacity in Oral Reading." *Quarterly Journal of Speech Education*. 12:176–82. 1926.

Bassett, Lee Emerson. "Adapting Courses in Interpretation to the Academic Mind." *Quarterly Journal of Speech*. 18:175–87. 1932.

Brooks, Keith and Bielenberg, John E. "Readers Theatre as Defined by New York Critics." *Southern Speech Journal*. 29:288–302. 1964.

Brooks, Keith and Wulftange, Sr. I. Marie. "Listener Response to Oral Interpretation." *Speech Monographs*. 31:73–79. 1964.

Bryan, Earl C. "Speech Training in Texas Colleges." *Quarterly Journal of Speech*. 18:261–9. 1932.

Cobin, Martin and Clevenger, Theodore. "Television Instruction, Course Content and Teaching Level: An Experimental Study in the Basic Course in Oral Interpretation." *Speech Monographs*. 28:16–20. 1961.

Coger, Irene. "Interpreter's Theatre: Theatre of the Mind." *Quarterly Journal of Speech*. 49:157–164. 1963.

Cunningham, Cornelius. "Interpretative Reading As a Fine Art." *Journal of Expression.* 2:78–9. 1928.

Dennis, Ralph. "One Imperative Plus." *Quarterly Journal of Speech Education.* 8:218–23. 1922.

Dusenbury, Delwin and Knower, Franklin H. "Experimental Studies of the Symbolism of Action and Voice." I, II *Quarterly Journal of Speech.* 24:424–35. 1938. 25:67–75. 1939.

O'Neill, J. M. *Quarterly Journal of Public Speaking.* 1:55–8. 1915.

Edwards, Davis. "Interpretation." *Quarterly Journal of Speech.* 21:561–4. 1935.

Ewbank, Henry L. " 'The Rhetorical Reader' by Ebenezer Porter.' " (A review.) *Quarterly Journal of Speech Education.* 13:474. 1927.

Fiske, Bertha V. "A Pioneer in Speech Training." *Emerson Quarterly.* 15:7–8. 1934.

Fritz, Charles Andrew. "From Sheridan to Rush: The Beginnings of English Elocution." *Quarterly Journal of Speech.* 16:75–88. 1930.

Geiger, Don. "Oral Interpretation in the Liberal Arts Context." *Quarterly Journal of Speech.* 40:137–144. 1954.

Hayworth, Donald. "The Development of the Training of Public Speakers in America." *Quarterly Journal of Speech.* 14:489–502. 1928.

Jeffrey, Robert C. "The History of the Speech Association of America 1914–1964." *Quarterly Journal of Speech.* 50:432–444. 1964.

Johnson, Gertrude. "Literature and Vocal Expression." *English Journal.* 3:533–7. 1914.

Kleinau, Marion L. and Marvin D. "Scene Location in Readers Theatre: Static or Dynamic." *Speech Teacher.* 14:193–199. 1965.

Klyn, Mark S. "Potentials for Research in Oral Interpretation." *Western Speech.* 29:108–114. 1965.

Kramer, Magdalene and McCarthy, Margaret M. "The Development of Personality." *Emerson Quarterly.* 16:16+. 1936.

Lahman, Carroll P. "Speech Education in Teacher-Training Institutions." *Quarterly Journal of Speech.* 16:42–61. 1930.

Linn, James R. L. "A Historical Study of Oral Interpretation as a Form of Professional Theatre in London, 1951–1962." *Speech Monographs.* 32:287–288. 1965.

Lyon, Clarence E. "The English—Public Speaking Situation." *Quarterly Journal of Public Speaking.* 1:44–50. 1915.

McCoard, William B. "An Interpretation of the Times." *Quarterly Journal of Speech.* 35:489–495. 1949.

Marcoux, Paul Albert. "An Analysis of Current Trends Concerning Certain Basic Aspects of Oral Interpretation as Evidenced in Selected Writings in the Field, 1950–1963, with Implications for Speech Education." *Speech Monographs.* 32:288–289. 1965.

O'Neill, James M. "After Thirteen Years." *Quarterly Journal of Speech.* 14:242–53. 1928.

Parrish Wayland Maxfield. "Implications of Gestalt Psychology." *Quarterly Journal of Speech.* 14:8–28. 1928.

Robb, Mary Margaret. "Trends in the Teaching of Oral Interpretation." *Western Speech.* 14:8–12. 1950.

Shepherd, John R. and Scheidel, Thomas M. "A Study of Personality Configuration of Effective Oral Readers." *Speech Monographs.* 23:298–304. 1956.

Simon, Clarence T. "Appreciation in Reading." *Quarterly Journal of Speech.* 16:185–93. 1930.

———. "Graduate Study in Speech." *Quarterly Journal of Speech.* 36:462–470. 1950.

Snidecor, John C. "An Objective Study of Phrasing in Impromptu and Oral Reading." *Speech Monographs.* 11:97–104. 1944.

Tallcott, Rollo Anson. "Teaching Public Reading." *Quarterly Journal of Speech Education.* 9:53–66. 1923.

Trueblood, Thomas C. "A Chapter on the Organization of Courses in Public Speaking." *Quarterly Journal of Speech Education.* 12:1–2. 1926.

Weaver, J. Clark. "A Survey of Speech Curricula." *Quarterly Journal of Speech.* 18:607–12. 1932.

Werner's Magazine. New York. 1895, 1897, 1899.

Wilds, E. H. "Public Speaking in the Early Colleges and Schools." *Quarterly Journal of Speech Education.* 2:31–8. 1916.

Wilson, Garff B. "The Growth of Oral Interpretation at the University of California." *Speech Teacher.* 1:187–192. 1952.

Wilson, Helene. "Some Statistics Concerning Interpretation Courses." *Quarterly Journal of Speech.* 12:342–52. 1926.

Winans, James A. "Report of the Eastern Public Speaking Conference." *Public Speaking Review.* 4:12. 1914.

Woolbert, Charles H. "Psychology." *Quarterly Journal of Speech.* 16:9–18. 1930.

C. Catalogues of Special Schools of Speech

School of Practical Rhetoric and Oratory. Boston. 1844.

National School of Elocution and Oratory. Philadelphia. 1875.

School of Expression. Boston. 1888.
Curry College. Boston. 1939–40.
Emerson College of Oratory. Boston. 1896–97.
Emerson College. Boston. 1939–40.
Leland Powers School of the Theatre. Boston. 1939–40.
Columbia College of Expression. Chicago. 1939–40.

II. MATERIALS ON GENERAL HISTORICAL BACKGROUND

A. Books, Monographs, and Pamphlets

Adams, John Quincy. *Lectures on Rhetoric and Oratory*. Cambridge, Hilliard and Metcalf. 1810. 2 vols.

Amherst College Annals. 1827.

Aristotle. *The Works of Aristotle*. ed. W. D. Ross. Oxford, Clarendon Press. 1924. vol. 11.

Babbitt, Irving. *Rousseau and Romanticism*. Boston, Houghton Mifflin. 1930. Sixth ed. 398p.

Baldwin, Charles Sears. *Ancient Rhetoric and Poetic*. New York, Macmillan. 1924. 247p.

Beard, Charles A. and Beard, Mary. *America in Midpassage*. New York, Macmillan. 1939. vols. 2, 3.

———. *The Rise of American Civilization*. New York, Macmillan. 1927. 2 vols.

Bode, Boyd Henry. *How We Learn*. Boston, D. C. Heath. 1940. 308p.

Boyd, William. *From Locke to Montessori*. London, George H. Harrap. 1914. 268p.

Brooks, Van Wyck. *The Flowering of New England*. New York, E. P. Dutton. 1936. 537p.

Burke, Kenneth. *Counter-Statement*. New York, Harcourt, Brace and Co. 1931. 219p. 2nd ed. Los Altos, Cailf., Hermes Publication. 1953.

———. *The Philosophy of Literary Form*. rev. ed. New York, Random House. 1957. 330p.

Butts, R. Freeman. *The College Charts Its Course*. New York, McGraw-Hill. 1939. 416p.

Channing, Edward. *A History of the United States*. New York, Macmillan. 1920. vols. 4 and 5.

Channing, William Ellery. "The Importance and Means of a National Literature" *in Character of Napoleon and Other Essays*. London, Charles Tilt. 1837. vol. 1.

Chesterfield, Philip Dormer Stanhope. *Letters to His Son.* New York, Dutton, 1929. 314p.

Cicero, Marcus Tullius. *De Oratore.* ed. J. S. Watson. Philadelphia, David McKay. 1897. 283p.

Clap, Thomas. *The Annals or History of Yale College.* New Haven, Hotchkiss and Maconi. 1766. 124p.

Darwin, Charles. *The Expression of the Emotions in Man and Animals.* New York, D. Appleton. 1896. 367p.

Dewey, John. *Democracy and Education.* New York, Macmillan. 1916. 434p.

Dictionary of American Biography. ed. Dumas Malone. New York, Charles Scribner's Sons. 1935. vols. 2 and 14.

Dictionary of National Biography. ed. Sidney Lee. New York, Macmillan. 1899. vols. 18, 20, 57, and 59.

Dwight, Timothy. *Travels in New England and New York.* New Haven, T. Dwight. 1821–1822. vol. I.

Evans, Charles. *American Bibliography.* vols. 5, 9, 11, and 12.

Flügel, John Carl. *A Hundred Years of Psychology,* 1833–1933. New York, Macmillan. 1933. 362p.

Foerster, Norman. *American Poetry and Prose.* Boston, Houghton Mifflin. 1934. 1472p.

Hartman, George W. *Gestalt Psychology.* New York, Ronald Press. 1935. 325p.

Heidbreder, Edna. *Seven Psychologies.* New York, Century. 1933. 450p.

Hicks, Granville. *The Great Tradition.* New York, Macmillan. 1933. 306p.

James, William. *Briefer Course of Psychology.* New York, Henry Holt. 1893. 478p.

————. *Talks to Teachers on Psychology.* New York, Henry Holt. 1939. new ed. 238p.

Jastrow, Joseph. "Psychology" in *Encyclopedia of the Social Sciences.* eds. Edwin R. Seligman and Alvin Johnson. New York, Macmillan. 1934. vol. 12. p. 588–96.

Kazin, Alfred. *Contemporaries.* Boston, Little, Brown and Co. 1962. 513p.

Low, Seth. *The Trend of the Century.* New York, Thomas Y. Crowell. 1899. 31p.

McLaren, Gay. *Morally We Roll Along.* Boston, Little, Brown. 1938. 308p.

Morison, Samuel Eliot. *The Founding of Harvard College.* Cambridge, Harvard University Press. 1935. 472p.

Morison, Samuel Eliot and Commager, Henry Steele. *The Growth of the American Republic.* New York, Oxford University Press. 1937. vol. II.

Murphy, Gardner. *An Historical Introduction to Modern Psychology.* New York, Harcourt, Brace. 1932. Third ed. 471p.

Nevins, Allan. *The Emergence of Modern America 1865–1878.* New York, Macmillan. 1935. 407p.

A New English Dictionary. ed. James Murray. Oxford, Clarendon Press. 1901. vol. 7.

Noble, Stuart G. *A History of American Education.* New York, Farrar and Rinehart. 1938. 429p.

Oberholtzer, Ellis Paxson. *A History of the United States Since the Civil War.* New York, Macmillan. 1926. vol. 3.

Old South Leaflets. Boston, Directors of The Old South Work. vol. 3, no. 51.

Parrington, Vernon Louis. *Main Currents in American Thought.* New York, Harcourt, Brace. 1927. 3 vols.

Perry, Bliss. *The Heart of Emerson's Journals.* Boston, Houghton Mifflin. 1914. 357p.

Pierce, Benjamin. *A History of Harvard College.* Cambridge, Brown and Shattuck. 1833. 159p.

Present State of Learning in the College of New York (Columbia College). New York, T. and J. Swords. 1794. pam.

Quincy, Josiah, Jr. *Figures of the Past from the Leaves of Old Journals.* Boston, Roberts Bros. 1896. 400p.

Quintilian. *The Institutio Oratoria.* trans. H. E. Butler. London, William Heinemann. 1921. vol. IV.

Reports on the Course of Instruction in Yale College by a Committee of the Correction and Academical Faculty. New Haven, Hezekiah Howe. 1830.

Rice, Emmett A. *A Brief History of Physical Education.* New York, A. S. Barnes. 1926. 269p.

Rousseau, Jean Jacques. *Emile.* trans. Barbara Foxley. London, J. M. Dent. 1911. 444p.

Sandburg, Carl. *Abraham Lincoln, The Prairie Years.* New York, Harcourt, Brace. 1926. 2 vols.

Smith, Preserved. *A History of Modern Culture.* New York, Henry Holt. 1930. vol. 1. 608p.

Snow, Louis Franklin. *The College Curriculum in the United States.* New York, Teachers College Contributions to Education. 1907. 186p.

Spingarn, J. E. *Creative Criticism and Other Essays*. New York, Harcourt, Brace. 1931. 221p.

Sullivan, Mark. *Our Times*. New York, Charles Scribner's Sons. 1927. vol. 2.

Swift, Jonathan. *Works*. ed. Thomas Sheridan. London, J. Johnson. 1803. vol. 8.

Thwing, Charles F. *A History of Higher Education in America Since the Civil War*. New York, D. Appleton-Century. 1906. 347p.

Trilling, Lionel. *A Gathering of Fugitives*. Boston, Beacon Press. 1956. 167p.

Tynan, Kenneth. *Curtains; Selection from the Drama Criticism and Related Essays*. New York, Atheneum. 1961. 405p.

West, Ray B., ed. *Essays in Modern Literary Criticism*. New York, Holt, Rinehart and Winston. 1961. 611p.

Zabel, Morton D., ed. *Literary Opinion in America*. New York, Harper, Row. 1961. Vols. I, II, 3rd. ed. 903p.

B. PERIODICALS

Clurman, Harold. "Review of *Ages of Man*." *The Nation*. 188:39–40. 1959.

Eiseley, Loren. "Science and the Unexpected Universe." *American Scholar*. 35:415–429. 1966.

Fromm, Erich. "The Present Human Condition." *American Scholar*. 25:29–35. 1955.

Grove, Richard. "National Foundation on the Arts and Humanities Act." *U. S. Department of Health, Education and Welfare Indicators*. Nov., 1965.

Hicks, Granville. "Liberalism in the Fifties." *American Scholar*. 25:283–296. 1956.

Langbaum, Robert. "This Literary Generation." *American Scholar*. 25:87–94. 1955.

Welty, Eudora. "Must the Novelist Crusade?" *Atlantic*. 216:104–108. 1965.

INDEX

Abruptness, 87, 92, 93, 104, 115, 173
Academic Speaker, 32
Accent, 44-49, 59
Acting, 198, 205
Adams, John Quincy, 21; Boylston professor, 76, 77
Aesthetics, 194, 195, 223
"Age of Criticism," 215
Aggertt, Otis J., 221, 238
Alberti, Eva Allen, 205
American Elocutionist, 113
American Preceptor, 26
Amherst College, 24, 25
Analysis of Principles of Rhetorical Delivery as Applied in Reading and Speaking, 41, 42, 55
Analysis of Vocal Inflections as Used in Reading and Speaking, 41, 85
Analytic Elocution, 117
Ancient Rhetoric and Poetic, 20
Appreciation of literature, 141, 174, 191, 207, 232
Aristotle, 20
Armstrong, Chloe, 222, 238
Art of Acting and Public Reading, 200
Art of Choral Speaking, 191
Art of Delivering Written Language, 37
Art of Elocution, 114, 116
Art of Interpretation, 223, 225, 238
Art of Interpretative Speech, 197, 221
Art of Speaking, 26, 35, 133
Articulation, 44, 58-61, 104, 119, 157
Arts and Humanities Act, 212
Aspirate quality, 115
Atonics, 88, 90
Audience, 119, 205-206, 223, 227, 228
Austin, Gilbert, 40, 63-67, 80, 133, 137, 150, 234, 235, 238; notations for gesture, 63-67
Avery, Elizabeth, 190

Babbitt, Irving, 187-188
Babcock, Maude May, 198, 200, 201, 218, 221, 235, 236
Bacon, Albert M., 133, 136, 137, 160
Bacon, Wallace, 219, 223, 225, 236, 238
Baldwin, Charles S., 20
Baldwin, James, 214
Barber, Dr. Jonathan, 101, 103-106, 234

Barnes, John, 196
Barry, James J., 233
Basic Principles of Speech, 190
Bassett, Lee Emerson, 138, 169, 177, 197, 198
Bayly, Anselm, 18
Beard, Charles A., and Mary, 17, 123, 125, 128
Beecher, Henry Ward, 125
Bell, Alexander Melville, 153-160
Beloof, Robert, 223, 224, 225, 226, 238
Bibliography of Speech Education, 192, supplement, 237
Bingham, Caleb, 26
Bishop, Emily, 130, 148
Blair, Hugh, 80
Blake, William H., 209
Blanks, Anthony F., 12, 24, 101
Blanton, Smiley, 169
Boardman, Gail, 237
Bode, Boyd H., 194
Boston University, 130
Bowen, Elbert R., 221, 238
Bowyer, Frances E., 234
Boy Growing Up, 227
Boyd, William, 28
Brandes, Paul D., 222, 238
Breathing, 40, 107-109, 157, 162, 165-167, 196
Breen, Robert S., 220, 223, 225, 233
Briefer Course of Psychology, 203
Bronson, Dr. C. P., 102, 107-108
Brooks, Emerson, 129
Brooks, Van Wyck, 72, 77, 213
Brown, Moses True, 130, 148-151
Brown University, 25
Browning and the Dramatic Dialogue, 166
Bulwer, John, 36-37, 133, 234, 236
Burgh, James, 26, 35-37, 61-62
Burke, Kenneth, 215, 224
Burns, Kenneth, 234
Button, John, 43
Butts, R. Freeman, 17, 19, 25, 75, 135, 136
Byron King School of Oratory, 130

Cadence, 44, 99
Caesural pause, 57, 58, 205-6

Caldwell, Merritt, 102, 111-112
Campbell, George, 55, 80
Campbell, Paul N., 238
Capote, Truman, 214
Carpenter, Thomas, 43
Cather, Willa, 188
Chamber Theatre, 220
Chamberlain, William B., 171
Channing, Edward, 71
Channing, William Ellery, 73
Chautauqua, 126-129, 191, 234
Chesterfield, Philip D. S., 18
Chicago University, 188, 189
Chirologia . . . Chironomia, 36, 133, 234, 236
Chironomia, 40, 63-67, 133, 148, 150, 234, 238
Choice Readings, 182
Choral reading, 191
Chromatic scale, 96
Cicero, 20
"Circumsession," 143
Clap, Thomas, 23
Clark, Solomon H., 171-176, 198, 221
Clarke, John, 21
Cleary, James W., 234, 236
Clurman, Harold, 227
Cobin, Martin, 220, 222, 238
Coburn, Mr. and Mrs., 129
Cockin, William, 37-38, 50
Coger, Leslie Irene, 228, 234
College Charts Its Course, 17
Columbia College, 25, 234
Columbia School of Expression, 130, 191
Columbia University, 189
Columbia Orator, 26
Commager, Henry S., 131
Commission on the Humanities, 212
Communication theory, 222-223
Communicative Reading, 222, 238
Compere, Moiree, 237
Comstock, Andrew, 106-107
Concrete scale, 96
Consonants, 59, 60, 103; Rush's list of, 90; Sheridan's list of, 60
Content of the Teaching of Speech in the American College Before 1850, 12
Conversational style, 90, 173, 181
Cooke, Edmund Vance, 129
Cornell University, 160, 176
Corson, Hiram, 176-178, 198, 235
Coulton, Thomas E., 12, 77-79, 136, 137, 190
Course of Lectures on Elocution, 30, 59
Crain, Harold C., 238

Critical Pronouncing Dictionary of the English Language, 33
Criticism, 215-216
Crocker, Lionel G., 221, 237
Cumnock, Robert McLean, 130, 181-182
Cunningham, Cornelius Carmen, 195, 224, 225, 237
Curriculum, early period, 23-24; enlarged, 190-191, 219; reaction against classics in, 136-137
Curry, Samuel Silas, 11, 130, 137, 163-169, 171, 233, 234, 235, 237
Curry School of Expression, 138, 169, 192
Cushman, Charlotte, 168

Dartmouth College, 79
Darwin, Charles, 134, 135, 148, 149
Davis, Estelle H., 199-200
Davis, Olive B., 237
Day, Henry N., 114-117
DeBanke, Cecile, 191
Declamation, 21, 23-24, 77, 78, 79, 136; Latin and Greek, 22, 24
Delaumosne, L'Abbé, 144, 146
Delivery, 18, 19, 34, 109, 110, 116, 174-175, 180
Delsarte, François, 124, 133, 134, 137, 142-152, 164, 171, 181, 233
Delsarte Speaker, 147
Delsarte System of Oratory, 144
Delsarte system, 142, 143, 147, 163; basic principles of, 151-153; related to theology, 142
Delsarte System of Expression as Seen Through the Notes of Steele Mackaye, 142
Dennis, Ralph Brownell, 182, 208, 233, 235, 236, 237
Dewey, John, 132, 188, 192
Dialects, 58
Diatonic scale, 96
Dickens, Charles, 227
Dickinson College, 111
Diehl, Anna, 130
Dillport, Rayda W., 233
Discourse Delivered in the Theatre at Oxford, 30
Dodez, M. Leon, 234
Dolman, John Jr., 236, 238
Don Juan in Hell, 228
Donner, Stanley T., 236
Dorsey, Jane, 191
Dos Passos, John, 188
Drake, Anne Christine, 233
Dramatic Interpretation, 168
Dusenbury, Delwin, 196

Ear-training, 159
Eastern Public Speaking Conference, 139
Easy Lessons in Vocal Culture, 160
Eclectic method, 140, 179, 181, 182
Education, two theories of, 27-28
Effectiveness of Group Speaking on the Acquisition of Certain Speech Skills, 192
Eich, Louis M., 221, 237
Eiseley, Loren, 211, 212
Elements of Elocution, 32, 41, 202
Elocutio, 18, 21
Elocution, 13, 19, 21, 25, 41, 43, 58, 68, 78, 101, 102, 109, 113, 118, 136, 140, 153, 155, 174, 181; relation of rhetoric and poetic to, 20; two schools of, 28-29
Elocutionary movement, 22, 33-35, 43, 44
Emerson, Charles Wesley, 130, 137, 169-170
Emerson College of Oratory, 130, 169, 191
Emerson, Ralph Waldo, 127
Emotion, expression of, 134-135, 203-205, 206; expression of "passions," 36, 61
Emotional content, 203-205, 222
Emphasis, 44, 46, 47, 116, 157
Enfield, William, 26, 42
English, combining written with spoken, 77, 79, 139
English elocutionists, 19, 21, 35-40, 236
English oratory, 17-18
English Theories of Address, 1530-1828, 18
Equable concrete, 88
Essay on Elocution or Pronunciation, 21, 51
Exercises, alphabetic elements, 115; breathing, 107-108, 117, 157, 162, 165-167; physical, 106, 112; relaxation, 148; Rush's, 97-100; tone drills, 178, 179; with metronome, 106
Exercises in Elocution, 43
Expressional pharaphrasing, 172

Farma, William J., 198
Faulkner, William, 214
Fenno, Frank H., 160
First Principles of Speech Training, 191
Fiske, Bertha V., 171
Flügel, John Carl, 134
Foerster, Norman, 188
Force, 91, 93, 98, 115, 156
Forensics, 77
Formulae Oratoriae, 21
Foster, William T., 190

Foundations of Expression, 164, 167
Fredericks, Virginia, 224, 238
Frederickson, Ronald Q., 235
Fritz, Charles A., 12, 24, 26, 44, 85, 105
Fromm, Erich, 213
Frost, Robert, 188, 224
Fulton, Robert I., 160
Fundamentals of Speech, 197

Garrick, David, 53
Geiger, Don, 219, 223, 224, 242
General Dictionary of the English Language, 31
George Washington University, 79
Gesture, 44, 109, 153, 166, 169, 204; Austin's treatment of, 40; Bulwer's canons, 36-37; Delsarte, 144-145; early methods of teaching, 61-67, "trinity of restriction," 149
Gielgud, Sir John, 227
Gilbert, Edna, 237
Gillis, Herbert R., 234
Graduate degrees, 219, 220
Graduate studies, 218-220
Grammar of Elocution, 101, 103
Grammatical Institutes of the English Language, 25
Gray, Giles W., 235
Greeley, Horace, 127
Grimes, Wilma H., 223, 238
Grouping, 116, 221
Guide to Elocution, 43
Gullan, Marjorie, 19
Guthrie, Warren, 235
Gutteral quality, 115

Hadley, Dorothy S., 234
Hale, Lester Leonard, 233
Hamill, S., 160
Handbook of Oral Reading, 197
Hargis, Donald E., 236
Hartman, George W., 195-196
Hartung, Nancy, 235
Harvard College, 25, 78, 105, 188; Bolyston professor, 21, 76; commencement, 22, 23; electives introduced at, 75; instruction in elocution at, 19
Hawk, Sara Stinchfield, 169
Hayworth, Donald, 24
Heidbreder, Edna, 132-133
Henneke, Ben Graf, 238
Herendeen, Jane E., 237
Hersey, John, 214
Hicks, Granville, 188
Hints to Public Speakers, 42
History of Physical Education, 147
Hochmuth, Marie, 236

Holbrook, Hal, 227
Holbrook, Josiah, 75, 127
Holbrook, Nelson, 102
Hollatz, Edwin A., 235
How to Read, 205
Howell, Wilbur S., 236, 238
Humanism, 21, 188-189
Humanities, 219, 226, 229, 232
Hutchins, President, 188, 189
Illustrations of Rhythmus, 43
Imagination and Dramatic Instinct, 164
Immel, Ray K., 202, 203
Impersonation, 168, 218
Indiana University, 79
Inflection, key of, 54; harmonic, 47; kinds of, 54
International phonetic alphabet, 199
Interpretation of the Printed Page, 174, 175, 198, 201, 221
Interpretation: Reader, Writer, Audience, 223, 238
"Interpretative Reading As a Fine Art," 195
Interpretative Reading: Techniques and Selections, 221, 237
Intonation 85
Introduction to the Art of Reading with Energy and Propriety, 45
Introductory Study of the History of the Teaching of Public Speaking in the United States, 12, 102

James, William, 132, 164
Jarrell, Randall, 215
Jastrow, Joseph, 132, 194
Jefferson, Thomas, 75
Jeffrey, Robert C., 217, 236
John Brown's Body, 228
Johnson, Gertrude, 169, 198, 218, 221, 237
Jones, Lloyd S., 234

Kazin, Alfred, 216
Kendrick, William, 42
Kennedy, Charles Rann, 129
Keppie, Elizabeth E., 191
Kershner, A. G., 236
Kilpatrick, William H., 132
Kirby, Edward N., 179-181
Kirkland, Audrey S., 235
Kling, Janette, 129
Klyn, Mark S., 219
Knower, Franklin, 196
Knox College, 79
Knox, Thomas, 42
Kolch, Frederick L., 233
Kramer, Magdalene, 191, 237

Laird, Dugan, 234
Lamb, John Hall, 235, 236
Langbaum, Robert, 214
Language, sounds of, 79-60
Lardner, J. L., 189
Latham, Azubah, 169, 237
Laughton, Charles, 227, 228
Law of correspondence, 147, 149
Law of equilibrium, 147
Law of opposition, 147
Law of radiation, 150
Law of reaction, 150
Leavis, F. R., 216
Lectures on Elocution, 26, 27
Lectures on the Art of Reading, 31, 50
Lee, Charlotte, 223, 224, 225, 237
Leland Powers School of Oratory, 130, 191
Lessons in Elocution, 27, 39, 62-63
Leverton, Garrett, 82, 101
Liberal arts, 119, 218, 219, 229
Lincoln-Douglas debate, 79
Linn, James R., 22, 227, 238
Literature, appreciation of, 141, 173, 191, 195, 207; nonfiction, 214
Literature as Experience, 223, 238
Locke, John, 27-28
Logic, 77
Logical content, 200-203, 222
Lowell Institute, 75
Lowrey, Sara, 221, 237
Lyceum, 75, 127, 191
Lynch, Gladys E., 238

McCoard, William B., 229
McGuffey Readers, 102
McGuffey, William Holmes, 102, 233, 235
McLaren, Gay, 126, 127, 128, 130
McLean, Margaret P., 198, 199, 201, 202
Mackaye, Steele, 130, 142, 234
Maglachlin, Henry B., 102
Mammen, Edward W., 199-200
Man and Superman, 228
Mandeville, Henry, 160
Manning College, 130
Manual of Elocution, 160
Manual of Gesture, 131, 136, 160
Marcoux, J. Paul Albert, 221, 235
Marietta College, 107
Mark Twain, Tonight, 227
Mason, John, 21, 51
Matlon, Ronald John, 234
Matthison, Edith Wynne, 129
Mattingly, Alethea Smith, 223, 234, 238
Mayor, William, 42

Mechanical school, 29, 33, 49, 68, 82, 86, 153, 231
Mechanics of speech, 199-200
Melody, 47, 53, 91, 99, 175
Melody of Speaking Delineated or Elocution Taught Like Music by Visible Signs, 32
Memorization, 110, 181, 202, 203
Menchen, H. L., 187
Meter, 202
Miller, M. Oclo, 164, 166
Mind and Voice, 166
Mitchell, M. S., 160
Modern Literature for Oral Interpretation, 198
Modes of speech, 84, 87, 103
Modulation, 43, 49-54, 158; "tone color," 167
Monologue, 128, 168
Monroe, Lewis B., 130
Moody, Dwight L., 125
Morally We Roll Along, 127
Morison, Samuel E., 23, 131
Morris, Virginia, 233
Mouat, Lawrence H., 236, 238
Murdoch, James E., 85, 92, 101, 102, 105, 117-118, 234, 235
Murphy, Richard, 237
Murray, Lindley, 24-25
Music, relation of speech to, 51, 109; use in speech training, 115

Nathan, George Jean, 215
National Association of Academic Teachers of Public Speaking, 138, 183, 218
National Association of Elocutionists, 156
National Association of Teachers of Speech, 138
National School of Elocution and Oratory, 129
National Speech Arts Association, 138
Natural Drills in Expression, 178
Natural method, 198-199
Natural school, 29, 33, 45, 68, 84, 109, 179, 198, 230
Neely, George Albert, 233
Nelson, Severina E., 197, 198, 202, 204, 205, 221, 236
New Criticism, 223-224
New Speaker, 42
Newens, Adrian, 129
Newman, John B., 233, 236
Newman, Joseph, 131
Noble, Stuart G., 25

North, Dr. E. D., 109-111
Northrop, Henry D., 147
Northwestern University, 130, 181, 220
Notations, 51, 52; Bell, 156; Porter, 54; Steele, 38, 36; gesture, 63-67; intonation, 200

Oberholtzer, Ellis Paxson, 125
On the Use of Notations in Elocutionary Teaching, 159
O'Neill, James, 138
Oral English, 137
Oral Expression, 79
Oral interpretation, 14, 19, 44, 68, 78; modern textbooks, 197-198, 221-226; research in, 219-220
Oral interpretation, defined, 12; 223, 237
"Oral interpretation in the Liberal Arts Context," 219
Oral interpretation Interest Group, 216-217
Oral Interpretation of Fiction: A Dramatistic Approach, 224, 238
Oral Interpretation of Forms of Literature, 198
Oral Interpretation of Literature, 222, 238
Oral Reading, 221, 237
Oral Study of Literature, 197
Oration on the Influence of Elocution on Martial Enthusiasm, 43
Orations, 23, 77, 79, 136
Orator's Assistant, 26
Orator's Manual, 173
Oratory, 13, 25, 77, 78; English 17-18
"Orotund" quality, 92, 94, 115
Orthophony or Vocal Culture, 93, 112, 117, 148
Osgood, Lucius, 102

Packard, Vance, 214
Palmer, Erastus, 137, 139, 162
Pantomime, 153, 205
Pantomimes for Stage and Study, 209
Paperback books, 213, 214
Paraphrasing, 172, 202
Pardoe T. Earl, 205
Parrington, Vernon Louis, 72, 123, 126
Parrish, Wayland M., 198-199, 200, 201, 202, 203, 221, 236, 237
Pause, 44, 55-58
Pennsylvania State College, 79
The Performing Voice in Literature, 223, 225, 238
Perrin, Porter Gale, 12, 18, 19, 23
Perry, Bliss, 73

Phillips, Arthur Edward, 130, 178-179; tone drills, 178-179
Phillips, Helen K., 233
Phillips School of Oratory, 130, 178
Phillips, Wendell, 127
Philosophy, 81
Philosophy of Literary Form: Studies in Symbolic Action, 215
Philosophy of the Human Voice, 80, 81, 83, 92, 101, 103, 112, 173, 231
Philosophy of Rhetoric, 55
Phonetics, 60, 200
Physical culture, 171
Physical education, influence of Delsarte upon, 146
Physiology of speech, 140
Pierce, Benjamin, 25
Pitch, 44, 49-55, 87, 99, 109, 115, 156, 165, 199
Plan and Terms of Instruction for the Cure of Impediments of Speech, 43
Platform reading, 127, 191; lecture recital, 226, 229
Plea for Spoken Language, 85, 101
Portal to Rhetorical Delivery, 43
Porter, Ebenezer, 40-42, 50, 53-54, 55, 58, 60-61
Practical Elements of Elocution, 160
Practical Elocutionist, 102
Practical Manual of Elocution, 111
Practical Speaking as Taught at Yale, College, 109
Practice of Elocution, 43
Precís, 201
President's Commission on National Goals, 212
Princeton College, 107
Principles of Elocution, 42, 153, 154
Principles of Vocal Expression, 171
Professional schools, 129, 130, 166, 169, 178, 181, 191-192
Progressives, 188-189
Pronunciation, 44, 58-61
"Pronunciation or the Art of Just Speaking," 18
Pronuntiatio, 18, 20, 21, 29, 44, 230
Prose, Poetry, and Drama for Oral Interpretation, 198
Prosodia Rationalis, 38, 46, 51, 103
Province of Expression, 164
Psycho Vox, 170
Psychology, behavioristic, 193-194; functional, 131, 134; 192; gestalt, 193-194; 222-223
Public Speaking, 181
Public Speaking and Reading, 179

Public speaking, related to English, 139
Public Speaking Review, 139
Punctuation, 55-58

Quality, 54, 85, 93, 100, 103, 109, 115, 117, 158, 170, 172
Quarterly Journal of Public Speaking Review, 139
Quarterly Journal of Speech, 189
Quincy, Josiah, 71
Quintilian, 20

Radical movement, 89, 104; protracted radical, 88, 89
Rambin, Bill, 234
Rarig, Frank M., 224, 235, 237
Raymond, George L., 173
Raymond, Robert T., 168
"Readers," 24, 26, 102
Readers Theatre, 228-229
Reading Aloud, 198, 199, 221
Reading analysis necessary for 202; poetry, 58, 104, 112, 113, 168, 220, 225-226
Reading and Speaking, 160
Reading for Others, 198
Reading Programs, 226-229
Redpath, James, 127
Renshaw, Edyth, 233
Research, 196, 218-220, 229
Reynolds, Nydia J., 236
Rhetoric, 13, 68, 77, 78, 136, 153; classical, 20, 22; delivery a part of, 181; five parts of, 18-19
Rhetorical Grammar, 25, 27, 31, 32, 34, 42, 58
Rhetorical pause, 58
Rhetorical Reader, 41, 42, 49, 53, 61
Rhythm, 201-202
Rice, Emmett, 147
Rice, John, 45
Rice, Phidelah, 129
Richards, I. A., 225
Ridgeway, Katherine, 128
Riesman, David, 214
Rise of American Civilization, 17, 123
Roach, Helen Pauline, 233
Robb, Mary Margaret, 235, 237, 238
Robinson, Marion P., 235
Romanticism, 72
Rousseau, Jean Jaques, 28
Rush, Benjamin, 74
Rush, James, 11, 81-102, 103, 114, 118, 162, 163, 231, 233, 235
Russell, Francis, 112
Russell, William, 92, 102, 113, 114-117, 129, 136, 148

Sabine, John, 43
Sammis, Walter, 137, 162
Sandburg, Carl, 129
Sandford, William P., 18, 32, 33
Sarett, Lew, 129, 138, 190
Sargent, Epes, 102
Scales, 90, 96
School of Expression, 129, 166, 192
School of Practical Rhetoric and Oratory, 112, 129
School of Speech, 130, 181, 220
Schools. *See* Professional schools
School Speaker, 43
Science and Art of Elocution, 160
Scott, John R., 102
Scott, William, 27, 39-40, 62, 63, 108
Shaver, Claude L., 142, 143
Sheridan, Thomas, 12, 25, 27, 29, 30-31, 35, 36, 46, 57-59, 60, 61, 236
Shoemaker, J. W., 129
Shurter, Edwin D., 137, 179, 181
Sickels, Vera, 191
Siddons, Mrs., 95
Simon, Clarence T., 195, 219
Skill in Reading Aloud, 222
Sloan, Thomas O., 238
Smart, Benjamin, 43
Smith, Brainard G., 160
Smith, Joseph F., 222, 237
Smith, Preserved, 27, 29
Snow, Louis F., 24
The Sound, Sense, and Performance of Literature, 223, 238
Spalding, A. C. Bloomfield, 43
Speaker, 26, 42
Speaker, relation of audience to, 181, 222-223
Speech Association of America, 216-217
Speech, courses in 76-79, 189-191; exercises for improvement of, 97-100; relation of music to, 51, 108, 115
Speech departments, 77-78, 139, 216, 217
Speech mechanism, 117
Speech Monographs, 219, 220
Spoken English, 13
Spoken Word in Life and Art, 197, 199-200
Stahl, Margaret, 129
"Statue-posing," 147
Stebbins, Genevieve, 130, 147
Steele, Joshua, 34, 38-39, 46, 51-53, 103, 104, 233, 236
Story Telling, 190, 191
Stress, 92, 98, 115; "touch," 165
Studies in the Art of Interpretation, 218, 237

Subtonics, 88, 90
Sunday, Billy, 125
Swift, Jonathan, 18
Symbolism, of action and voice, 196; symbolic action, 215; symbols in literature, 224
Synthetic Philosophy of Expression, 148, 149
System of Elocution, 106, 107

Tallcott, Rollo A., 197
Talmadge, T. Dewitt, 125
Tassin, Algernon de V., 197, 198
Teacher Training Institutions, 190-191, 219
Teachers, Clark's rules for, 175; Emerson's requirements for, 170; function of 168; preparation of, 168, 218, 219, 220, 225, 226, 231
Teaching of Choric Speech, 192
Teaching of Rhetoric in the American Colleges Before 1750, 12, 18
Teaching, psychological theories of, 132, 182, 183
Technic of the Speaking Voice, 101
Textbooks, first, 26-27; following English elocutionists, 82; 1827-1870, 82, 110-111; 1870-1915, 136; modern, 197-198, 220-228, 237-238
Thelwall, John, 43
Theory and Technique of Interpretation, 222
"Think-the-thought," methods, 84, 163, 175
Thomas Alexander, 26
Thomas, Dylan, 227
Thompson, David W., 224, 237, 238
Thonssen, Dorothea, 237
Thonssen, Lester, 237, 238
Throat and Voice, 136
Thwing, Charles F., 19
Timing, 44, 94, 97, 156; early method of teaching, 55-58
Tone, pure, 172
Tone-color, 167
Tone drills, 178-179
Tonics, 88
Torsey, Kathleen, E., 235
Tousey, Gail Jordon, 233
Town, Salem, 102
Transitions, 105
Tremor, 91, 99
Tremulous scale, 96
Trends in Speech Education in American Colleges 1835-1935, 77-79
Tressider, Argus, 198, 200, 201, 237
Trilling, Lionel, 214

"Trinity of Restriction," 149
Trissolini, Anthony, 220
Trueblood, Thomas Clarkson, 137, 160, 217, 235
Twain, Mark, 127, 227
Tynan, Kenneth, 215

University of Alabama, 79
University of California, 219
University of Colorado Reading Program, 227-228
University of Michigan, 137; anniversary, 217
University of Minnesota, 196
University of North Carolina, 79
University of Pennsylvania, 79

Vandraegen, Daniel E. R., 233
Vanishing movement, 98; protracted vanish, 98, 99
Varnado, Alban F., 234
Vestibule of Eloquence, 43
"Visible speech," 153
Vocal and Polyglot Gymnasium, 129
Vocal apparatus, "trinity" of, 146
Vocal signs, 84, 111
Voice and Spiritual Education, 176
Voice science, 153, 207, 216
Volume, 115

Vowel wedge, 156
Vowels, 59, 60, 103

Walker-Austin-Rush tradition, 153-162
Walker, John, 12, 29, 32-34, 46-49, 50, 55-57, 58, 60, 61-62, 234, 235, 236
Wallace, Karl R., 6, 238
Waste Land, 188
Wave, 90
Weaver, J. Clark, 190
Webster, Daniel, 71-72
Webster, Noah, 25, 74
Weintraub, Stanley A., 234
Welty, Eudora, 214
Werner's Magazine, 130
West, Ray B., 224
Whately, Richard, 80, 198
Wiksell, Milton Joel, 233
William Butler Yeats, 232
Williams, Emelyn, 227
Wilson, Garff, 219
Wilson, Helene, 191-192
Wilson, John, 42
Winans, James A., 139, 181
Woolbert, Charles Henry, 195, 197, 198, 202, 204, 205, 221, 236

Yale College, 78, 105, 107, 188; commencement theses, 19; declamations, 23; mental discipline at, 76